POSTCARD HISTORY SERIES

Northeast Georgia

IN VINTAGE POSTCARDS

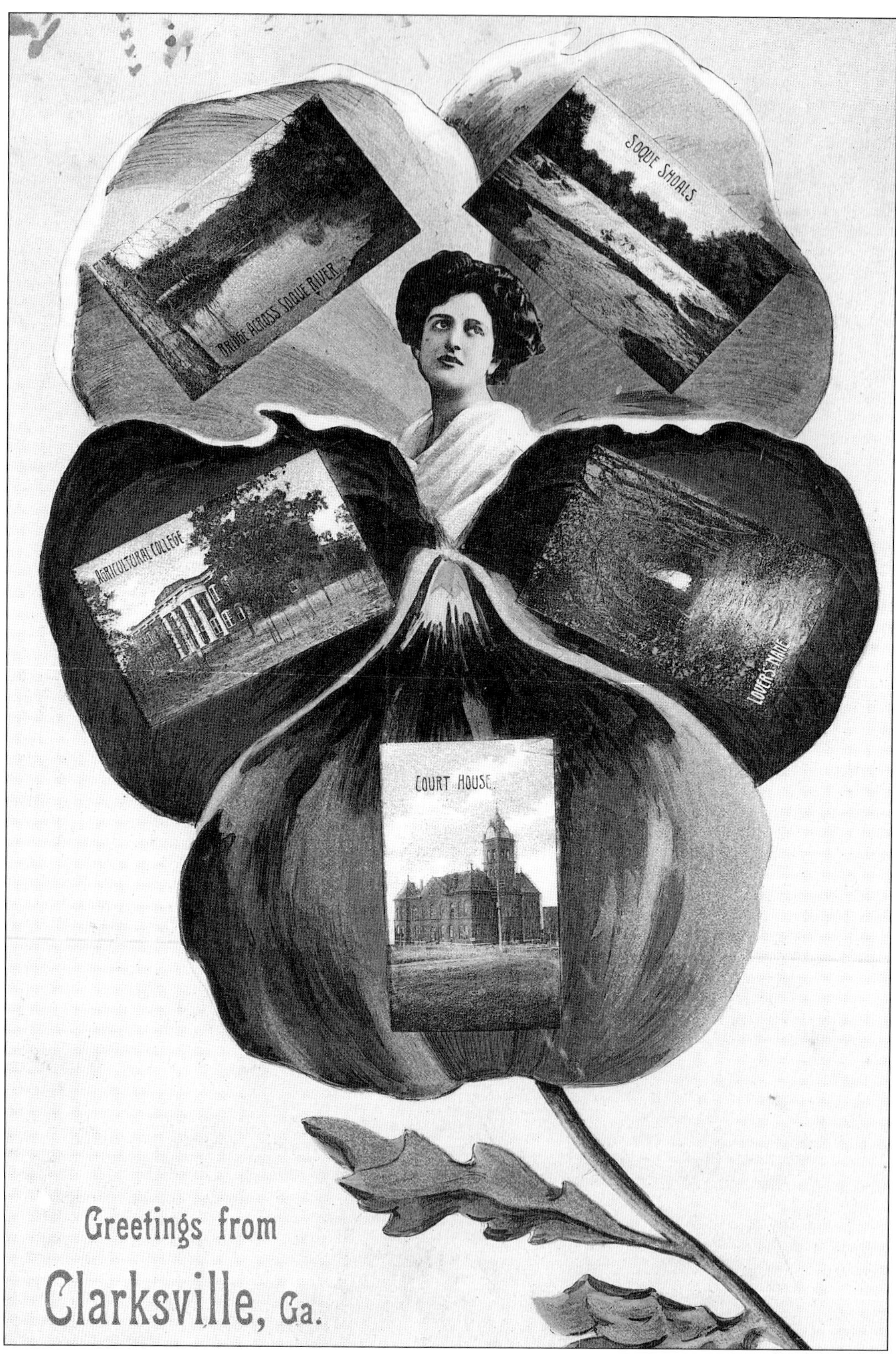
Bridge Across Soque River
Soque Shoals
Agricultural College
Lover's Made
Court House
Greetings from
Clarksville, Ga.

POSTCARD HISTORY SERIES

Northeast Georgia

IN VINTAGE POSTCARDS

Gary L. Doster

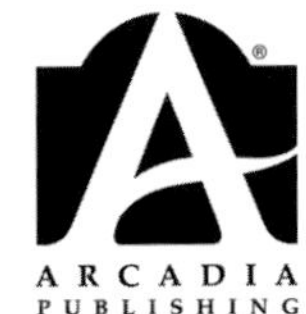

ISBN 978-0-7385-8990-9

Published by Arcadia Publishing
Charleston, South Carolina

Printed in the United States of America

Library of Congress Catalog Card Number: 98-86585

For all general information contact Arcadia Publishing at:
Telephone 843-853-2070
Fax 843-853-0044
E-mail sales@arcadiapublishing.com
For customer service and orders:
Toll-Free 1-888-313-2665

Visit us on the Internet at www.arcadiapublishing.com

For Faye Thomas Doster,
whom I have loved since she was 13 years old.

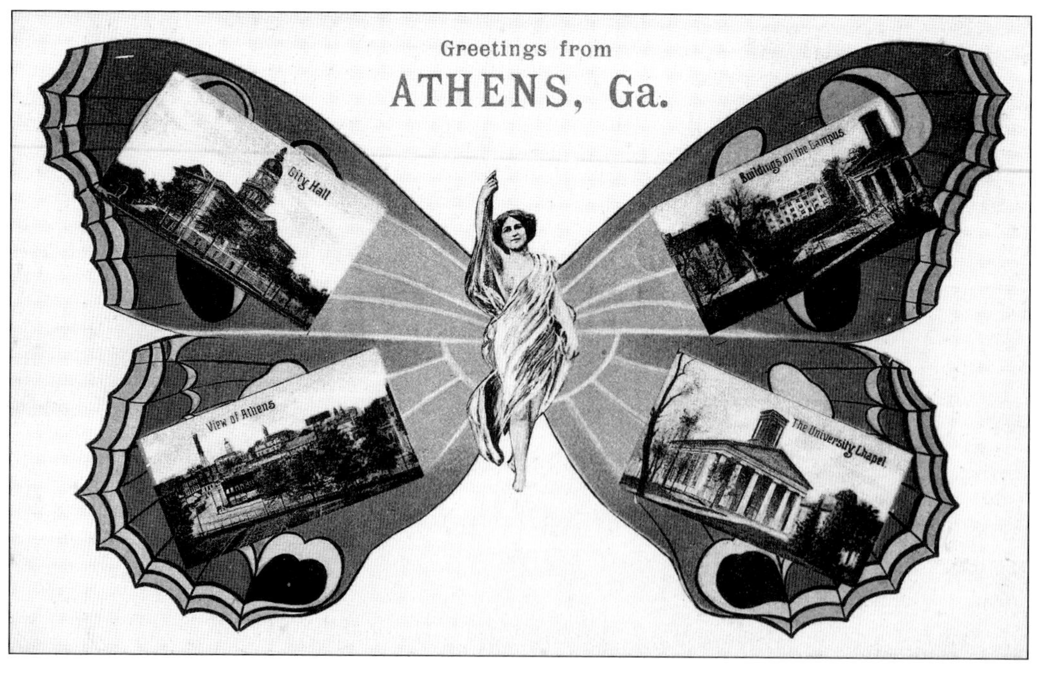

Contents

ACKNOWLEDGMENTS

For help in various ways, including advice, information, and post cards, I wish to thank the following people:

Carl Anderson
Bob Basford
Jim Dunn
Nell Dunn
John Kovalski
Jerald Ledbetter
Ernest Malcom
Dan Marshall
Bill Moffat
Edwin Oldham
Hershel Reeves
Gordon Sanford
SueFan Tate
Jeff West
Bill Wheless

Introduction

We are indeed fortunate that post cards* were invented and were so popular during the first several years of this century. In the clamor to satisfy the almost overwhelming demand for more and more post cards by the public, literally thousands of scenes were photographed that were never captured on film for any other reason. Over time, many of the homes, depots, court houses, stores, and other buildings so pictured have disappeared and these early post card views are the only images that remain. Two particularly interesting facts that were discovered while selecting and compiling the cards for these books concerned Georgia's Confederate monuments. A great many monuments were unveiled or dedicated on Confederate Memorial Day, April 26, and few of them remain on their original sites. The ladies of the United Daughters of the Confederacy and the old veterans themselves usually selected some prominent spot in the middle of town, almost always at the intersection of two main streets. Invariably, as automobile use increased over years, the monuments became traffic hazards and were moved to another part of town. Consequently, many of these post card views are the only pictures of them in their original locations.

Also of great interest are the views showing the intrusion of the automobile onto the scene. It is fun to note that the earlier post card views, those before 1907 or 1908, usually have horse- or mule-drawn wagons, buggies, or carriages in the street scenes (a few even show mule-powered streetcars!). Then, from that time to about 1912 or 1914, these views will typically show a mix of the animal-drawn vehicles and early automobiles. After this time, a wagon or buggy is only rarely seen, and the number of automobiles on the streets increased rapidly.

The collecting frenzy that swept the world began in Europe in the 1890s,

*Throughout the book, I have chosen to use the older spelling of the word, i.e. "post card" versus "postcard."

crept into this country before the turn of the century, and erupted a few years later. Many of the better quality post cards were produced in Europe, particularly Germany. Some of the post card factories in Germany were the size of cotton mills in this country, and they employed hundreds of people. For example, one German plant in 1909 had 112 cylinder printing presses and employed 1,500 workers. During the peak years of the post card collecting fad, more than a million people in Germany were employed in the post card business. In the three-year period from 1907 to 1909, more than 85,000 tons of post cards were imported into the United States from Germany.

In the Images of America book series published by Arcadia, the major effort has been to render pictorial books on individual towns or counties. And these are wonderful. Those of us who have an interest in preserving whatever we can of our past are hungry for books like this and they serve a valuable purpose. However, there are hundreds of smaller communities across every state that offer only a limited number of views of life of yesteryear that also are striking and important. Some medium-sized towns may have a handful of good views that show what their community and its people looked like nearly one hundred years ago. Many of the very small towns may have only one or two representative views. All of these are important, but none of them can support a book alone. Hence, this series of six volumes was conceived to provide a vehicle whereby a collection of early Georgia post cards from numerous small communities could be exhibited.

It is important to note here that this set of books is not intended to be any sort of scholarly work. It is merely an attempt to provide access to a selection of early views of Georgia that are not available in any other form, most of which have not been reprinted since their original publication. Many of the captions we provide in these books are no more than the caption printed on the cards when they were produced. Some additions have been made to some cards when the author had knowledge of some facts regarding the view in question. Other information came from the few reference books listed in the bibliography. To have researched each view and provided a comprehensive caption for each would have taken a lifetime of research, and then would still have been incomplete.

The author is a lifelong Georgian and has collected all manner of Georgiana for most of his life. Some of his other collecting interests are obsolete currency from the Colonial period through the War between the States, early letters and other documents, slave bills of sale and other items pertaining to slavery, Confederate letters and documents, old photographs, trade tokens, and Native-American relics.

One

Clarke and Madison Counties

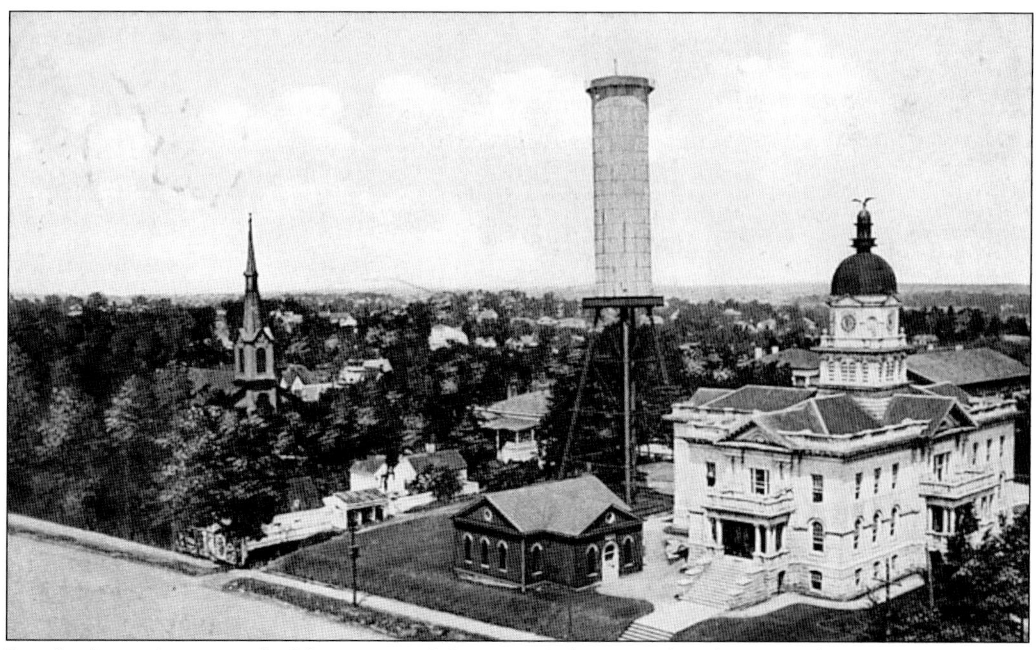

Besides being home to the University of Georgia, Athens is a lovely city with many historic and beautiful buildings. This bird's-eye view shows the Athens City Hall, jail, and water tower.

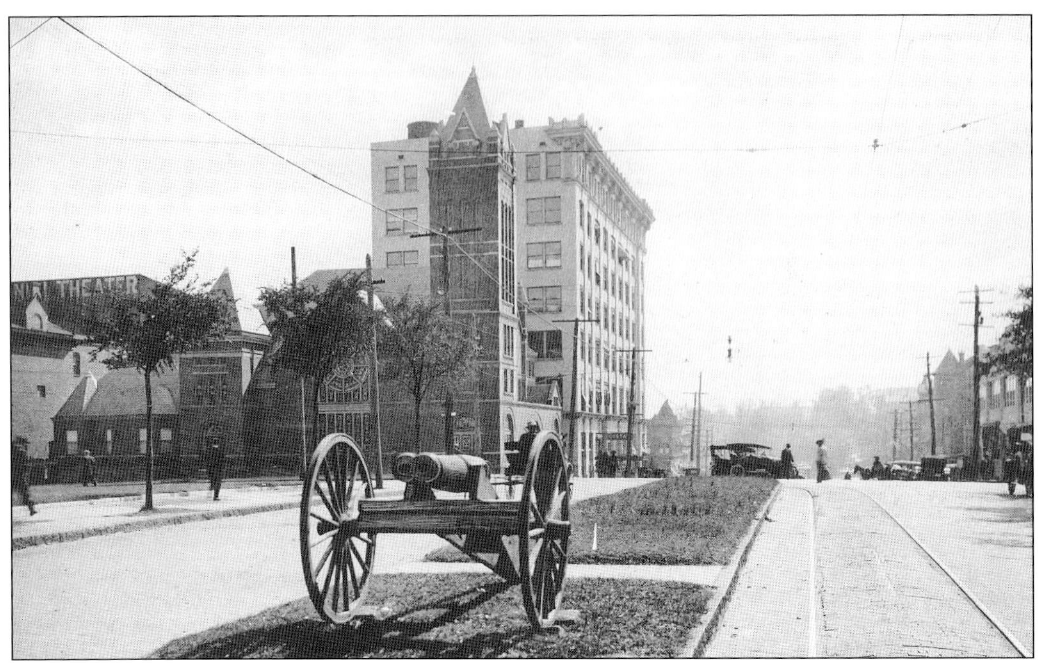

This view shows one of Athens' most unusual landmarks, a double-barrel cannon. The cannon was a unique, but unsuccessful, attempt to improve on existing weapons technology.

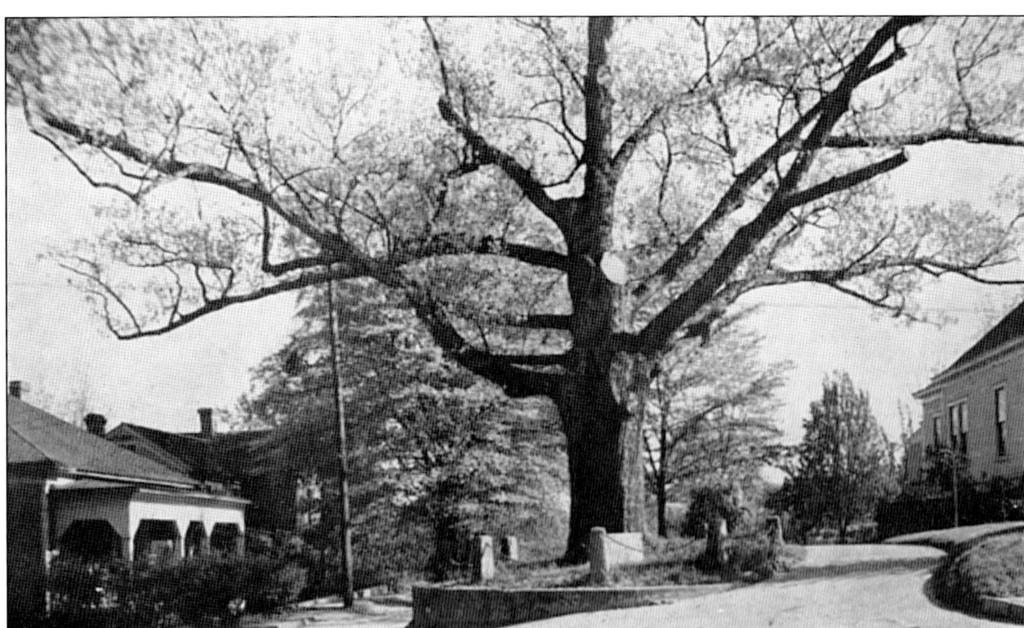

Athens can also boast of the only tree in the world that owns itself, even though the story is a myth, probably concocted by Athens newspaper man T. Larry Gantt in the 1890s. If Gantt didn't invent the story, he certainly is responsible for its perpetuation and spread. Regardless of its origin, the story has always delighted Athens citizens and no one has ever come forward to dispute the nonexistent deed or to attempt to claim the 16-foot-diameter piece of real estate at the corner of Dearing and Findley Streets.

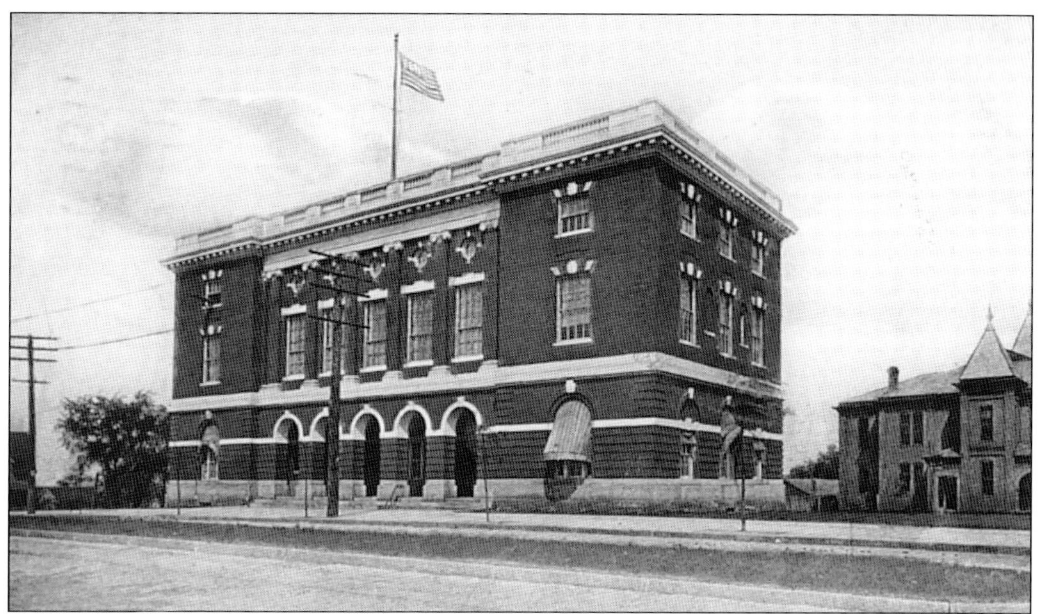

The Athens Federal Building and Post Office was built in 1907 across from the Athens City Hall on College Avenue. Part of the old Washington Street school can be seen at the right. The school was demolished in 1908 to make way for the Georgian Hotel.

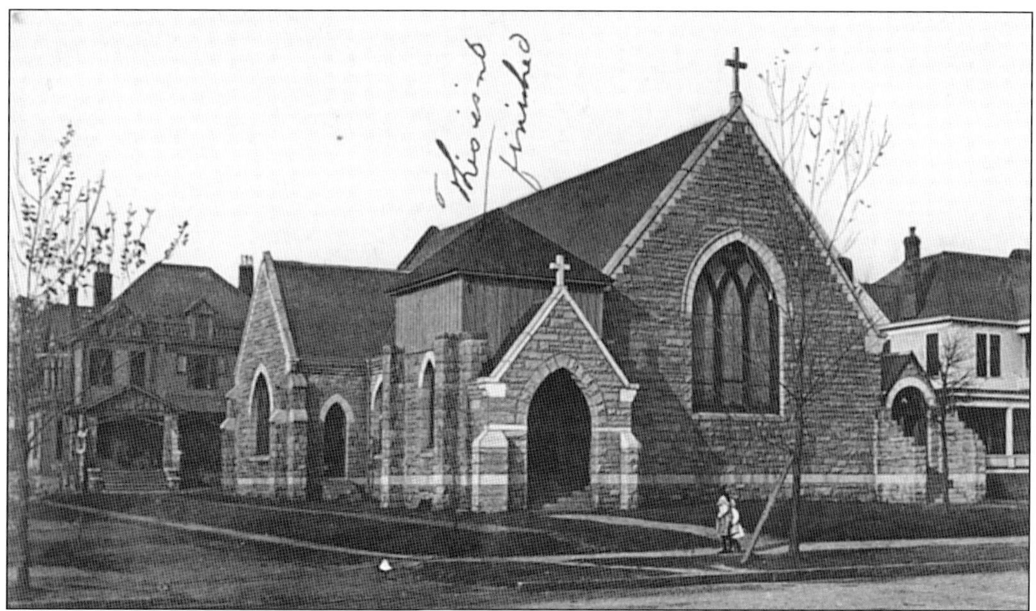

The buyer of this card showing the Episcopal church on Prince Avenue in Athens was evidently a stickler for details. He drew a line on the card pointing to a section of the church and noted "This is not finished." Actually, the church was completed and put into use in 1899, but the steeple was not added until 1925.

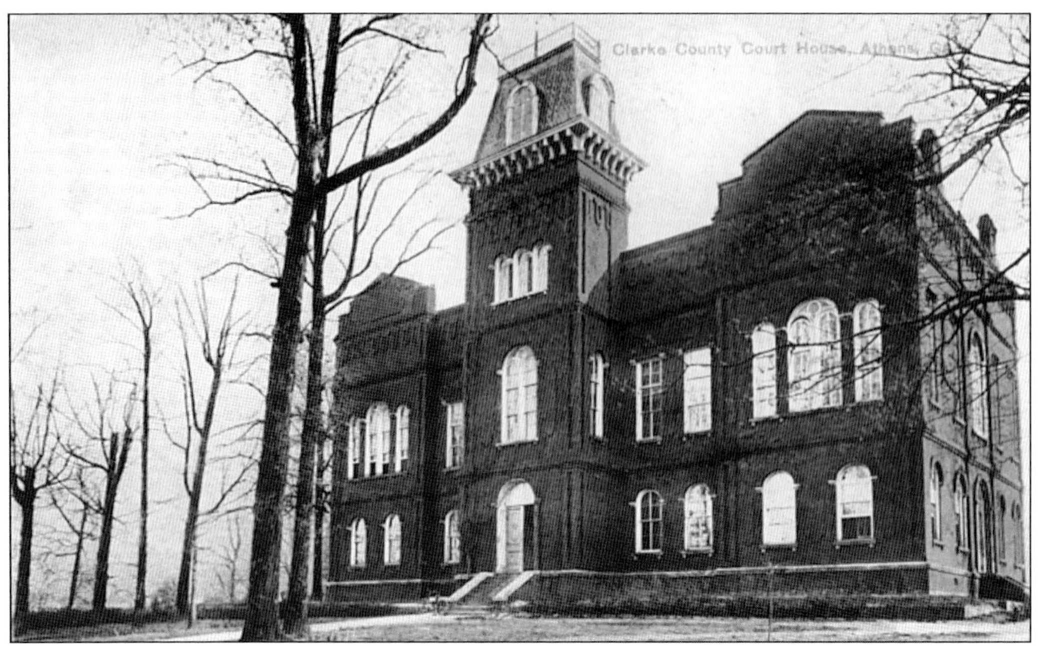

The Clarke County Courthouse was built on Prince Avenue in 1876. After the new courthouse was completed in 1913, the building was used as Athens High School from 1915 to 1953. The University Demonstration School occupied the building from 1953 to 1956. The building was demolished in 1959.

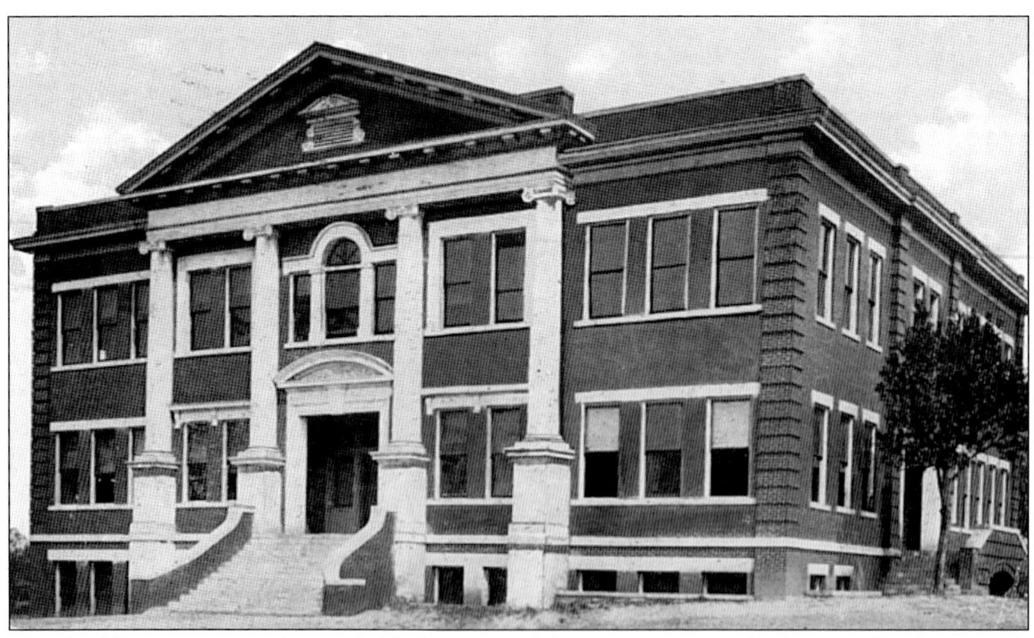

This building was erected on Childs Street in Athens in 1909 as the home of Athens High School. When the high school was relocated in the old courthouse building on Prince Avenue, this structure was converted to a junior high school and renamed Childs Street School. The school was burned down by two teenaged arsonists in 1966.

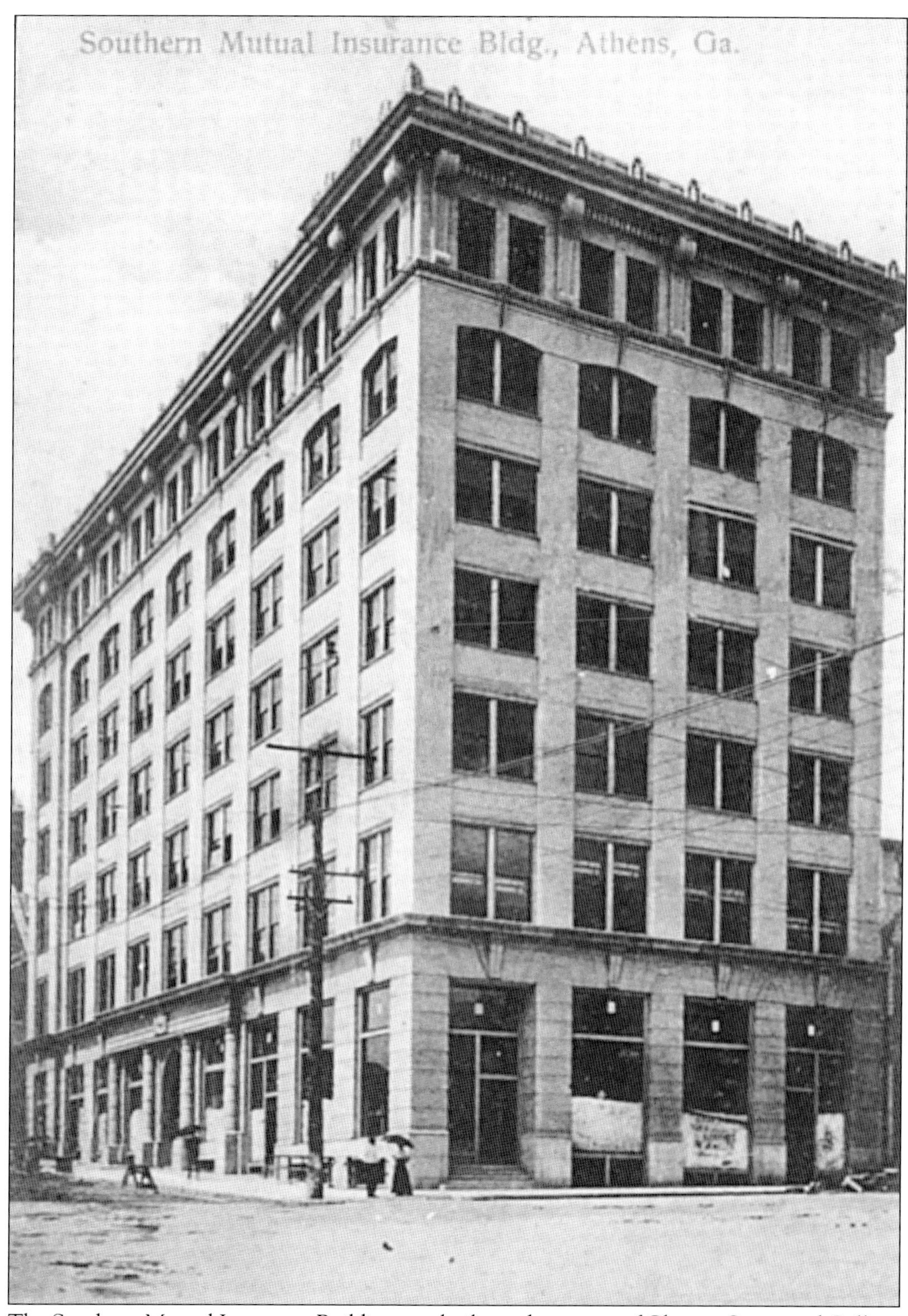

The Southern Mutual Insurance Building was built on the corner of Clayton Street and College Avenue in Athens in 1908.

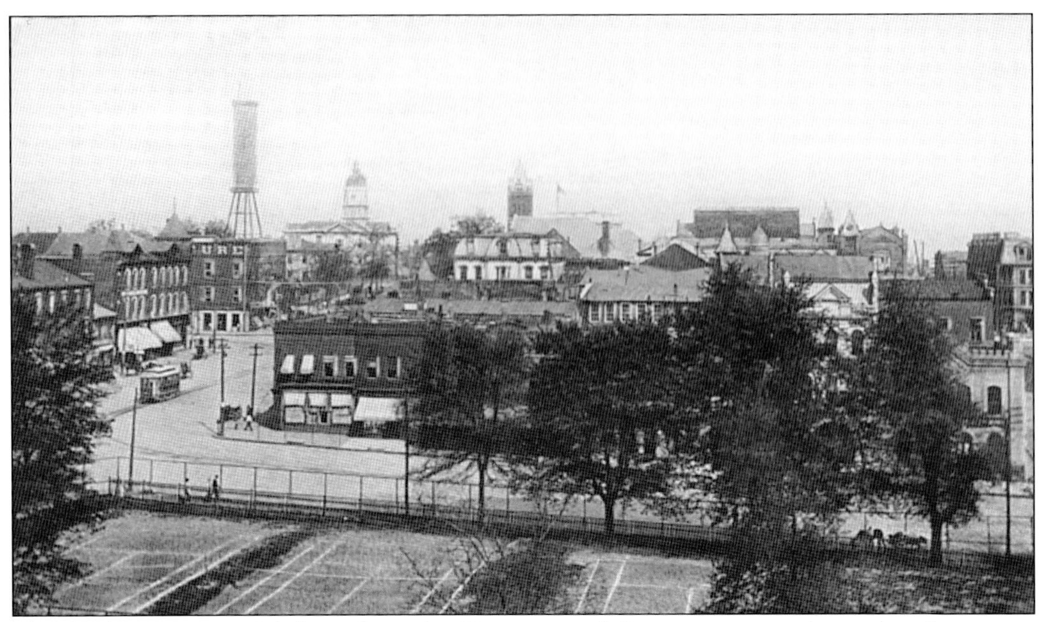

This bird's-eye view of Athens from the University of Georgia campus shows the clay tennis courts located just inside the fence along Broad Street.

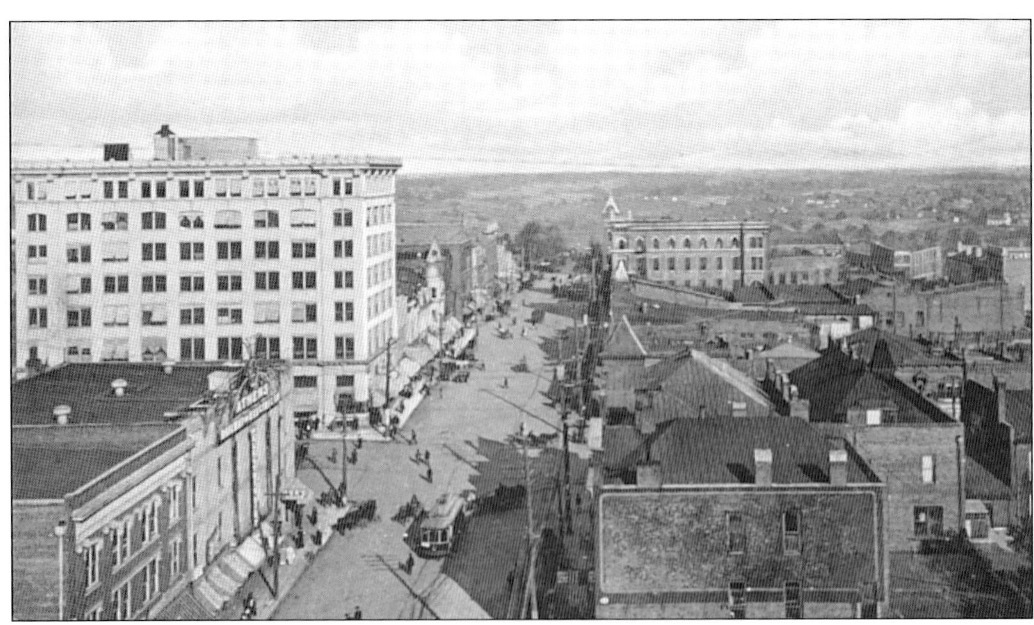

This bird's-eye view of Clayton Street in Athens was taken about 1914 from the top of the nine-story Holman Building on the corner of Clayton and Lumpkin Streets.

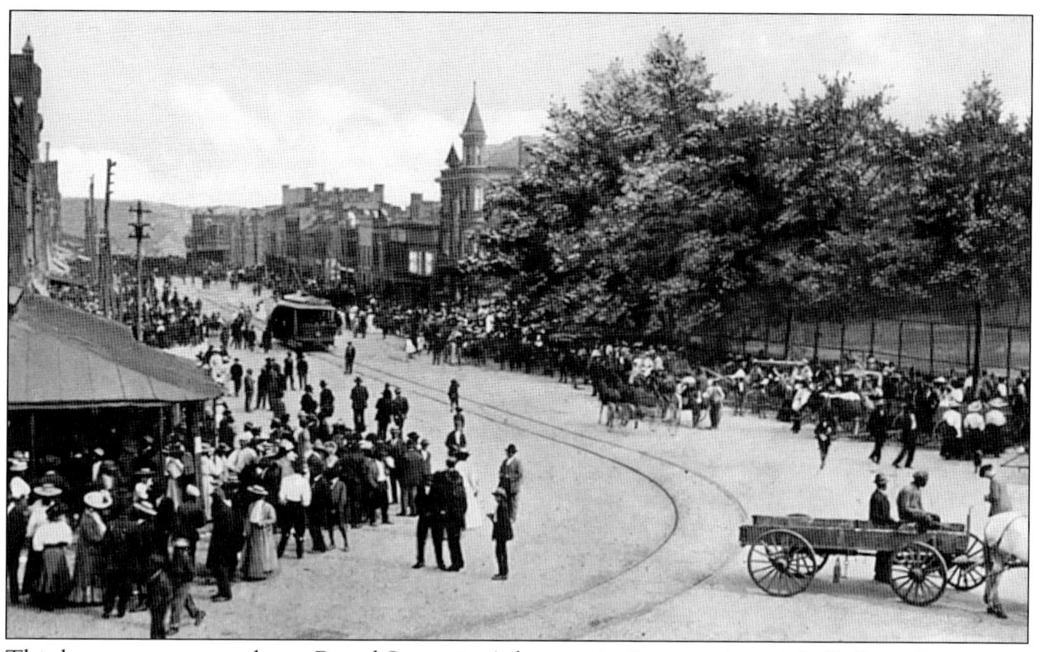

This busy street scene shows Broad Street in Athens at its intersection with College Avenue on what must have been a busy market day.

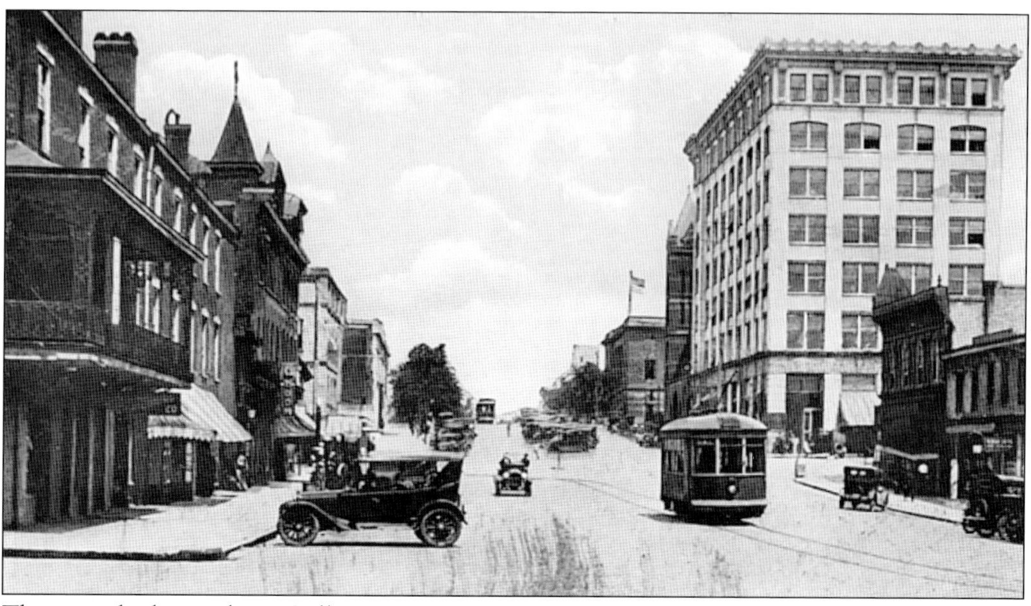

This view looks north up College Avenue in Athens from the Broad Street intersection. The hotel building on the corner on the left would become home to the Varsity restaurant in 1932.

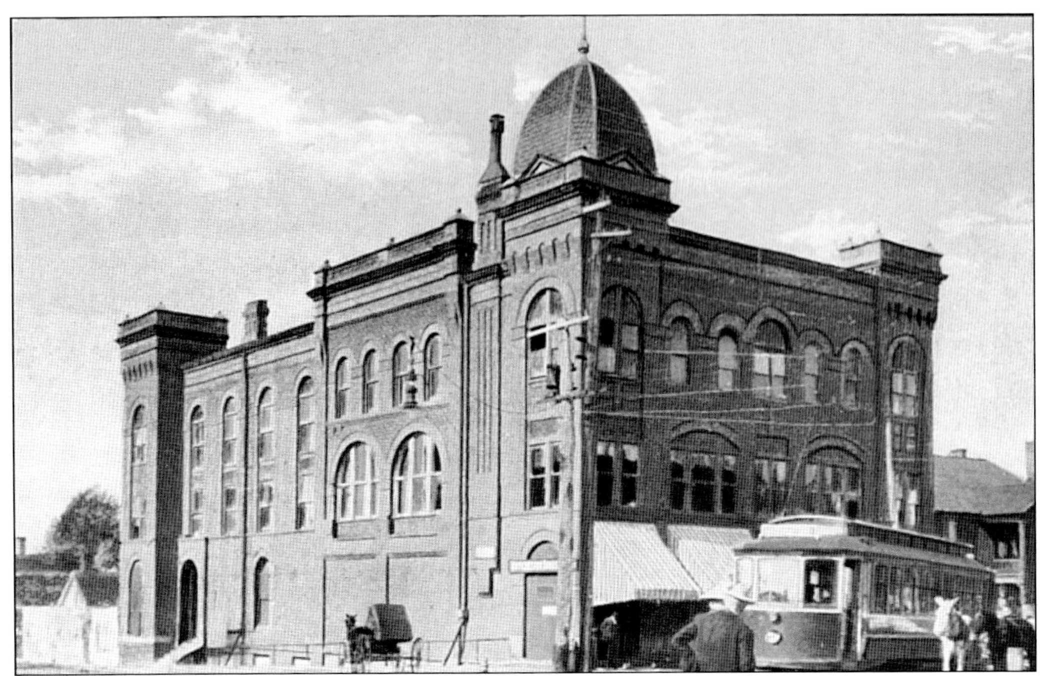

The Athens YMCA building was built on the corner of Clayton and Lumpkin Streets in 1889. It was torn down in 1920 and the Elite Theater (later the Georgian Theater) was built on the foundation.

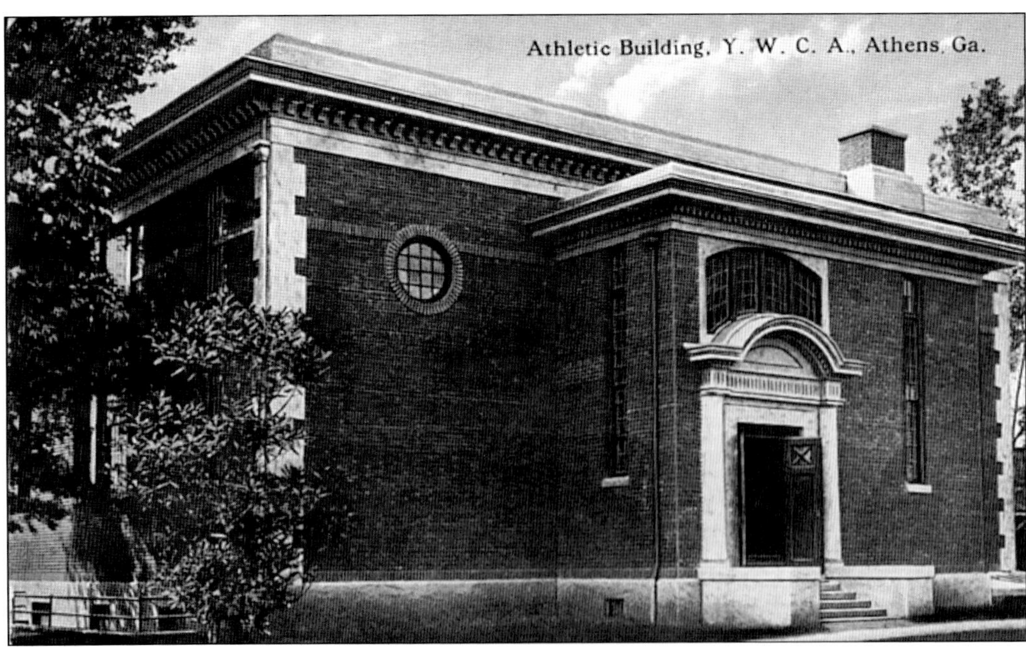

Along with the Young Men's Christian Association, Athens also had a Young Women's Christian Association. The Athletic Building of the YWCA, built in 1913 on Hancock Avenue at the intersection with Pulaski Street, is shown here.

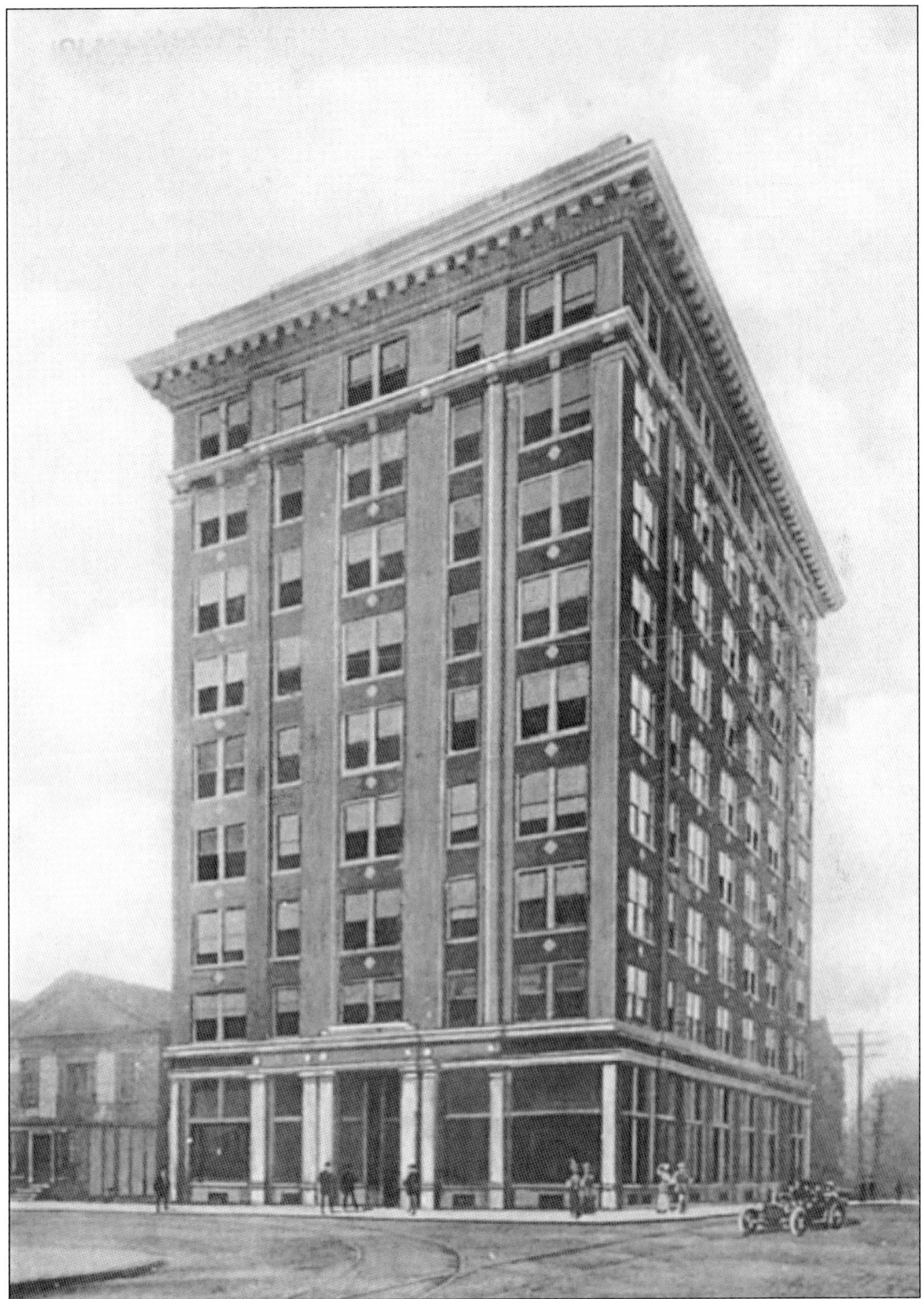

W.S. Holman's building was erected on the corner of Clayton and Lumpkin Streets in Athens in 1913. It was intended to be an office building, but was soon converted to a hotel. It is now home to NationsBank.

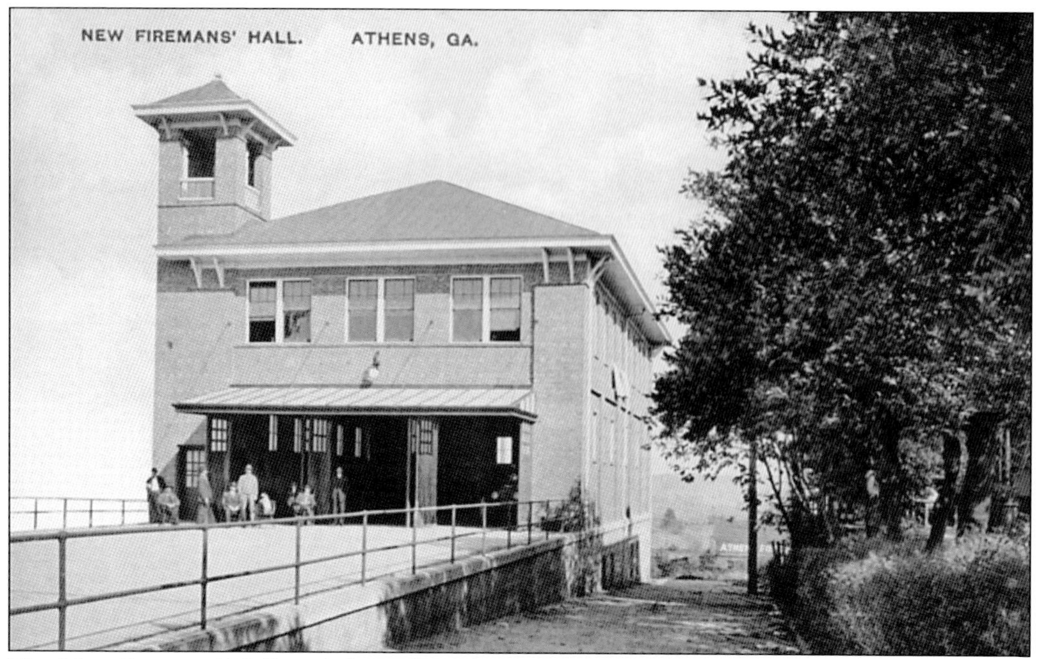

The New Firemans' Hall in Athens, later known as Station Number 1, was built on Thomas Street in 1910.

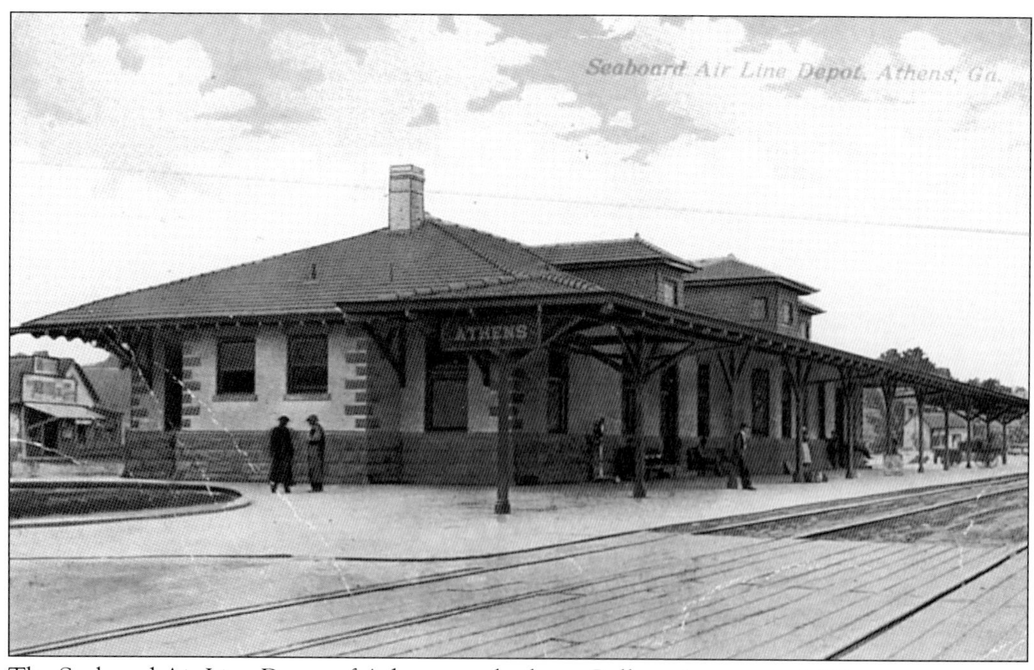

The Seaboard Air Line Depot of Athens was built on College Avenue in 1891.

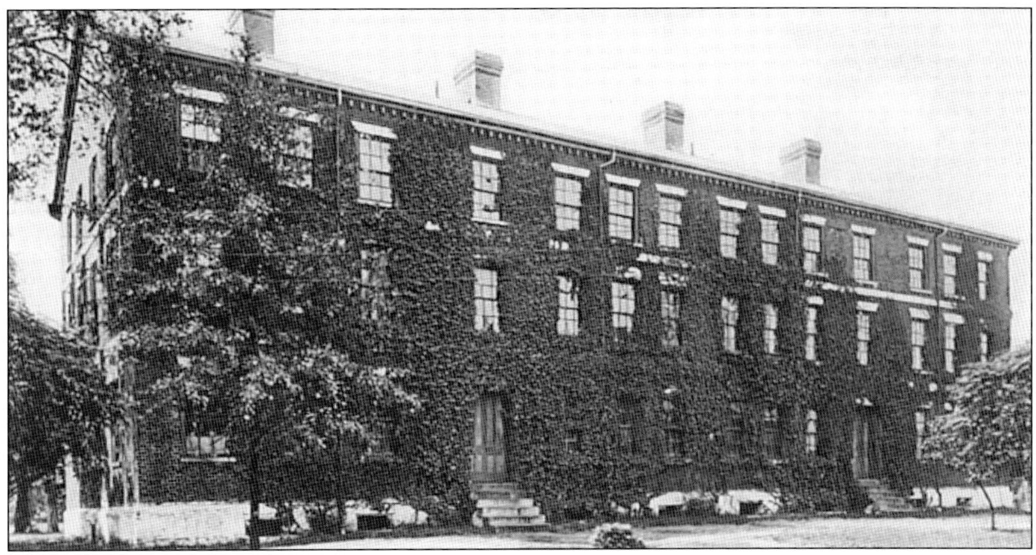

Old College, built on the University of Georgia campus in 1806, is the oldest structure in Athens.

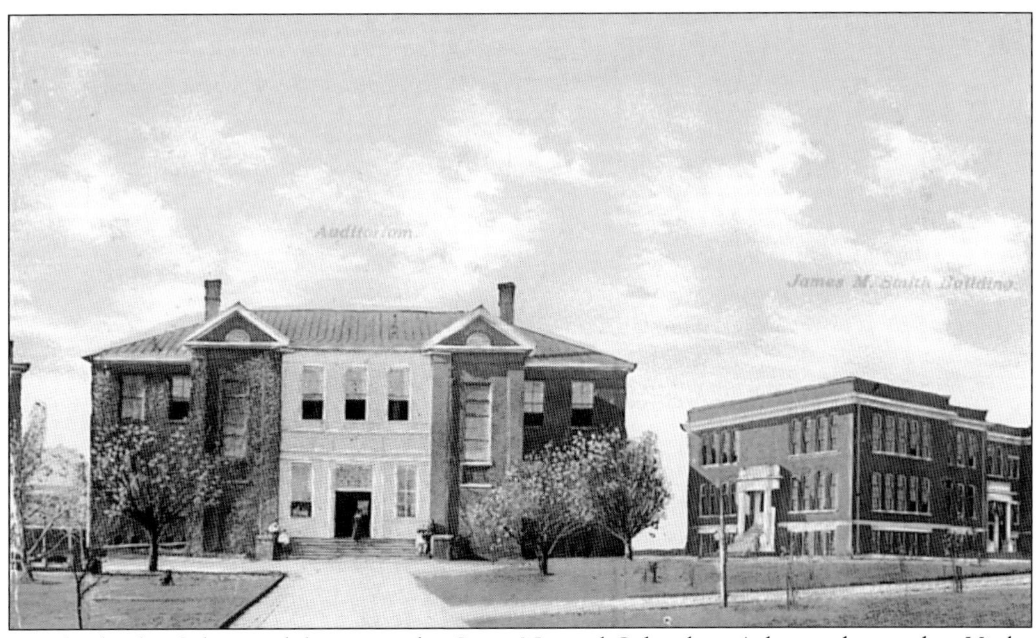

On the back of this card featuring the State Normal School in Athens, the sender, Viola, writes, "Dear Mother—Just a few lines to let you know I arrived safe & it did not rain it was very black here. Yesterday it rained some thing terriable & lighten. Thunder also. No one sleep hardly a wink. Mother said for you to try & come down it would do you good. by-by with love, Viola."

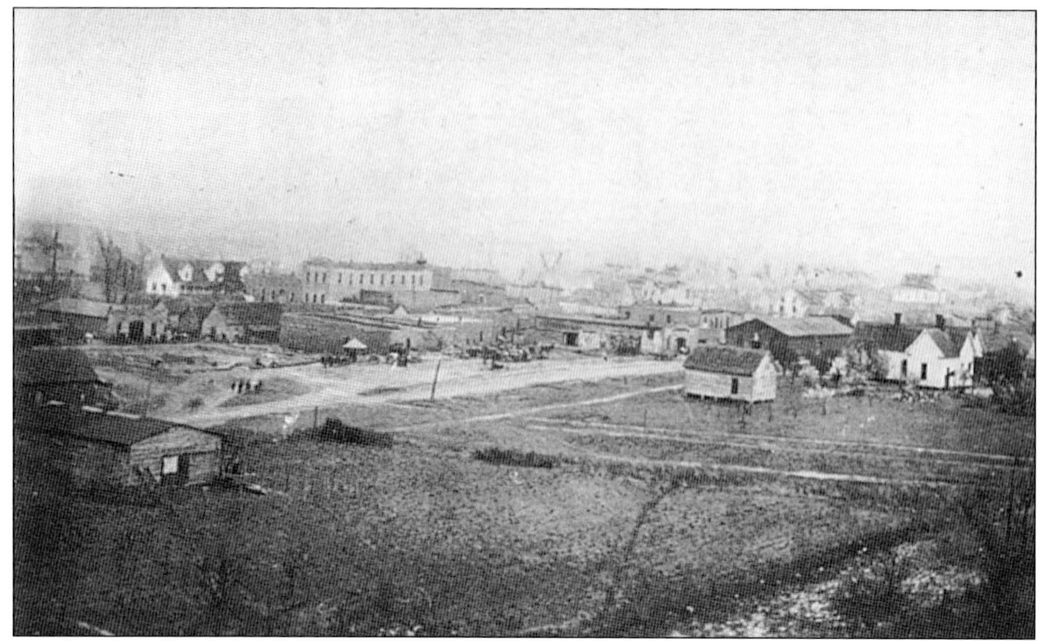

This bird's-eye view of Comer, Georgia, was made about 1908.

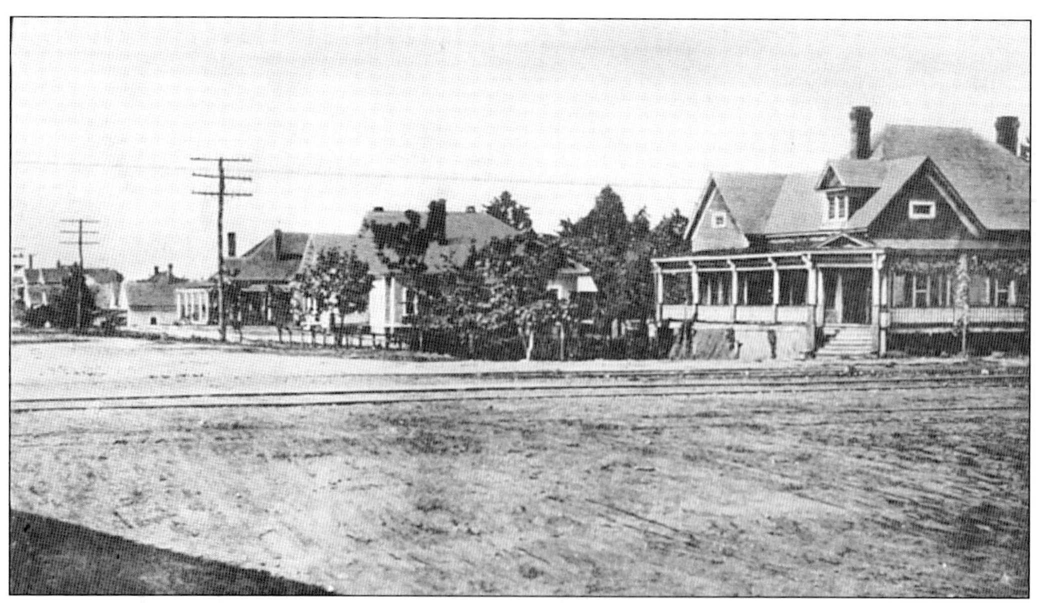

This view of the unpaved South Main Street in Comer was mailed to Miss Emily Dodge in Newcastle, Maine. The message from "Jane" read, "I am in this place now—having a wonderful time. Will see you about the seventh of September."

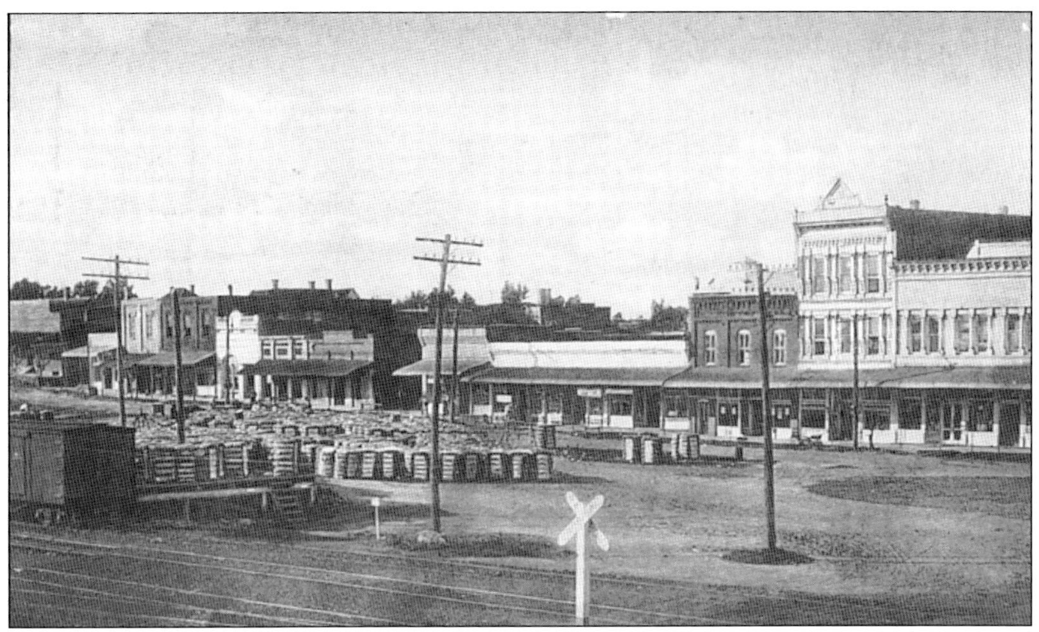

The large cotton bales stacked about in this view of Comer fill the railroad depot platform and overflow into the street.

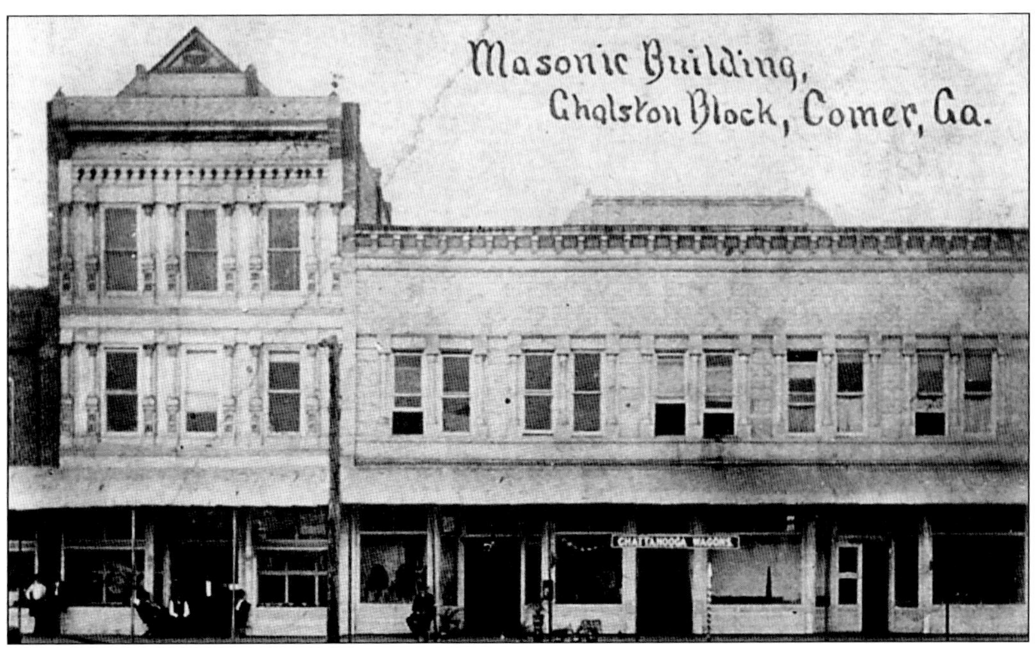

This view of the Masonic Building in Comer includes a sign advertising "Chattanooga Wagons."

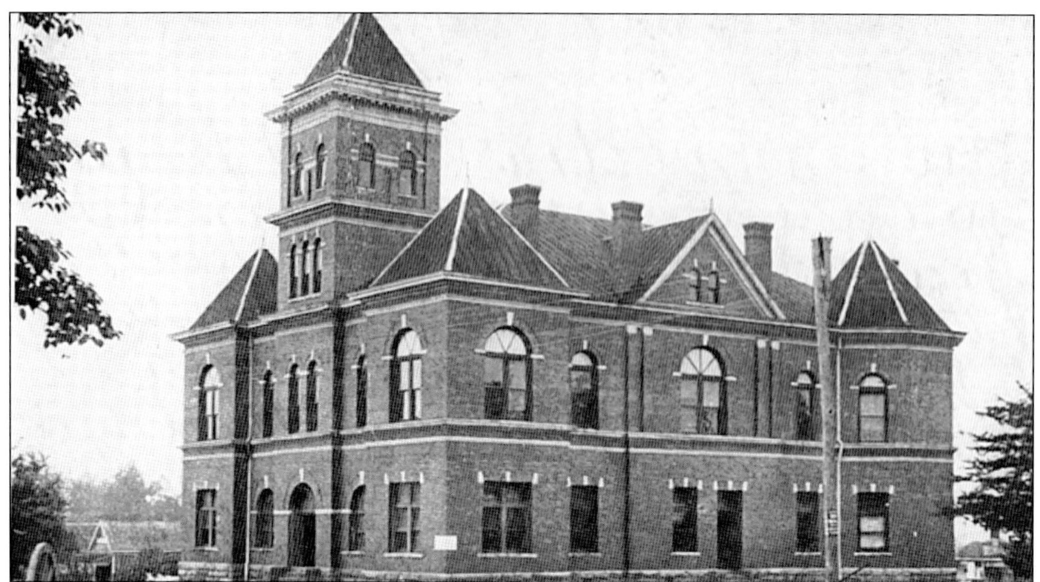

The Madison County Courthouse in Danielsville was built in 1901. The building still stands, but is no longer in use. The message reads, "Rufus my dear boy. I hope you are all well and happy. I have not been feeling well for a week or more that is why I have not wrote sooner. I have not sent for Will yet but I aim to. I have not got the money to spare now. Write as soon as you get this. Your Papa, J.C. Wright." Evidently, the card was never sent, as it bears no stamp or cancellation mark.

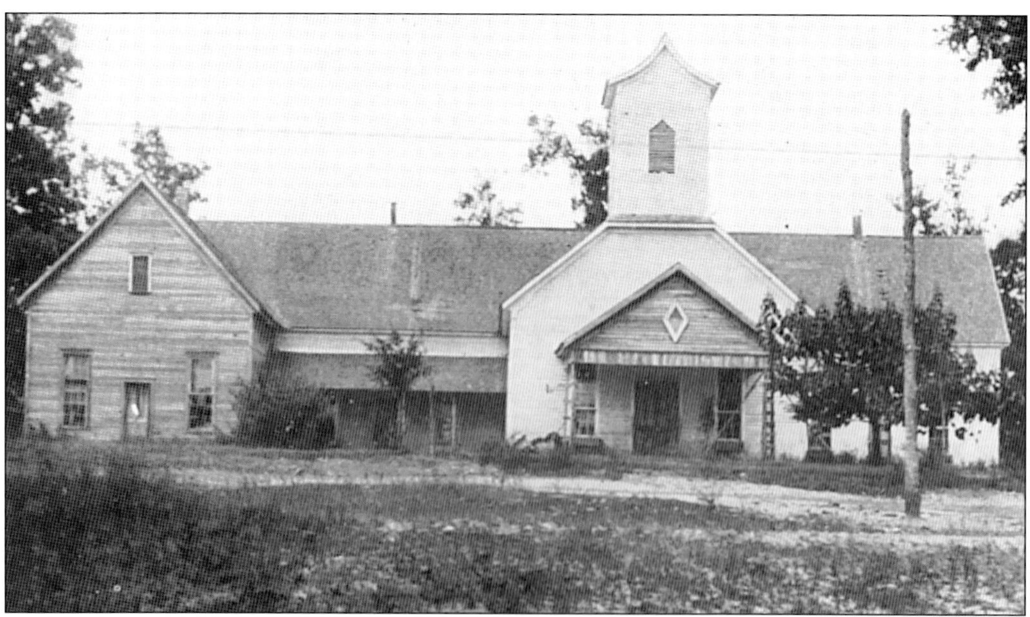

This real-photo post card shows the high school in Danielsville.

Two

Elbert, Franklin, and Hart Counties

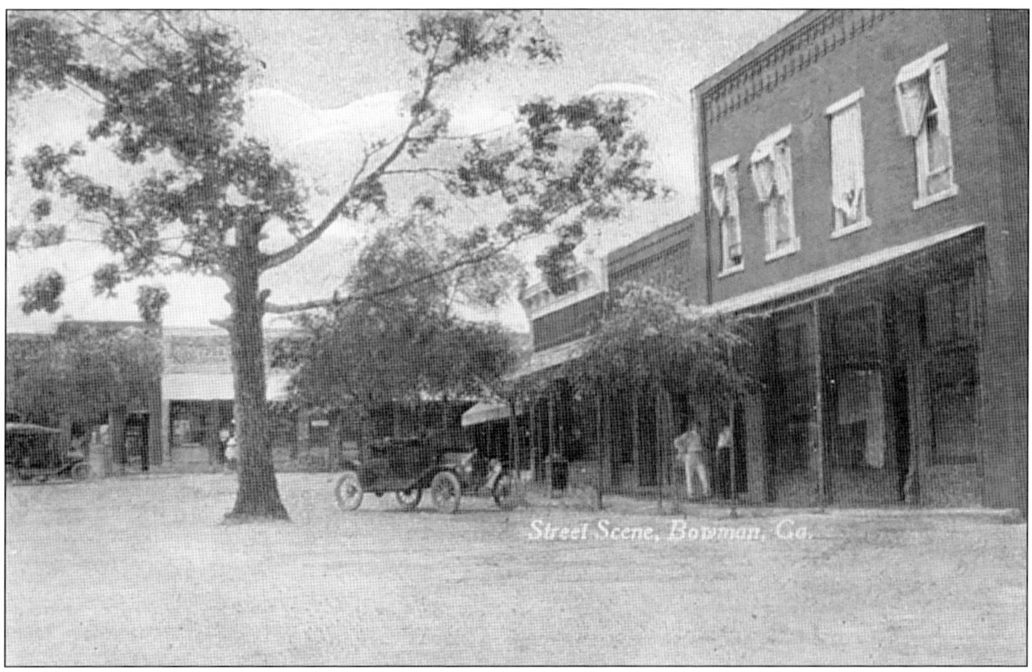

This view of an early street scene in Bowman was sent by R.B.M. to Miss Hazel Hill in Echo, Pennsylvania.

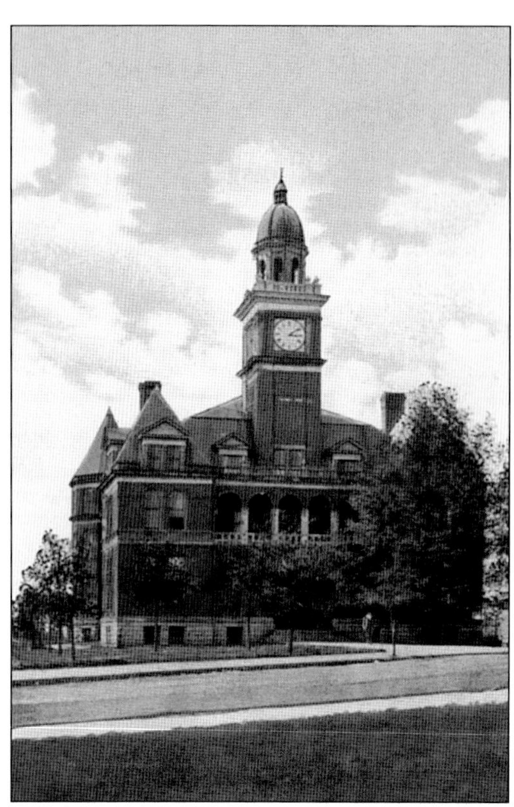

The courthouse in Elberton was built in 1894 at a cost of $35,000. The building was renovated in 1964 and still serves the town.

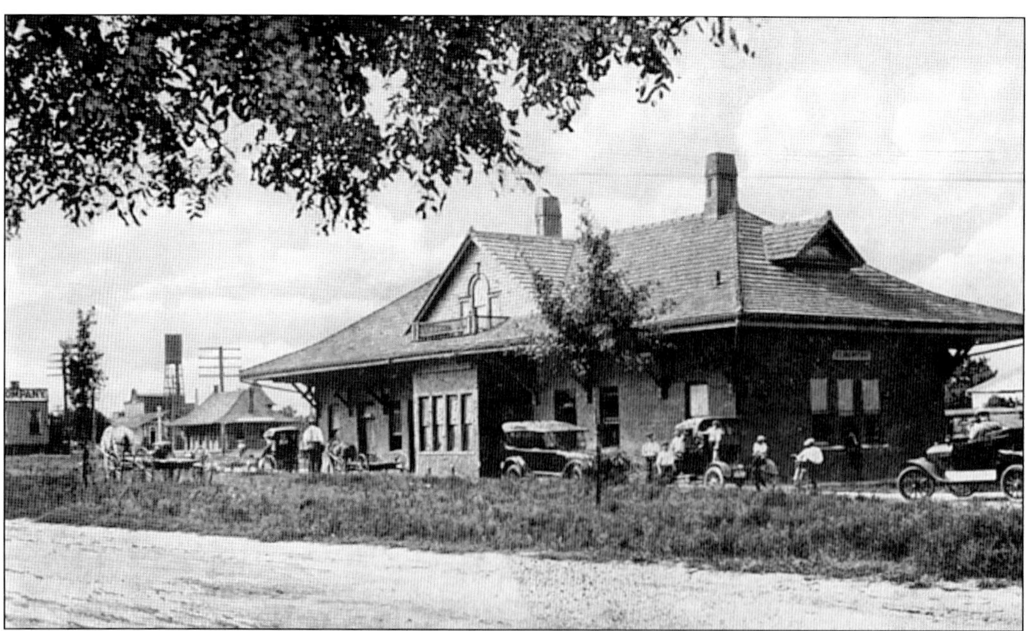

This card, published by the Todd Drug Company of Elberton, shows the Southern Air Line and Southern Railway depots in Elberton.

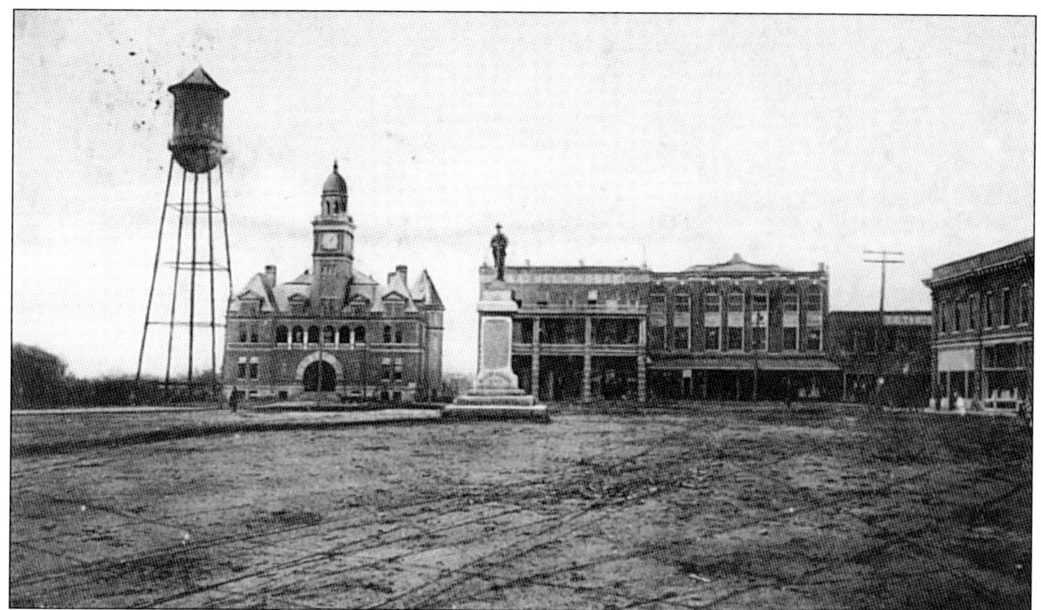

This *c.* 1908 view of Elberton shows the unpaved streets around the courthouse and Confederate Monument. The original monument was unveiled July 15, 1898, but local residents did not approve of its appearance. During the night of August 13, 1900, it was knocked from its base and broken. This replacement apparently pleased everyone and it stands today.

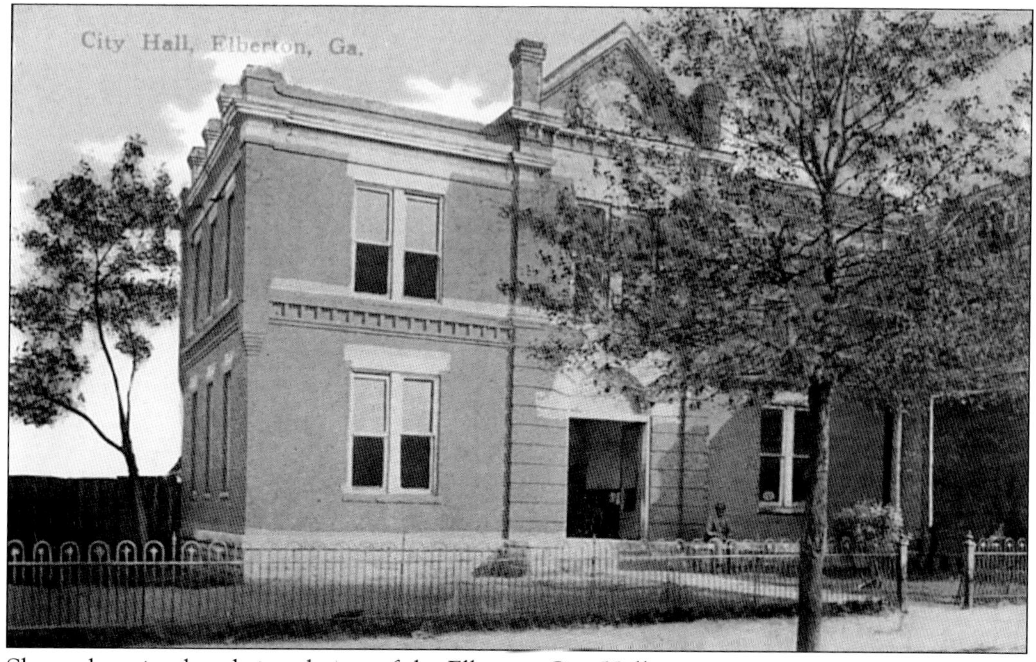

Shown here is a hand-tinted view of the Elberton City Hall.

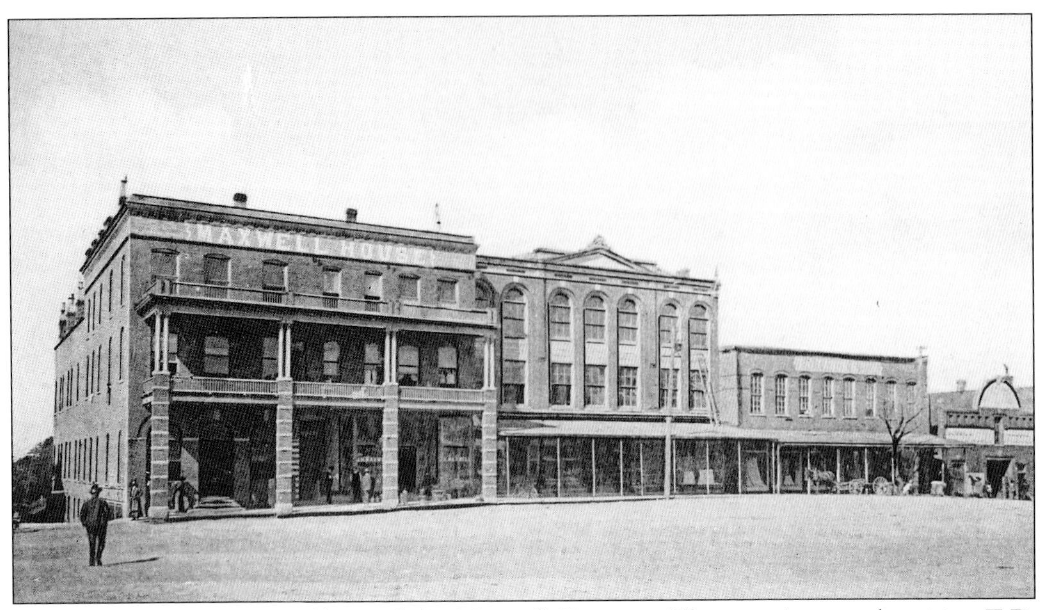

This view shows the post office and the Maxwell House in Elberton. A sign advertising T.D. Tabor and Son, dealers in general merchandise, can be seen to the right.

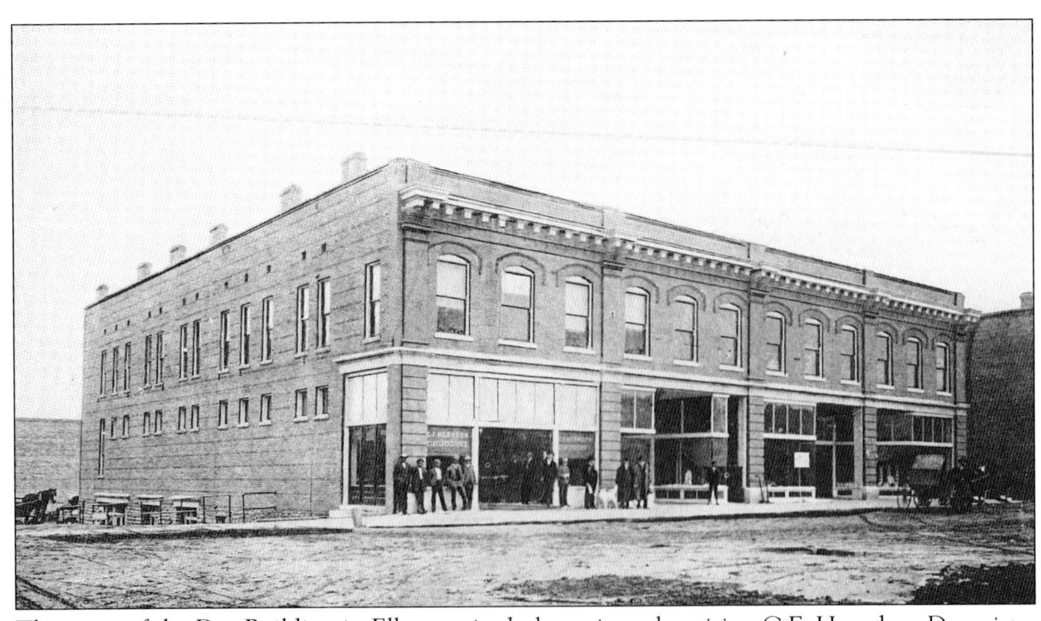

This view of the Day Building in Elberton includes a sign advertising C.F. Herndon, Druggist.

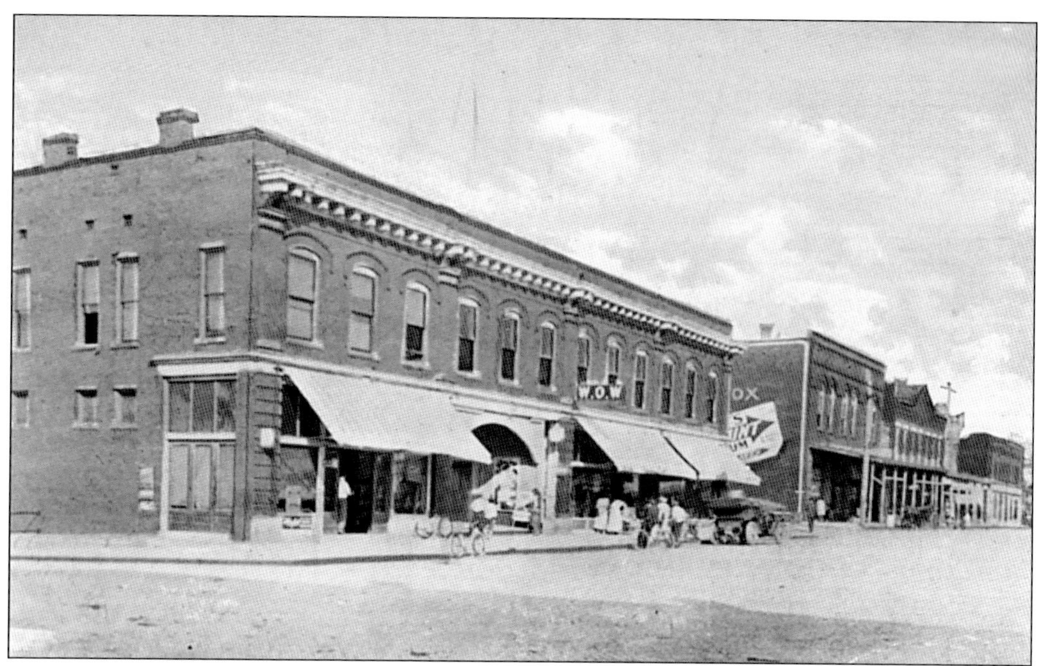

Shown here is the north side of the public square in Elberton. Part of an early advertisement for Wrigley's Spearmint Chewing Gum can be seen painted on the end of one building.

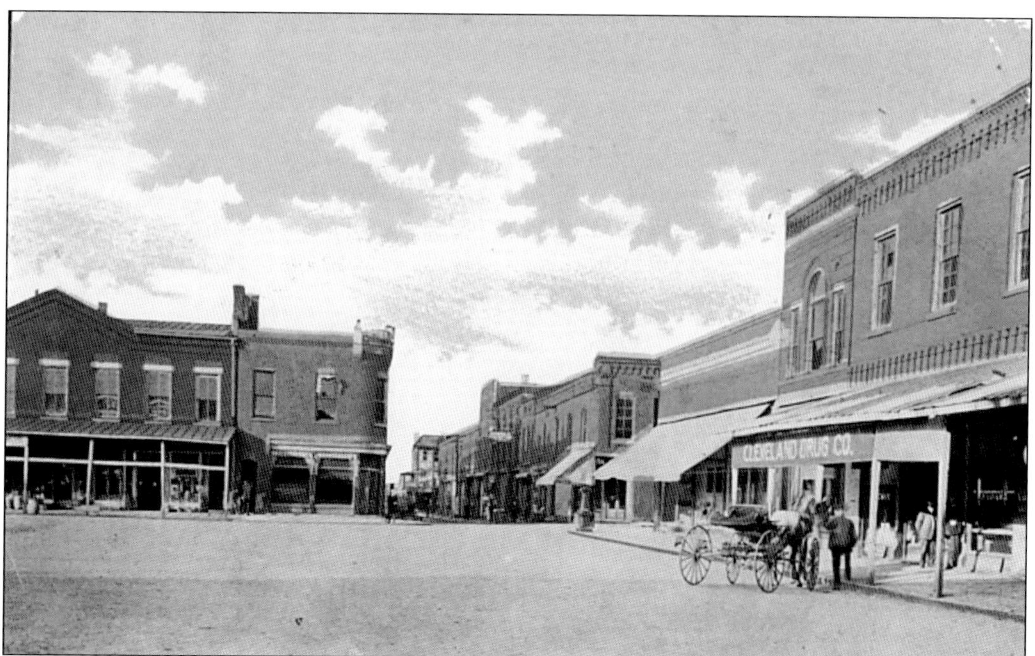

On the back of this post card featuring the east side of the Public Square in Elberton, the sender wrote, "Dear Clara: Got a letter from mama today. Will answer it tomorrow. It is warmer today. This is all the card I could get to send you. Mama says you did nicely at the recital. Good for you. Goodnight, Papa."

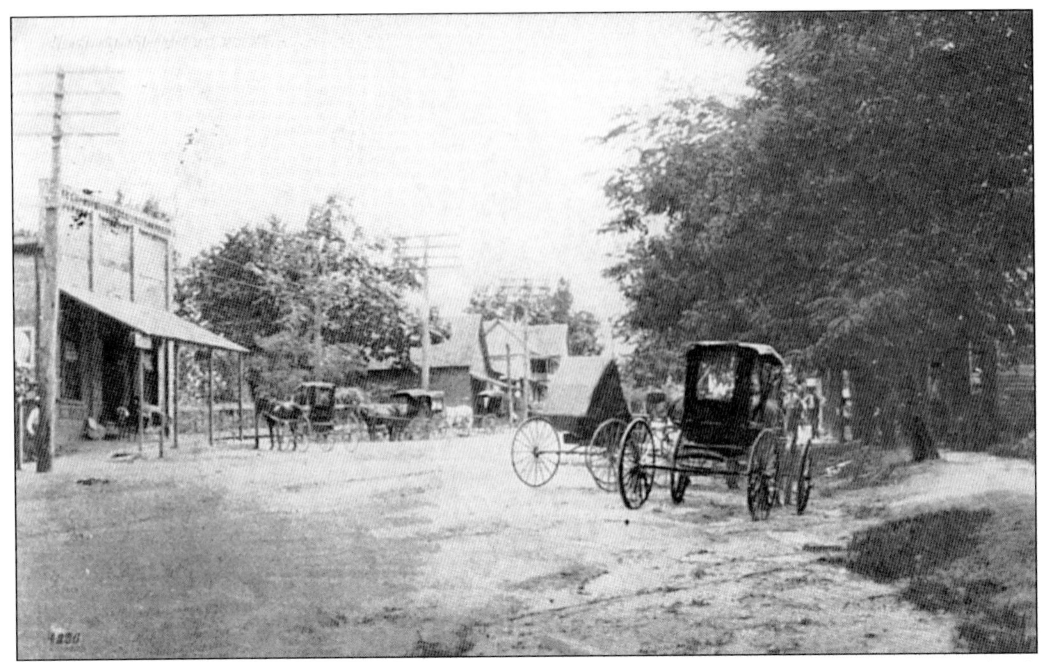

This *c.* 1913 card shows a view up Depot Street looking west in Canon, Georgia. On the back back the sender wrote, "My Dear Papa: How does this look for business. Hope to see you soon. Lots of love, lovingly, your daughter, Daisy Hedden."

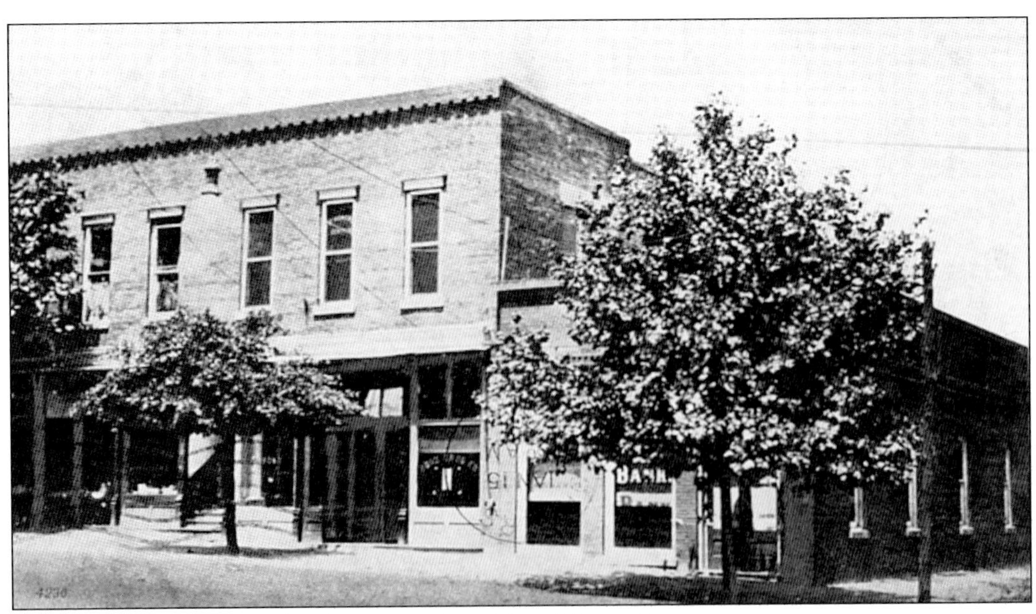

This *c.* 1911 card shows the Canon Bank and Bond Drug Company.

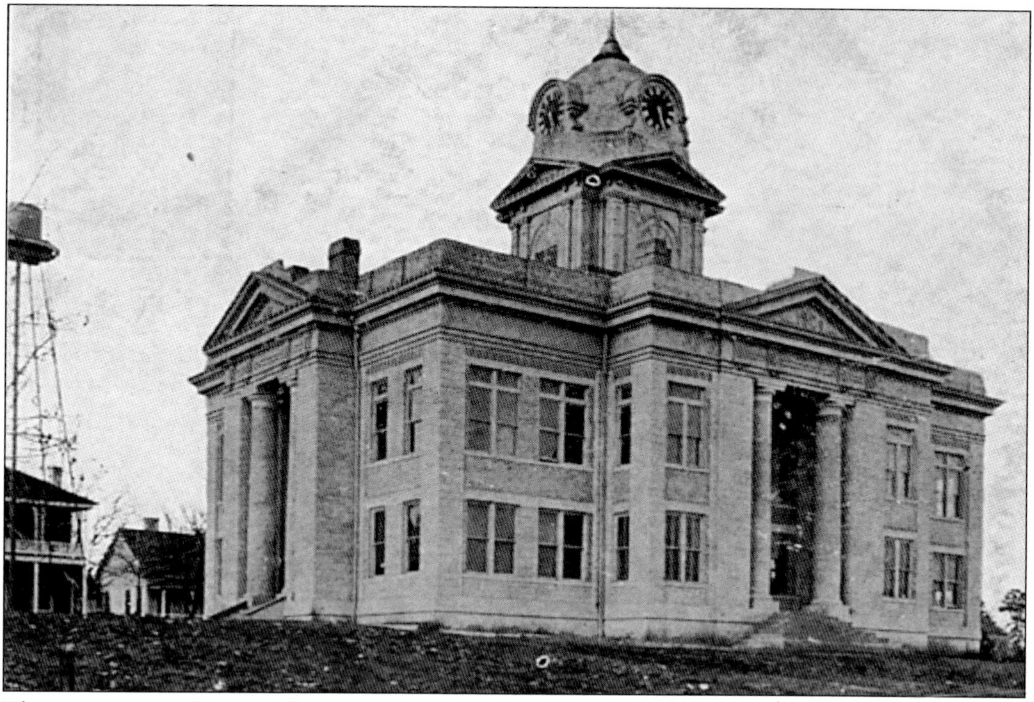

The message on this card featuring the 1906 Franklin County Courthouse in Carnesville and mailed to Lavonia, Georgia, reads, "Am having the best time. Say we are on our way to the mountains. Can't come tomorrow, don't get discouraged will come soon. How is dear old Lavonia? You all must plan for a good time when I come. I drive nearly all the time. Tell S.L. to 'howdy.' Give every body hello for me. A.M.G."

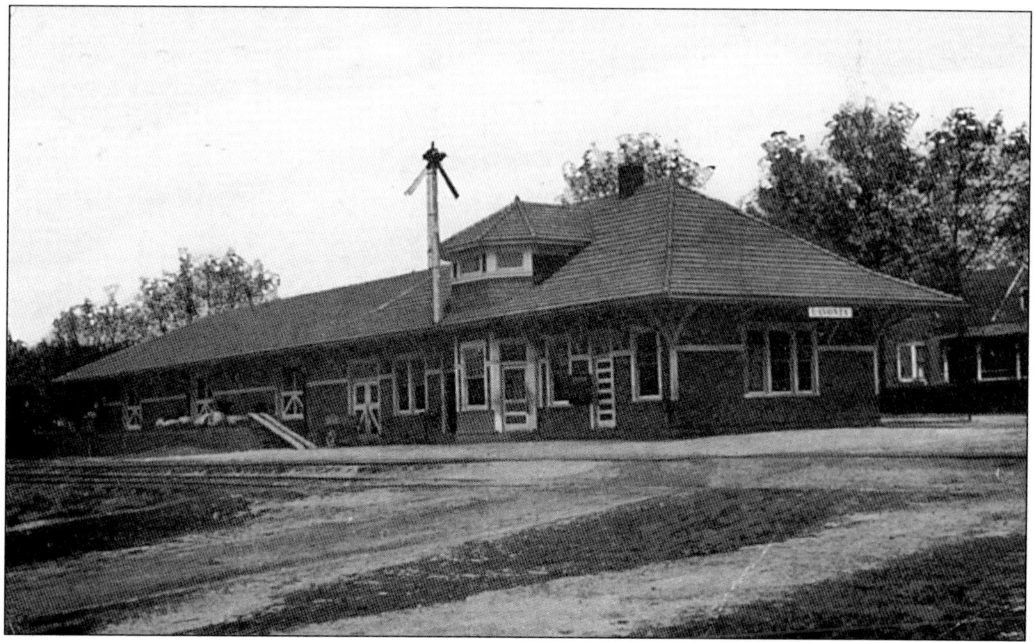

This *c.* 1914 post card shows the Southern Railroad depot in Lavonia.

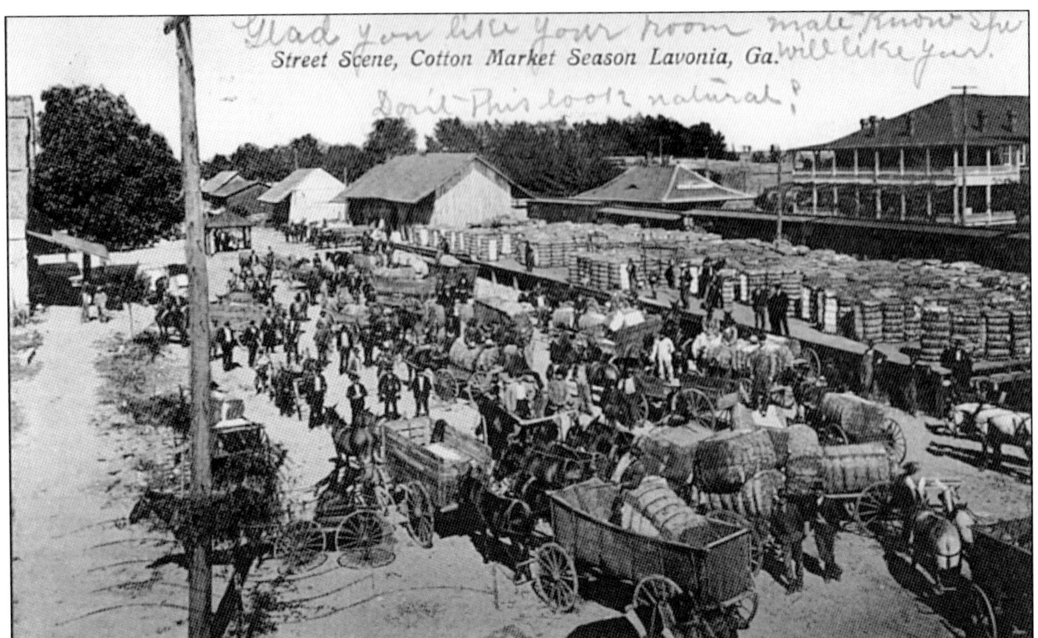

This card, aptly labeled "Street Scene, Cotton Market Season Lavonia, Ga.," shows the large number of wagons and cotton bales being brought to market. In the days before extensive fertilizing and modern farming practices, farmers would average one-half a bale of cotton per acre. To produce a 500-pound bale of ginned cotton, a worker would have to pick about 1,500 pounds of cotton. The large number of bales here represent hours of back-breaking work.

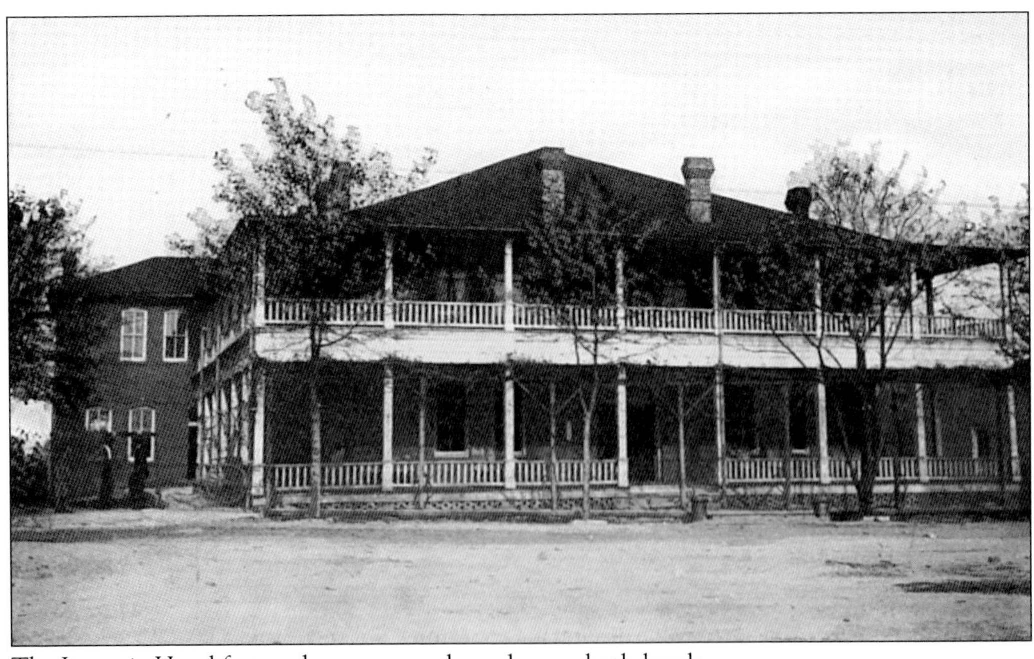

The Lavonia Hotel featured wrap-around porches on both levels.

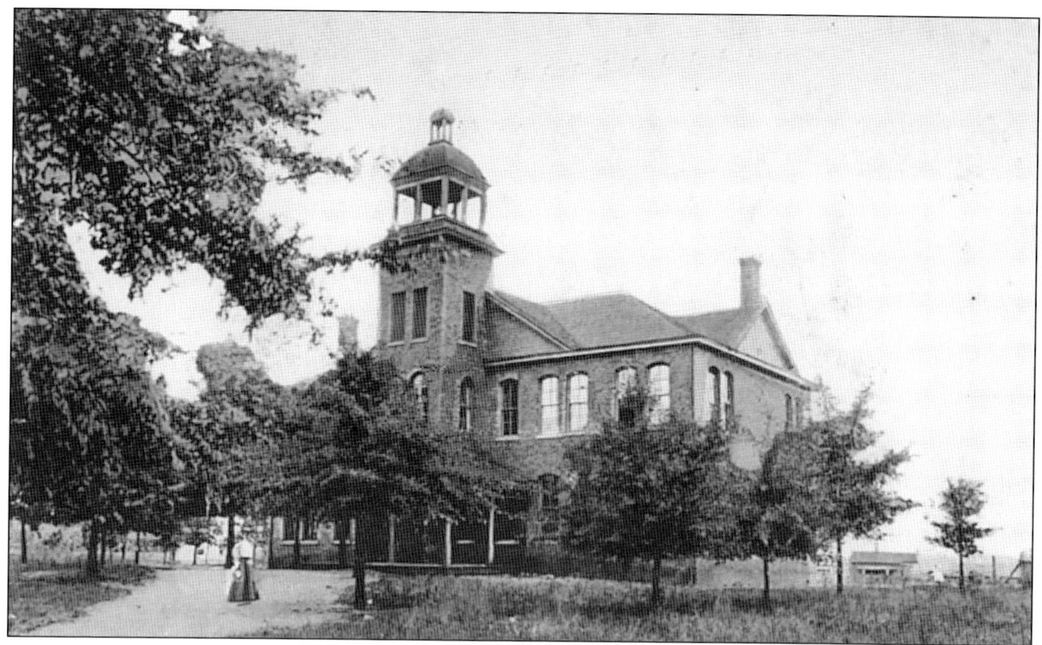

The Lavonia Graded School is shown in this *c.* 1909 post card.

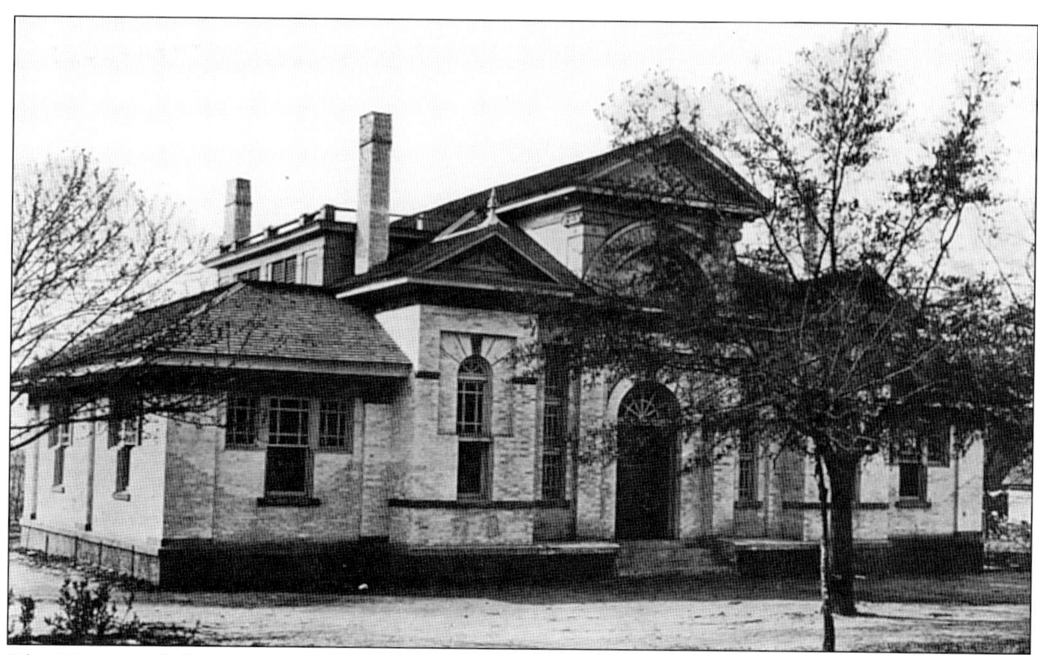

The Carnegie Library in Lavonia is shown in this post card. The library was one of many created across the country with money provided by Andrew Carnegie, the philanthropist.

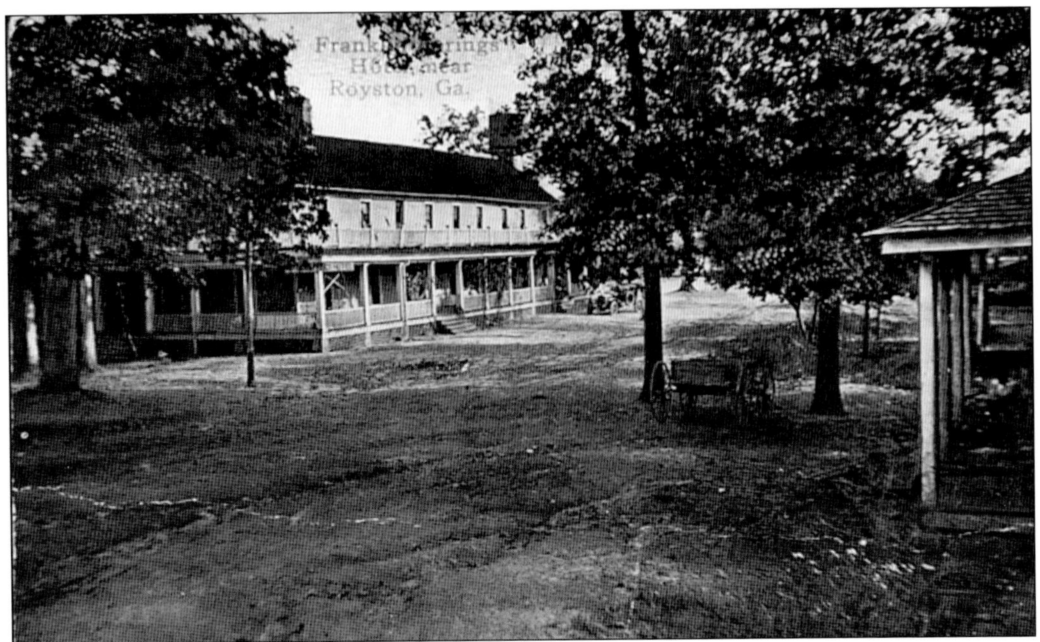

The Franklin Springs Hotel in Royston is shown in this scenic view, *c.* 1913.

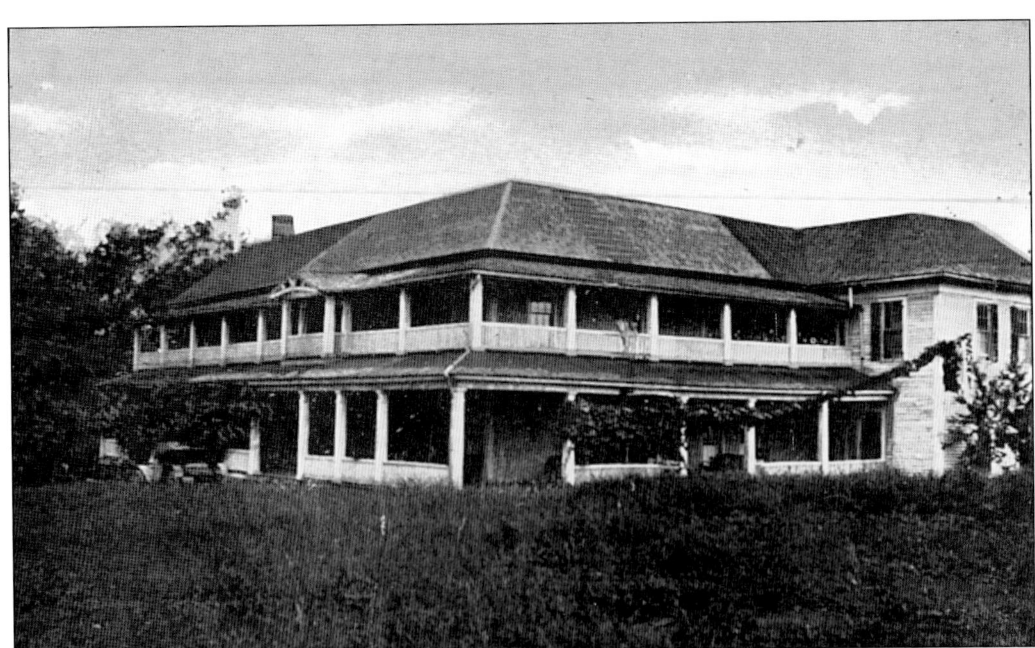

The relatively small community of Franklin Springs needed two hotels to accommodate the visitors who came to "take the waters" for their health. This one was named Spring View Hotel.

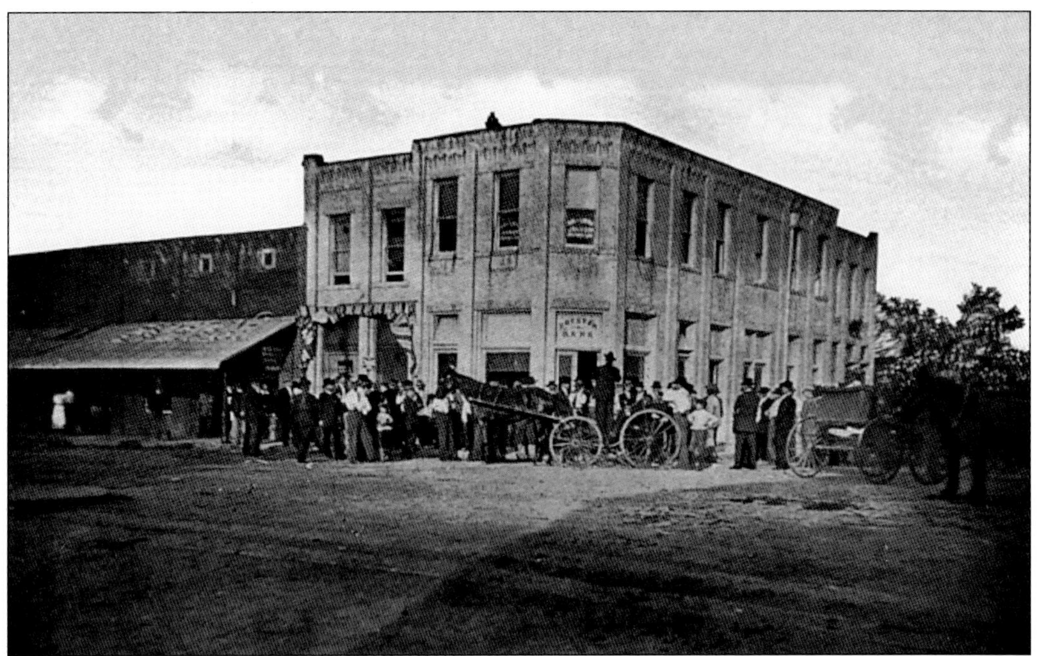

This Royston street scene, taken in front of the Royston Bank building, shows a crowd of people evidently listening to a speaker who is standing in the buggy. In 1910 the president of the Royston Bank was B.L. Bond and J.F. Lee was the cashier.

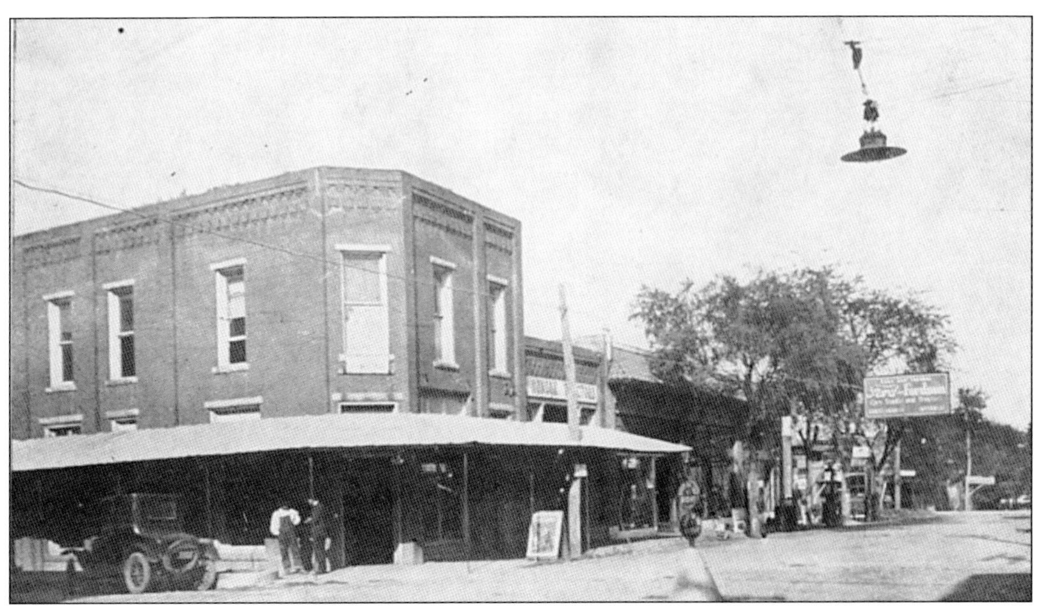

This post card features a concrete traffic sign in the middle of the street in Royston. Suspended across the street on the right is a sign advertising Ford and Fordson cars, trucks, and tractors.

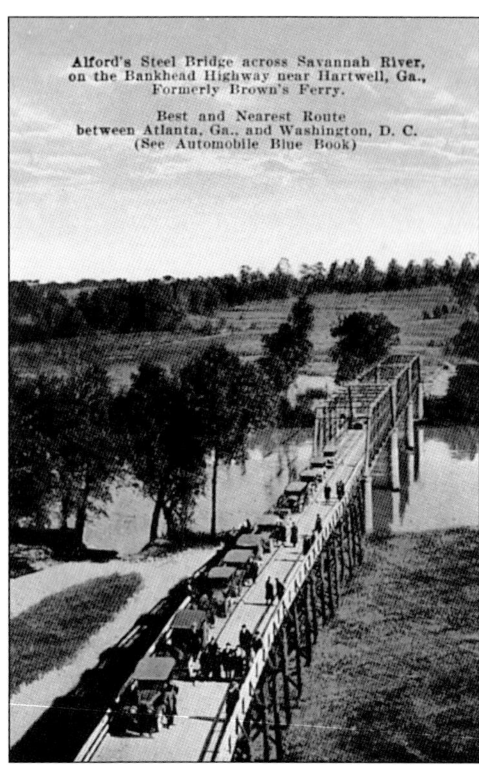

Early automobiles are shown here crossing the Savannah River near Hartwell via the new Alford's Steel Bridge, which replaced Brown's Ferry (pictured in the post card below).

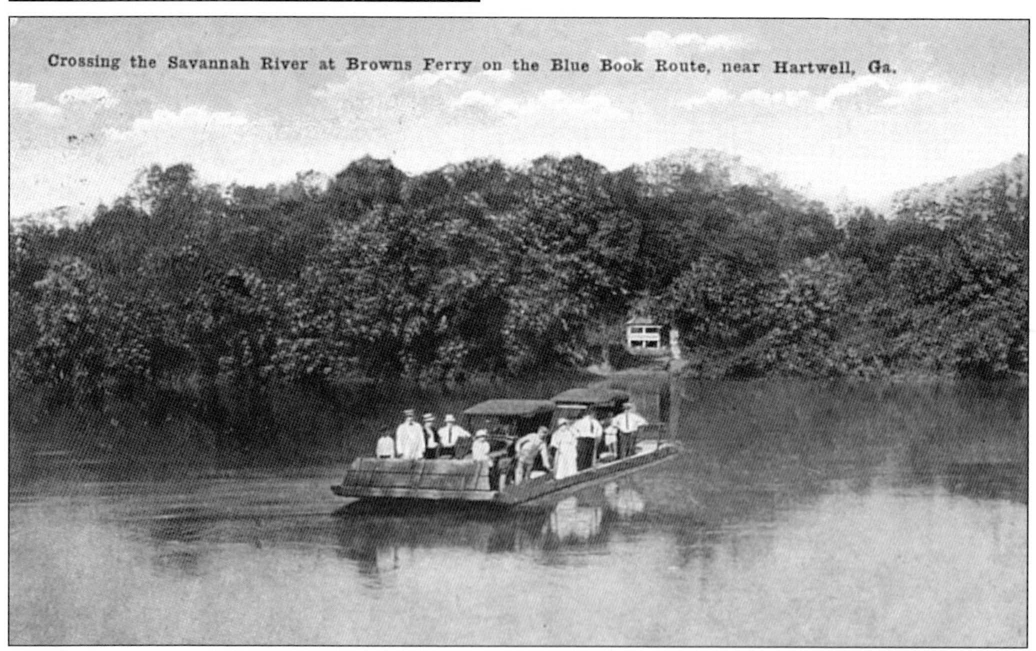

Automobile passengers cross the Savannah River at Browns Ferry, near Hartwell, in this *c.* 1916 post card. The message on the card mailed from Hartwell to Elberton reads, "Hello Lina, What are you doing these days? Going to school I guess. Didn't you enjoy the Friday I was there? I certainly did. O, you raisin! Our school closed Tuesday on account of measles and whooping cough. Write to me. Lovingly, Mildred."

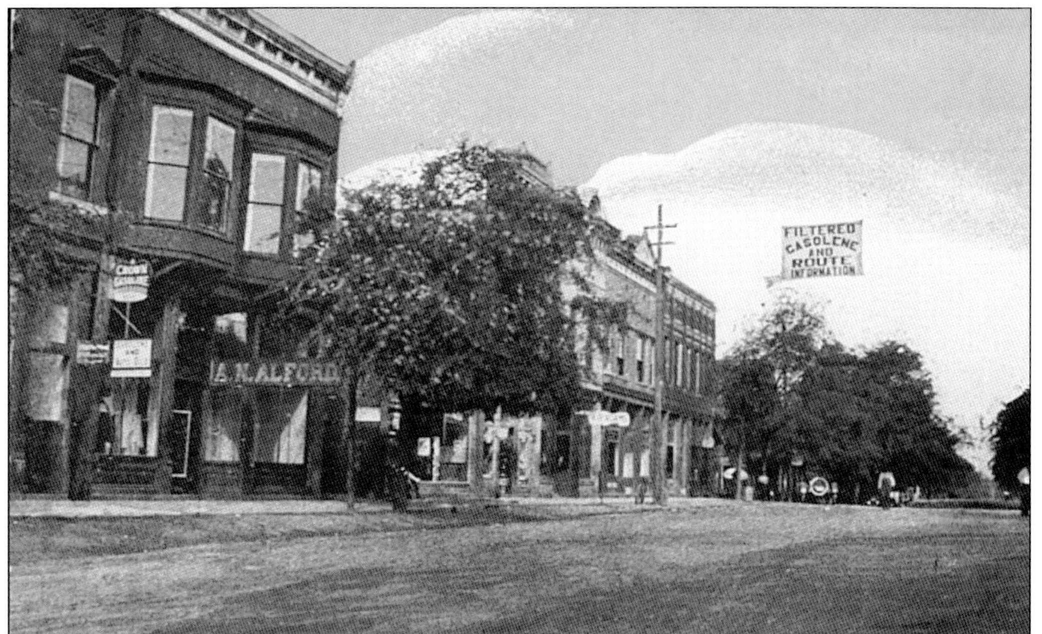

Notice the banner advertising "Filtered Gasolene and Route Information" in this view of the business section of Hartwell. A.N. Alford's store on the left side of this view dealt in general merchandise.

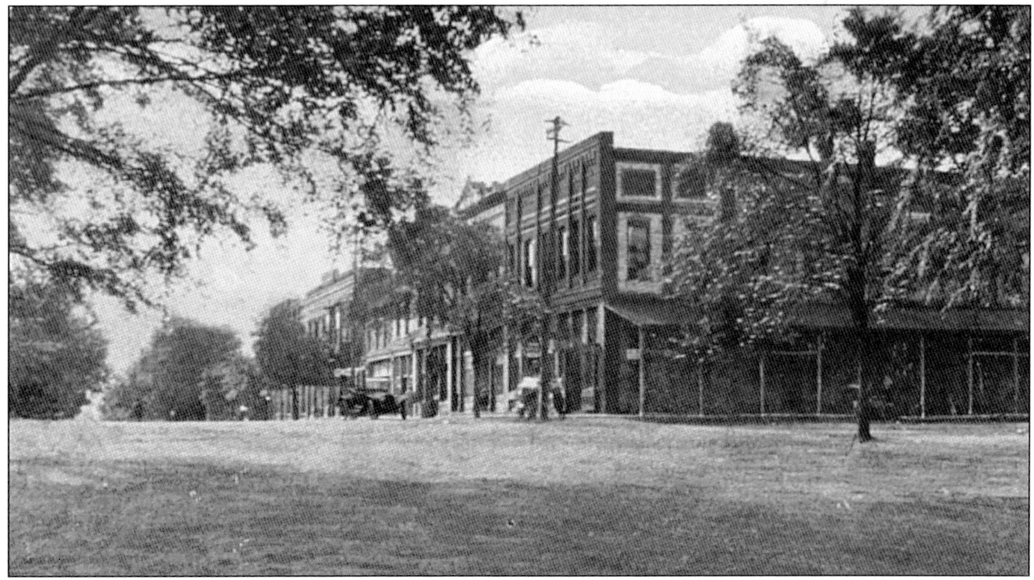

This post card, published by Herndon's Drug Store in Hartwell, shows another view of the business section of the town.

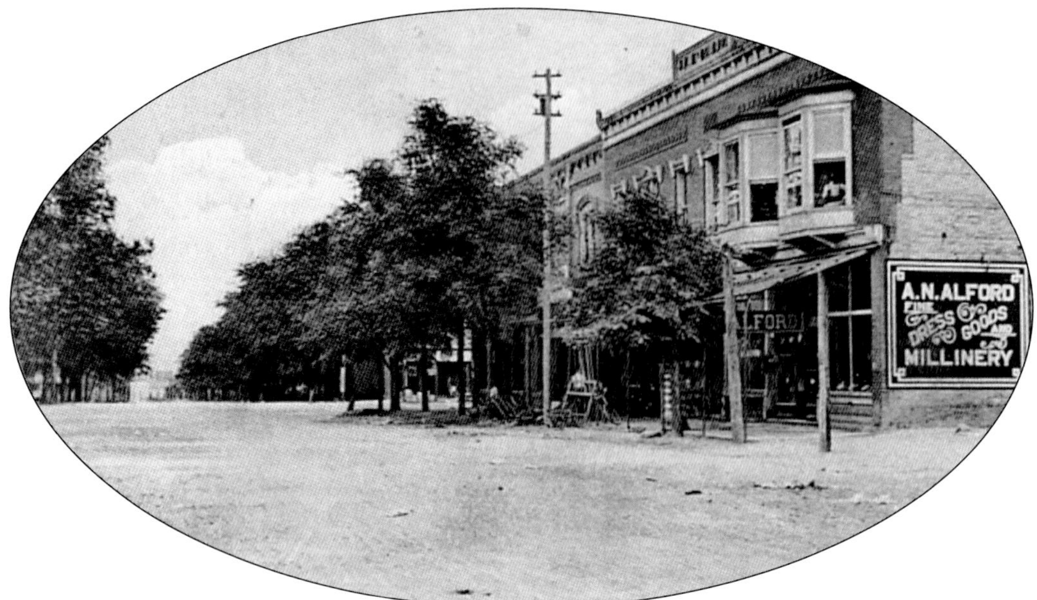

Business seems to be slow on Howell Street, Hartwell, in this *c.* 1913 post card. The street was named for Athenian Howell Cobb, the attorney who assisted local residents in having their town named county seat. Cobb served as governor of Georgia from 1852 to 1853, was the secretary of the treasury in President James Buchanan's cabinet, and was a major general in the Confederate Army during the War between the States.

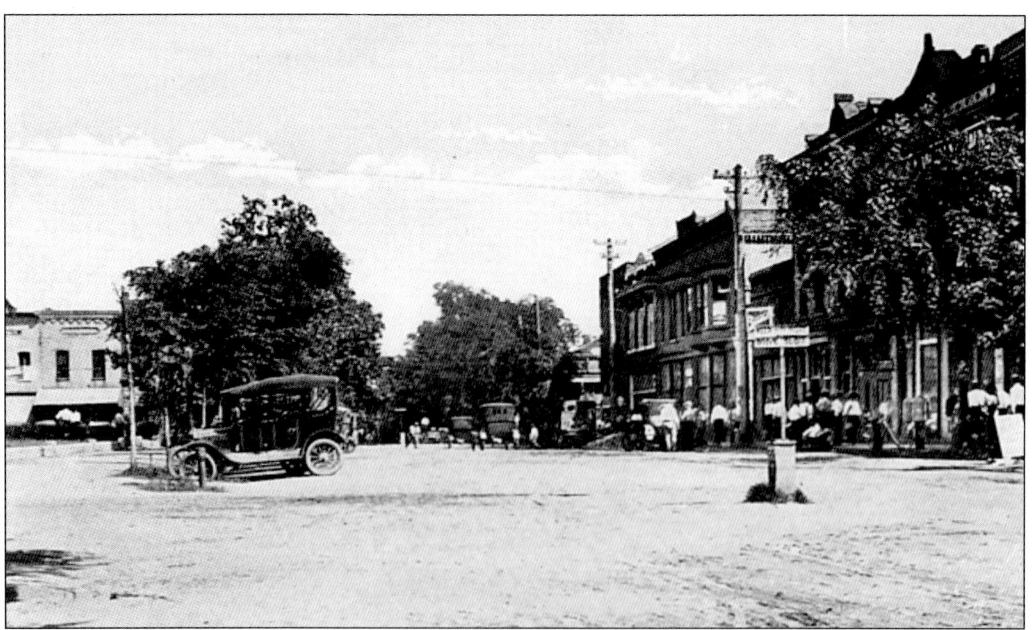

Hartwell's business district is a little busier in this post card, published by the E.C. Kropp Company, of Milwaukee.

Three

Greene, Oglethorpe, Taliaferro, and Wilkes Counties

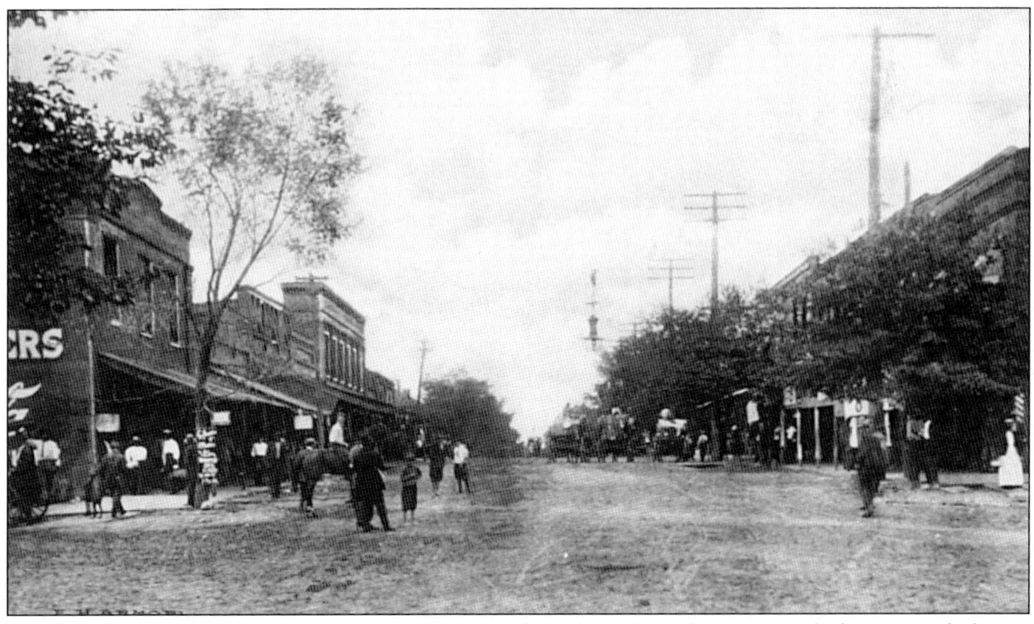

The bustling but unpaved main street in Greensboro has a "modern" street light suspended over it in this *c.* 1914 view.

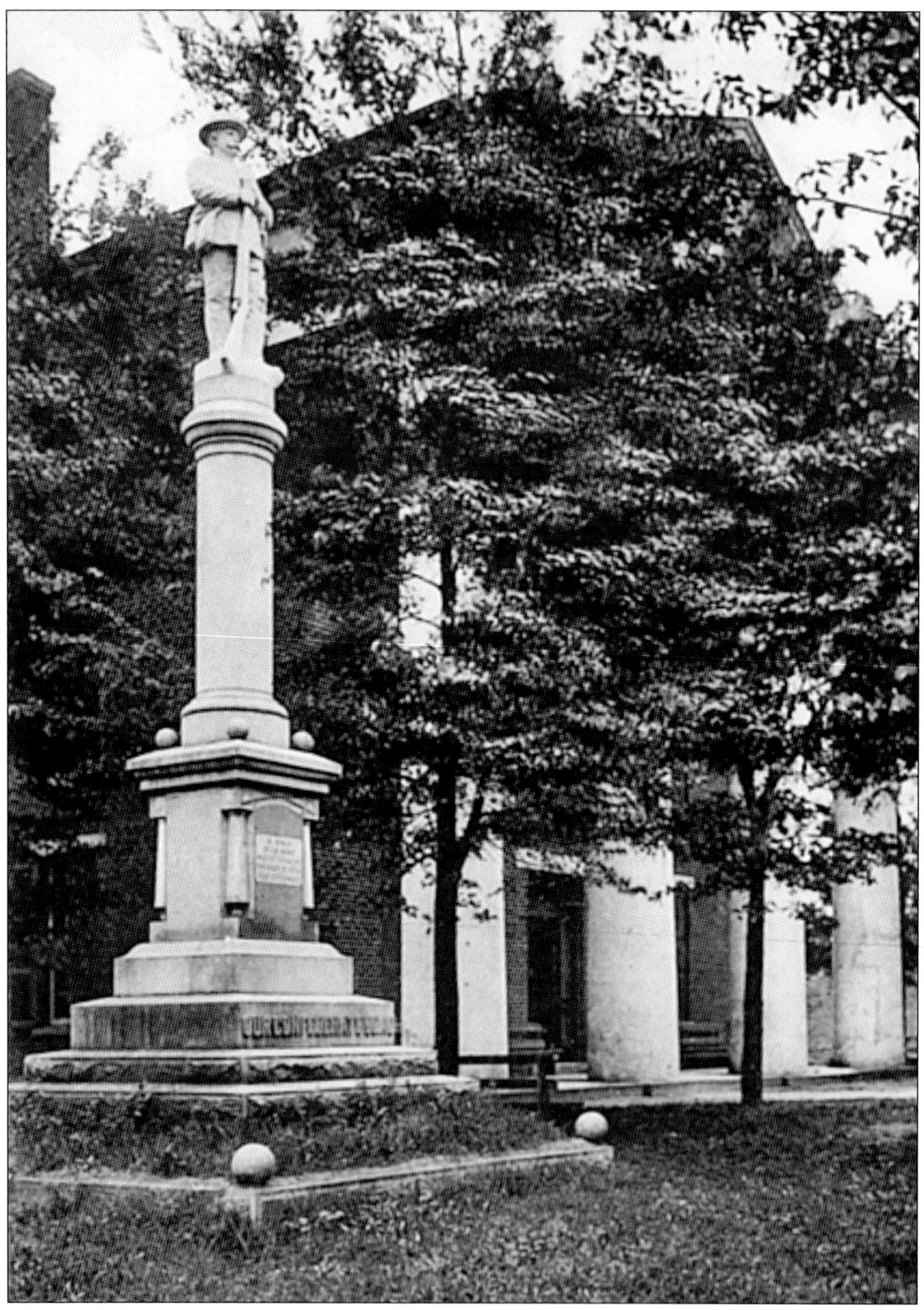

The Confederate Monument in Greensboro was unveiled on the lawn in front of the Greene County Courthouse in August 1898. The courthouse, built in 1849, is the third oldest in Georgia.

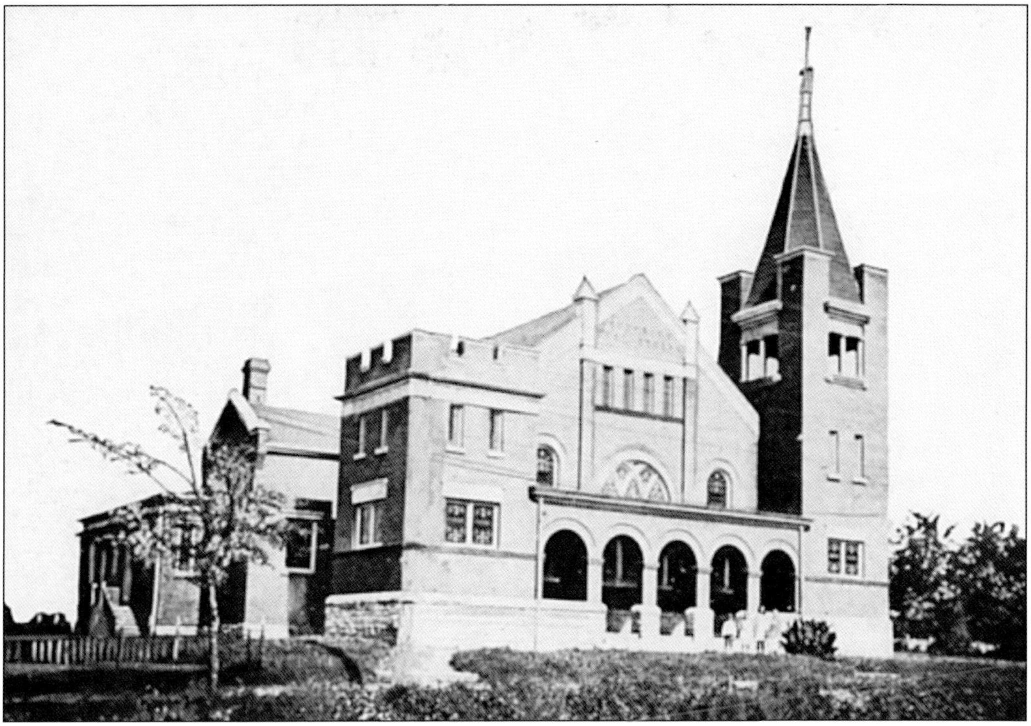

Yet another well-known publisher of post cards, Curt Teich & Company of Chicago, published this view of the Baptist church in Greensboro.

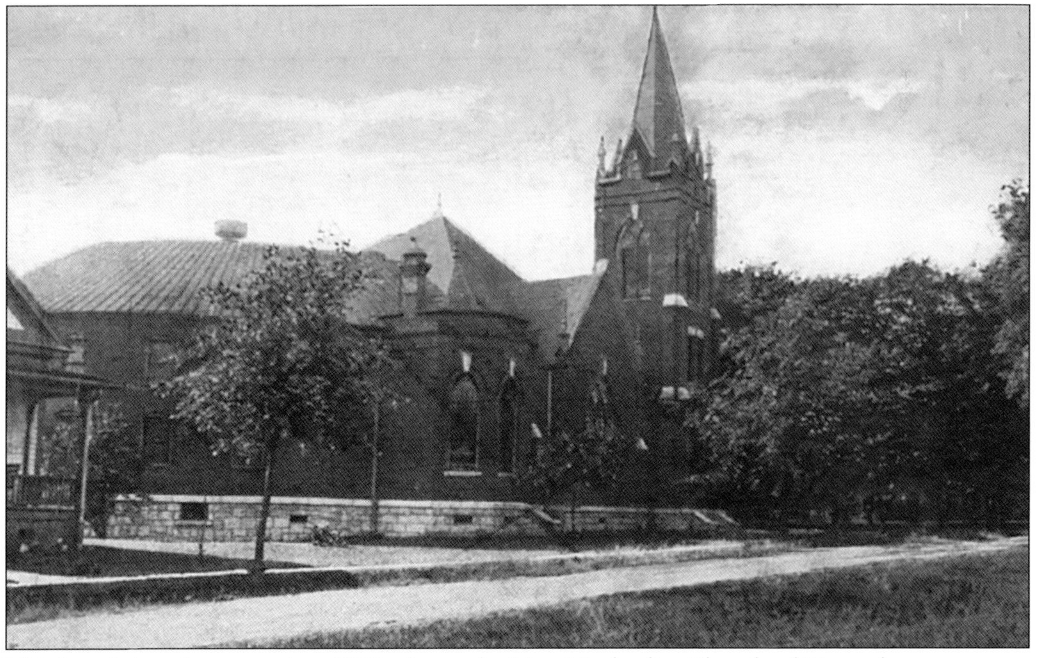

This hand-tinted post card, c. 1919, shows the First Methodist Church of Greensboro.

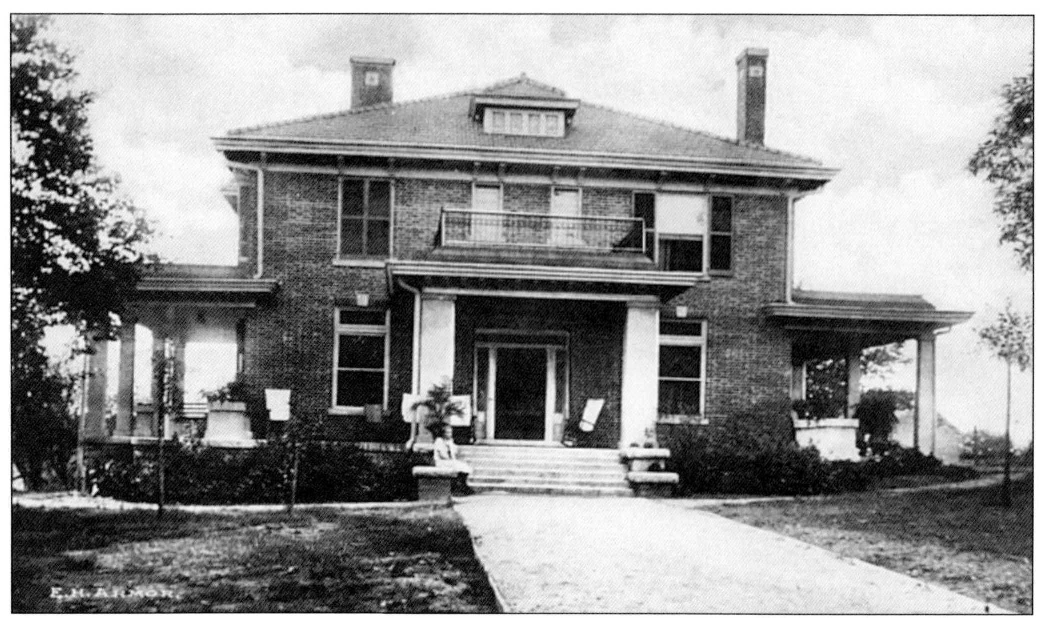

The home of the Honorable J.G. Faust, of Greensboro, is featured in this Albertype post card.

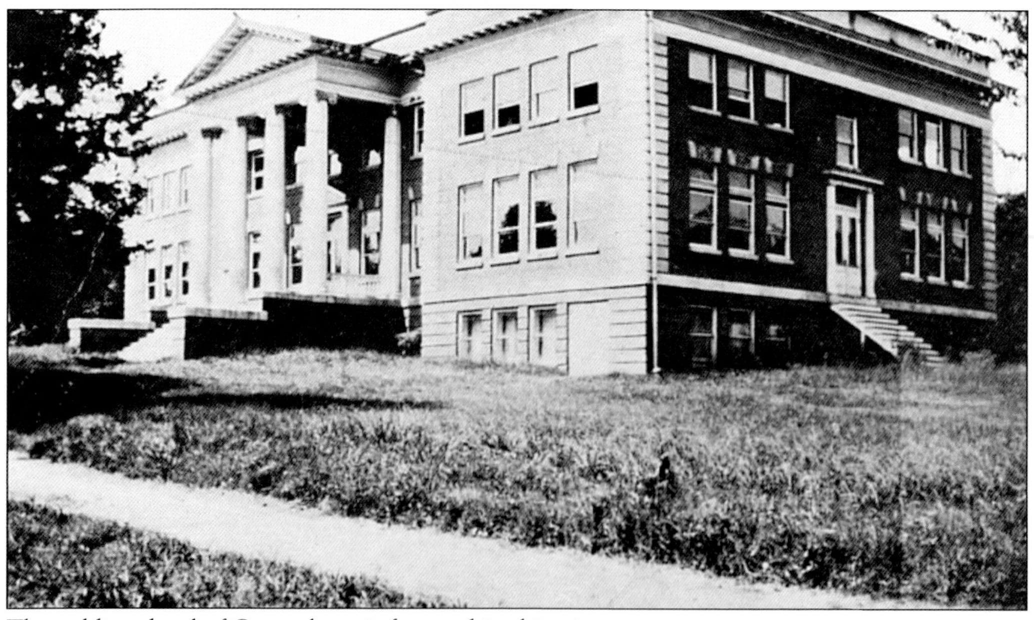

The public school of Greensboro is featured in this view.

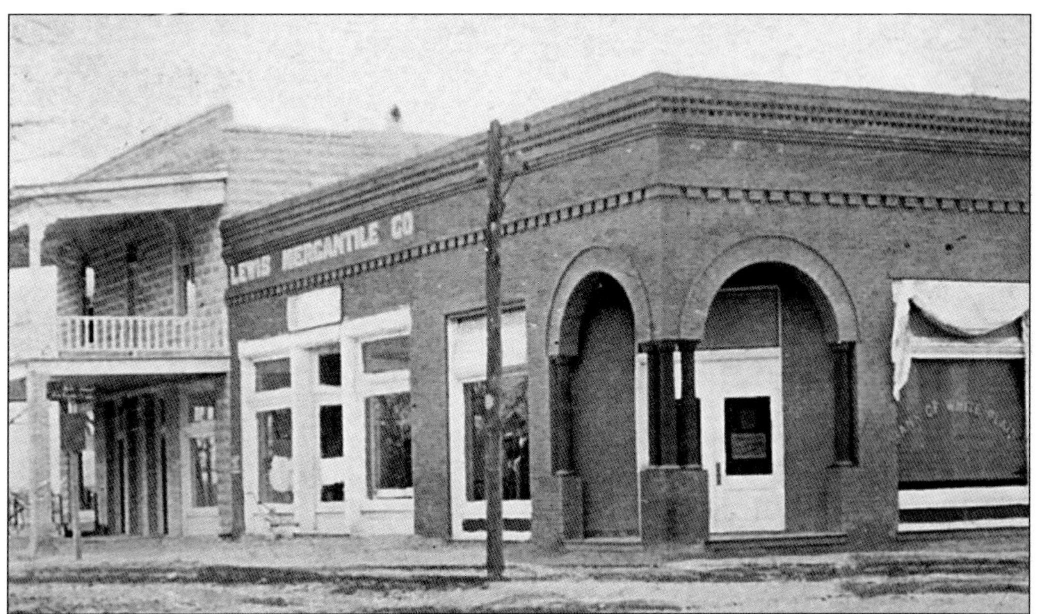

This *c.* 1908 card of White Plains includes three town landmarks—the Clark Hotel, the Lewis Mercantile Company, and the Bank of White Plains.

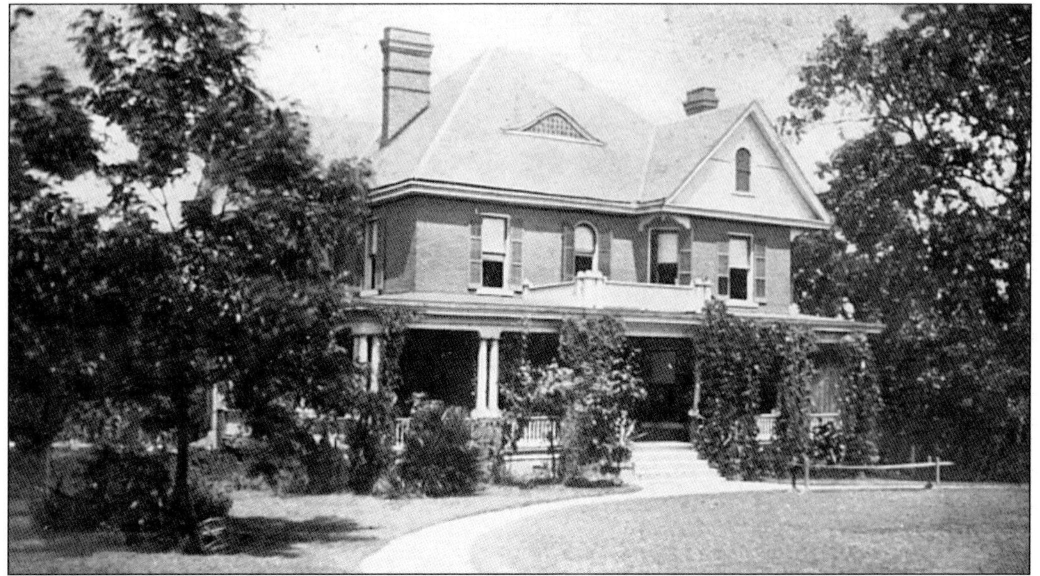

This is Judge Samuel H. Sibley's home in Union Point.

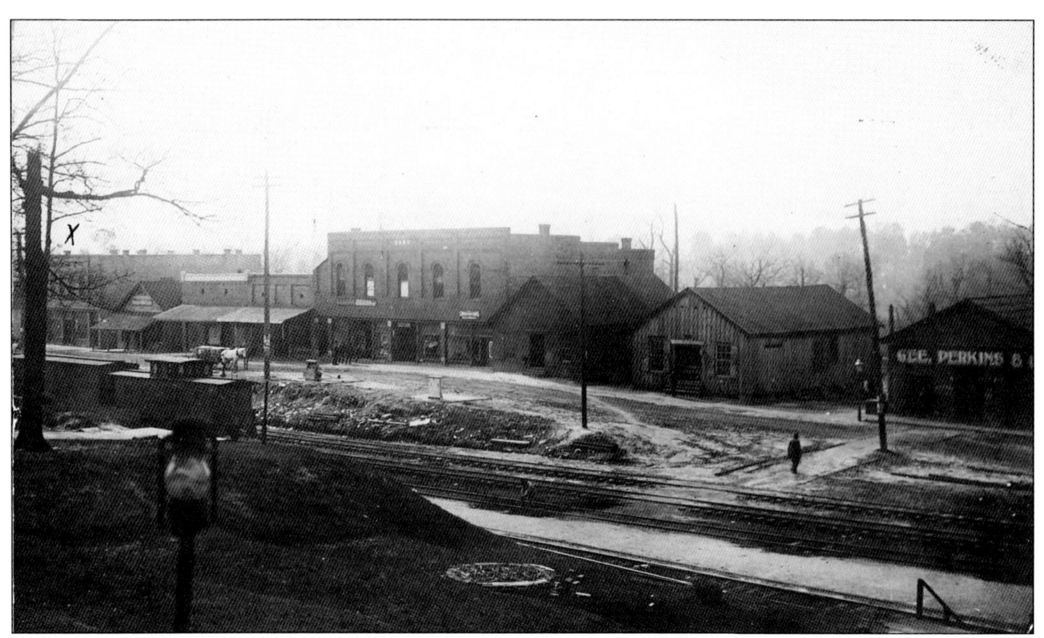

This 1906 real-photo view shows the business district of Union Point.

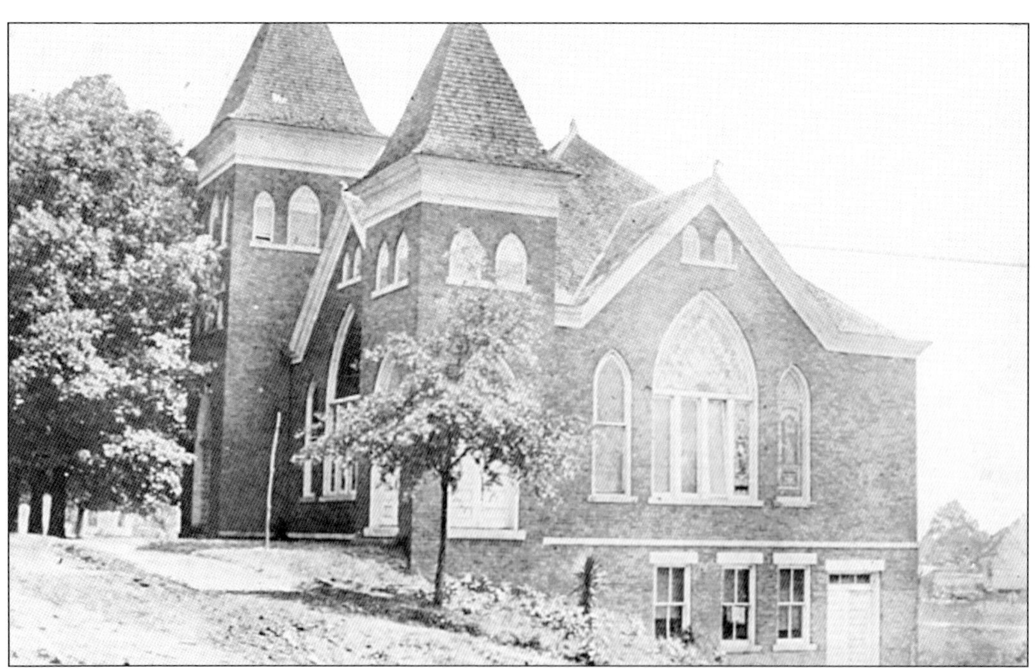

Churches have long been a favorite of post card photographers. This c. 1917 card shows the Presbyterian church in Union Point.

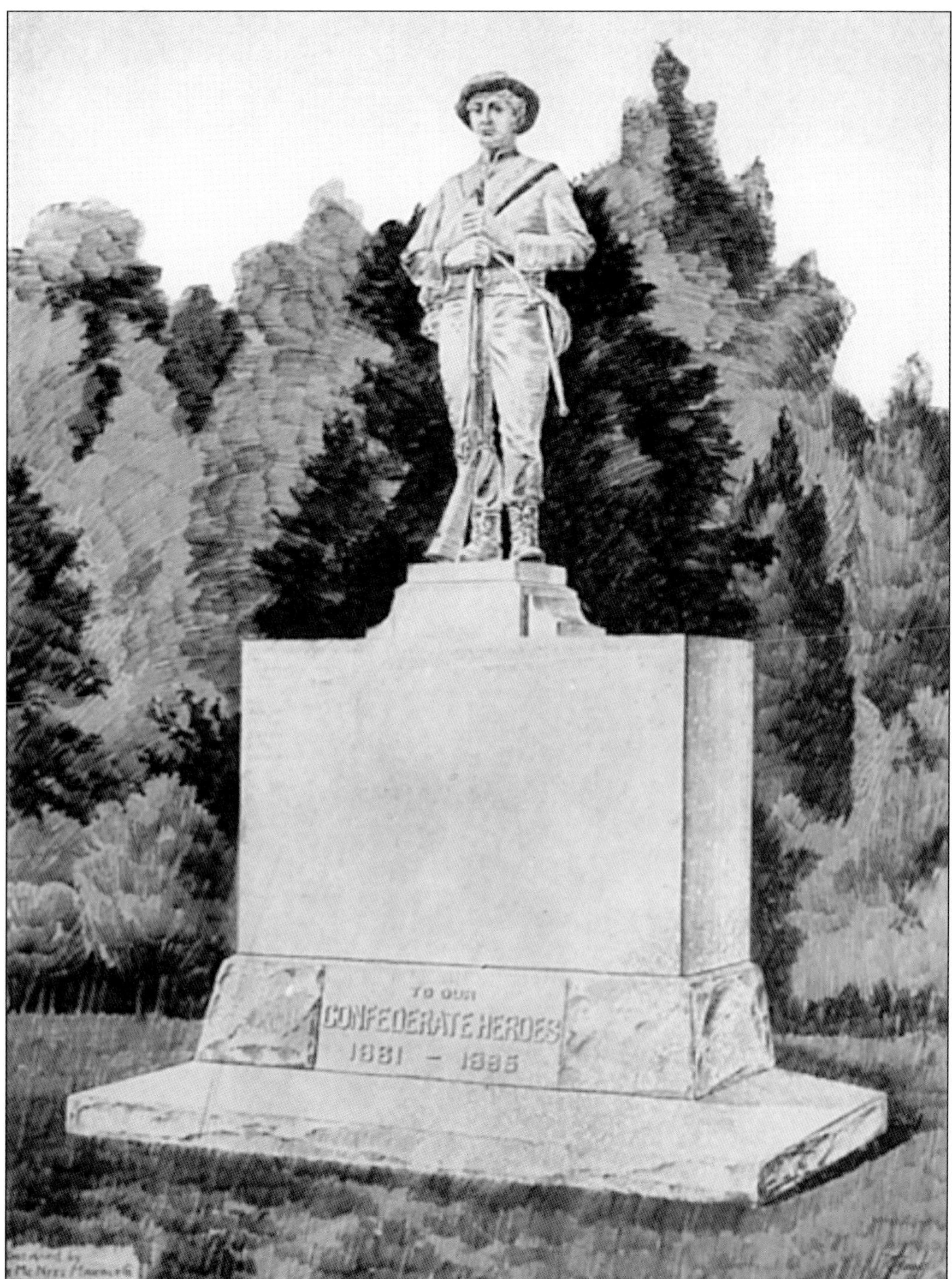

In a departure from the usual statuary featured on post cards, this *c.* 1912 card shows the proposed Lexington Confederate Monument. The monument came to fruition on Confederate Memorial Day, April 26, 1916, when the local ladies of the United Daughters of Confederacy held the unveiling on the lawn in front of the Oglethorpe County Courthouse.

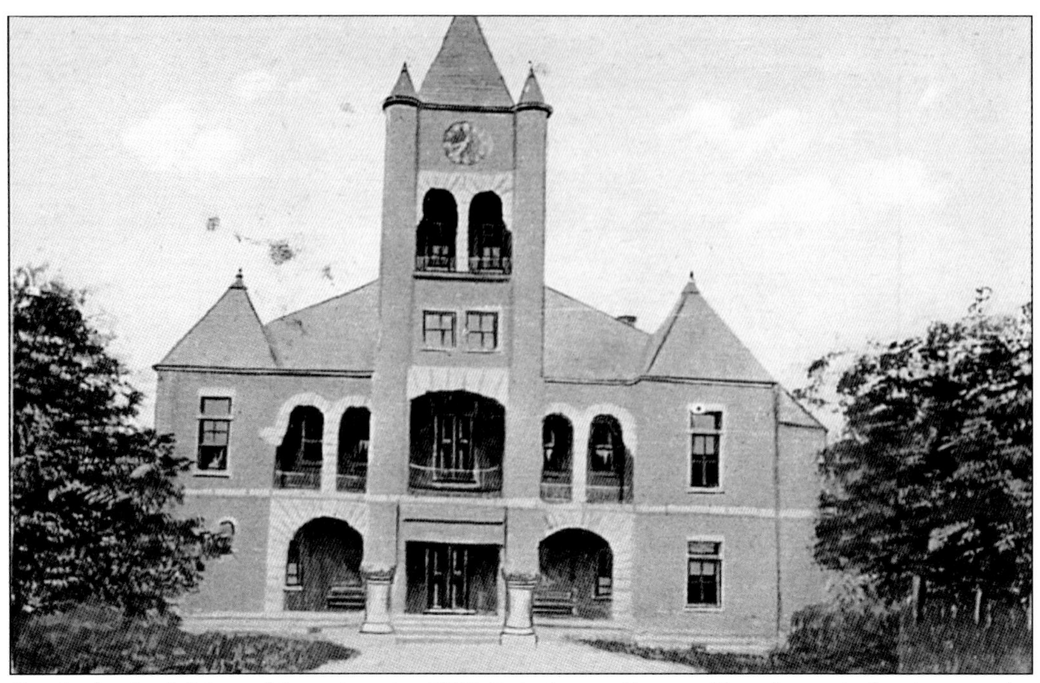

On the back of this card featuring the 1887 Oglethorpe County Courthouse in Lexington, the sender wrote, "I rec'd your card. don't suppose it seams like it did one year ago over at Lula's do it. I think Ethel is just fine she has moved now."

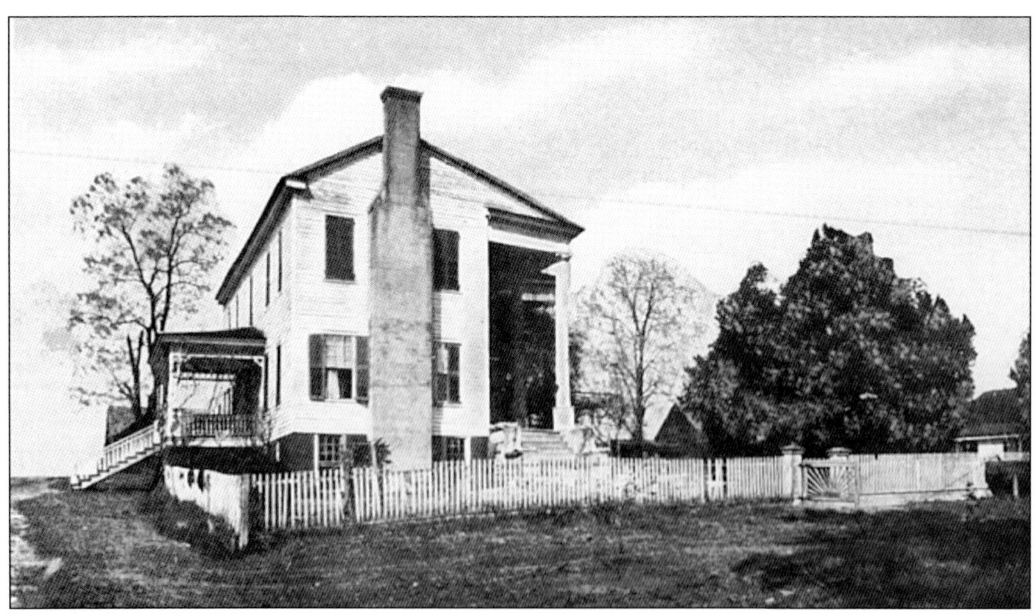

This card, published by the R.F. Brooks Company, features the former home of Governor Gilmer, in Lexington. The house was moved in modern times to adjoining Wilkes County for preservation and possible restoration.

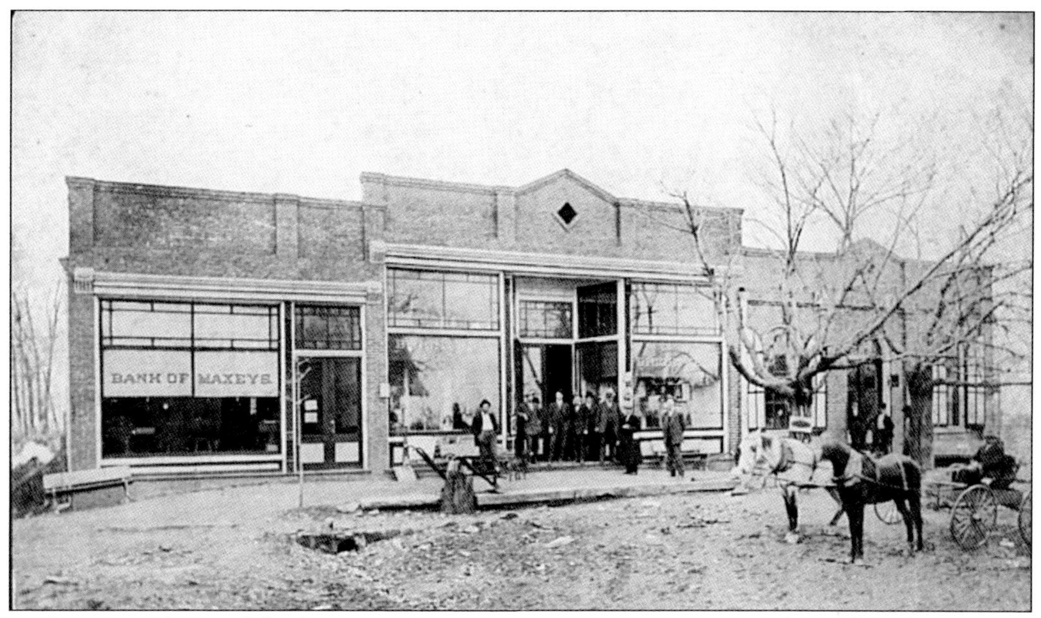

In this view of part of the business section in Maxeys, *c*. 1910, a crowd is gathered in front of the A.T. Brightwell and Sons store. The Brightwells sold general merchandise and lumber and were undertakers. The Bank of Maxeys is on the left. Guy R. Brightwell was president and W.H. Thomas was the cashier.

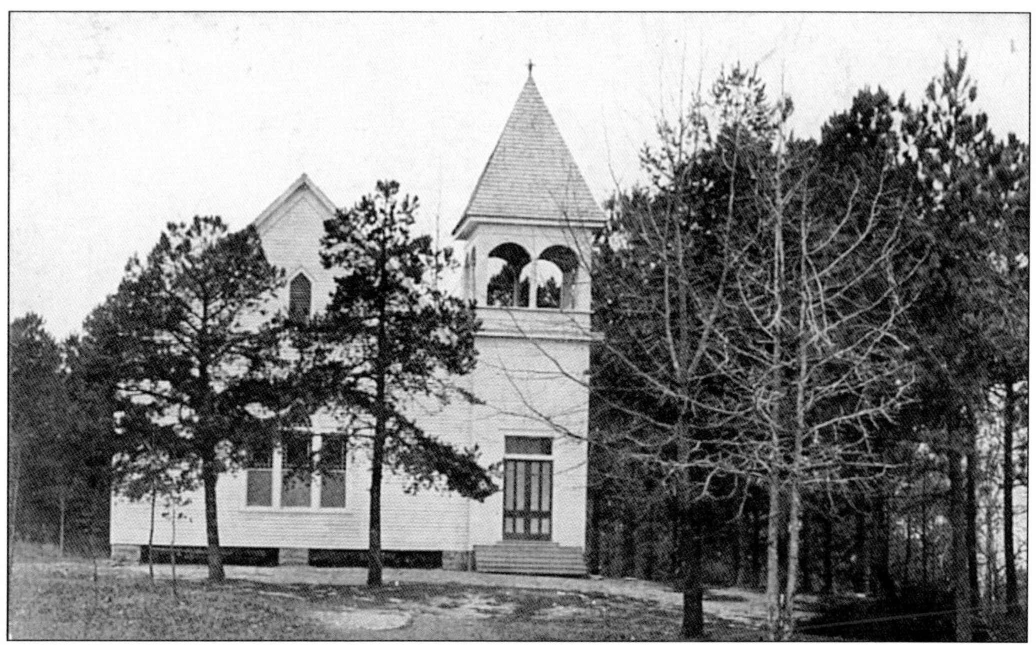

This real-photo post card shows the Christian church in Maxeys.

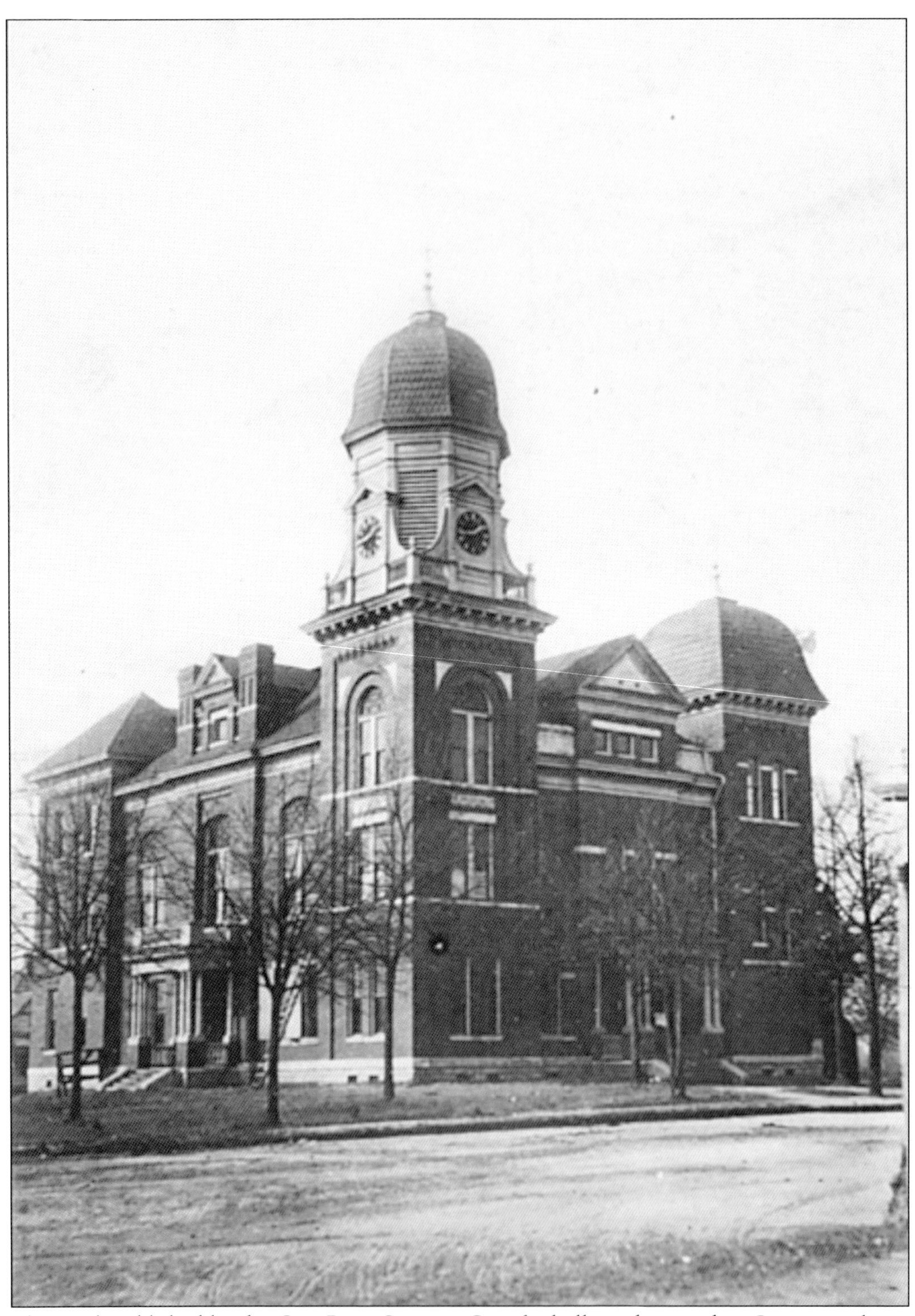

This card, published by the One Price Store in Crawfordville and printed in Germany, shows the courthouse in Crawfordville, which was built in 1902.

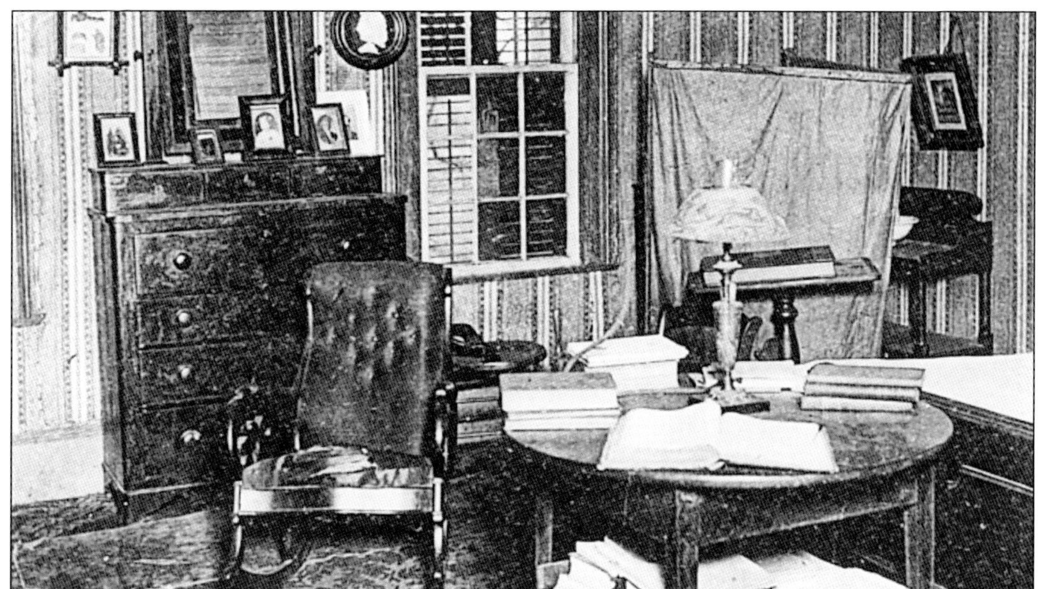

Alexander Hamilton Stephens, a Georgia congressman, governor, and vice president of the Confederacy during the War between the States, lived at Crawfordville. His home was named Liberty Hall. When Stephens died in 1883, his sitting room at Liberty Hall was preserved as he left it, and it remains so today as a museum.

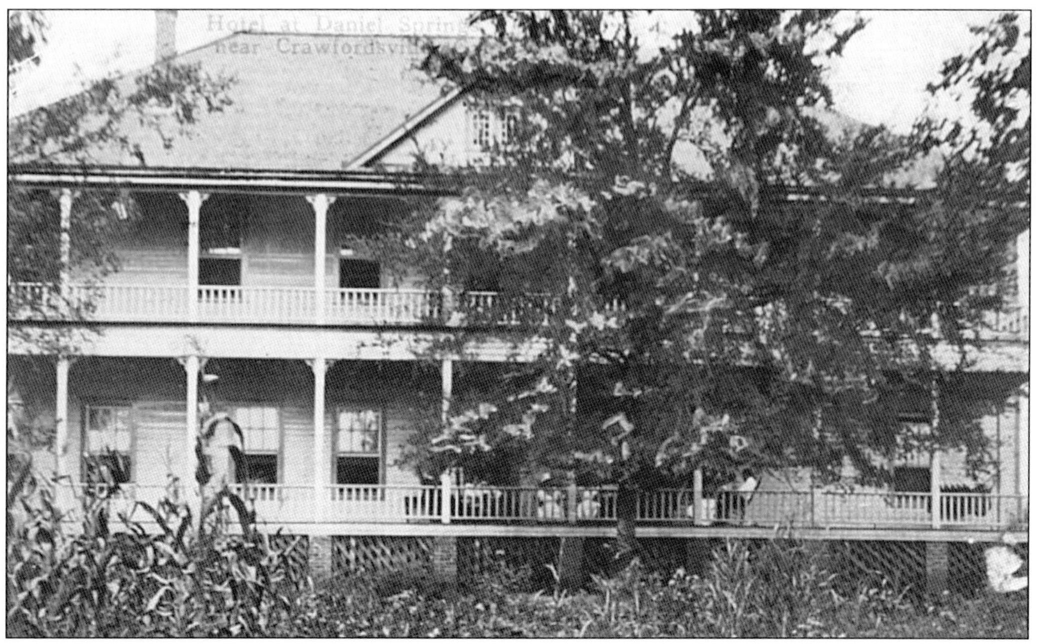

Guests enjoy themselves on the porch of the hotel at Daniel Springs, near Crawfordville, in this 1912 post card.

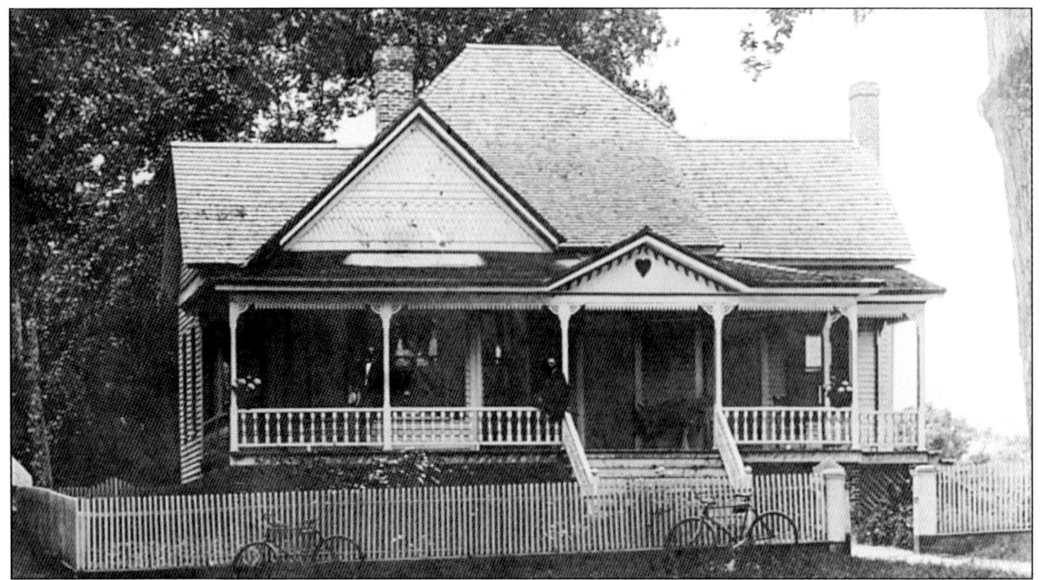

J.O. Gunn's residence in Crawfordville was captured by the photographer of this post card in 1912.

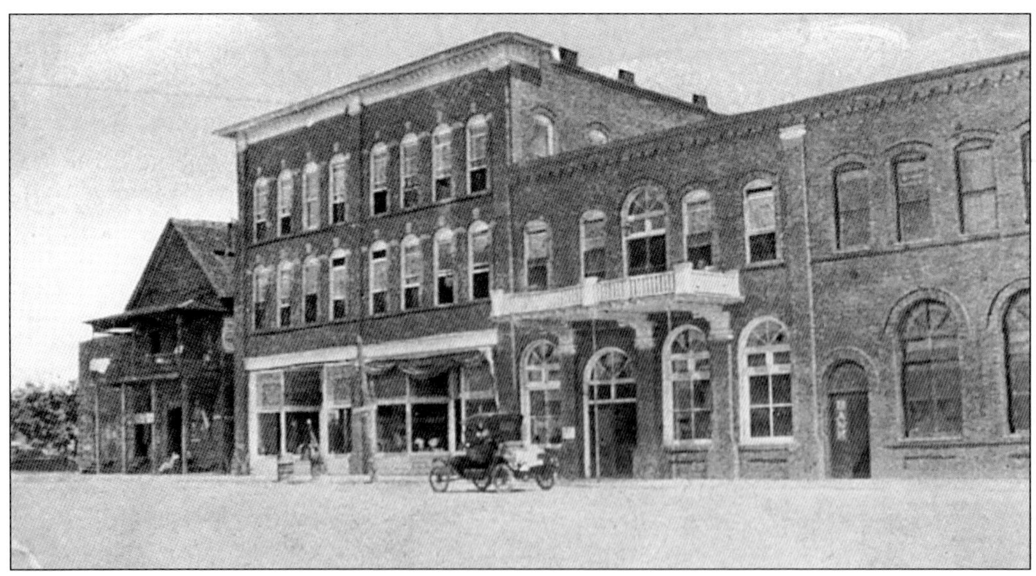

A lone automobile seems to have the street in front of the Hotel Tignal all to itself in this *c.* 1910 card.

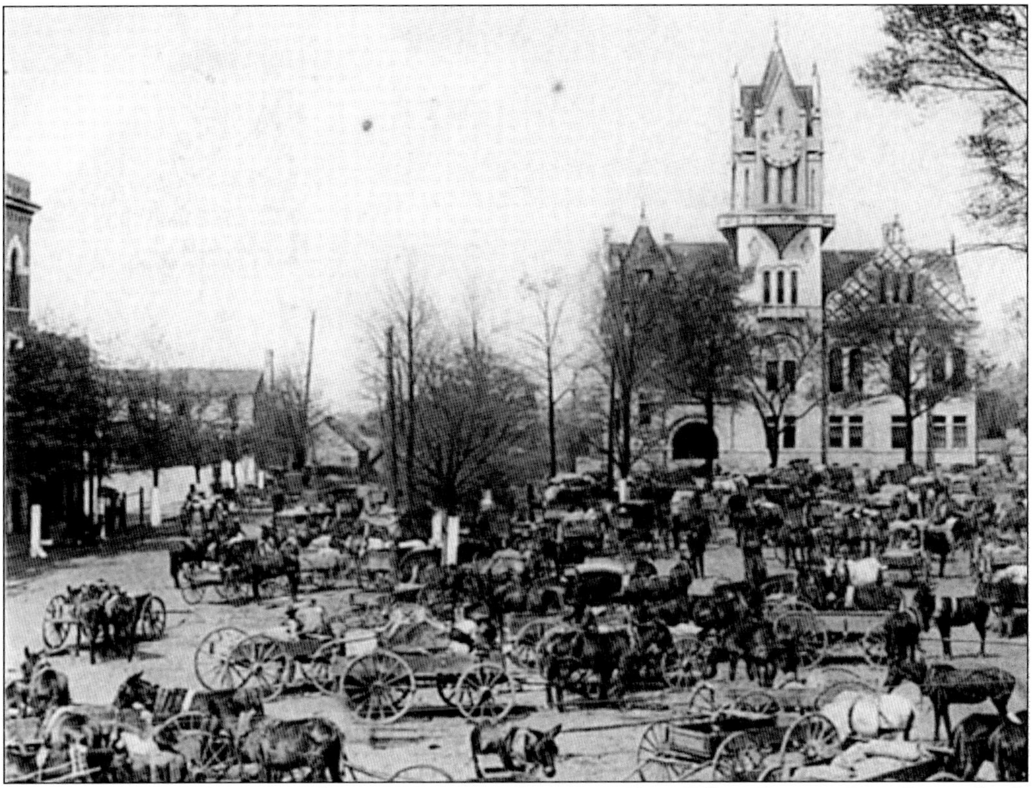

Cotton farmers gather in Market Square in Washington. The Wilkes County Courthouse, built in 1903, was severely damaged by fire in 1958 and no longer has the beautiful clock tower.

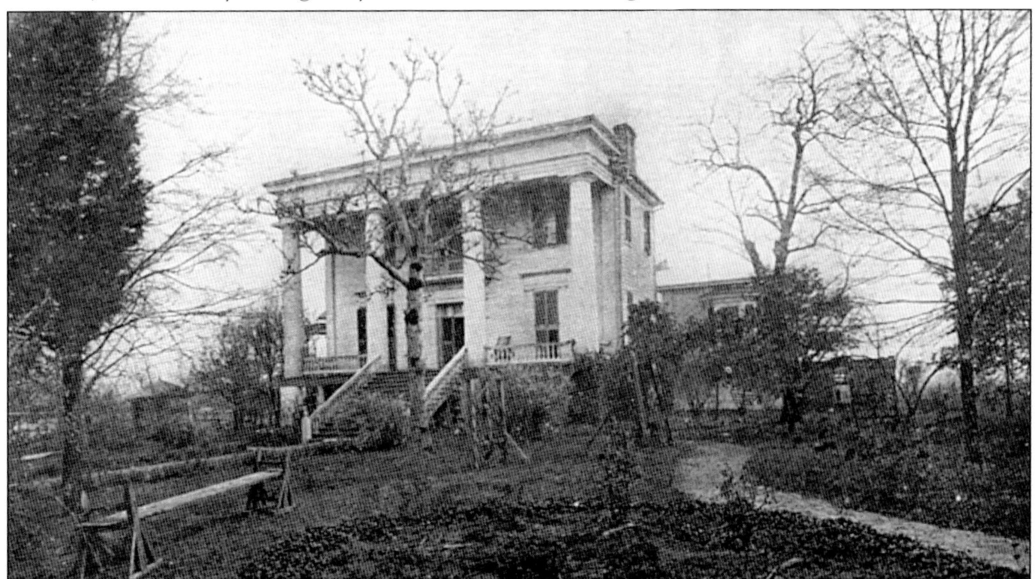

The Robert Toombs home in Washington now is a museum operated by the Georgia Department of Natural Resources. Toombs was a state legislator, state senator, U.S. Representative, U.S. senator, secretary of state of the Confederacy, and brigadier general in the Confederate Army.

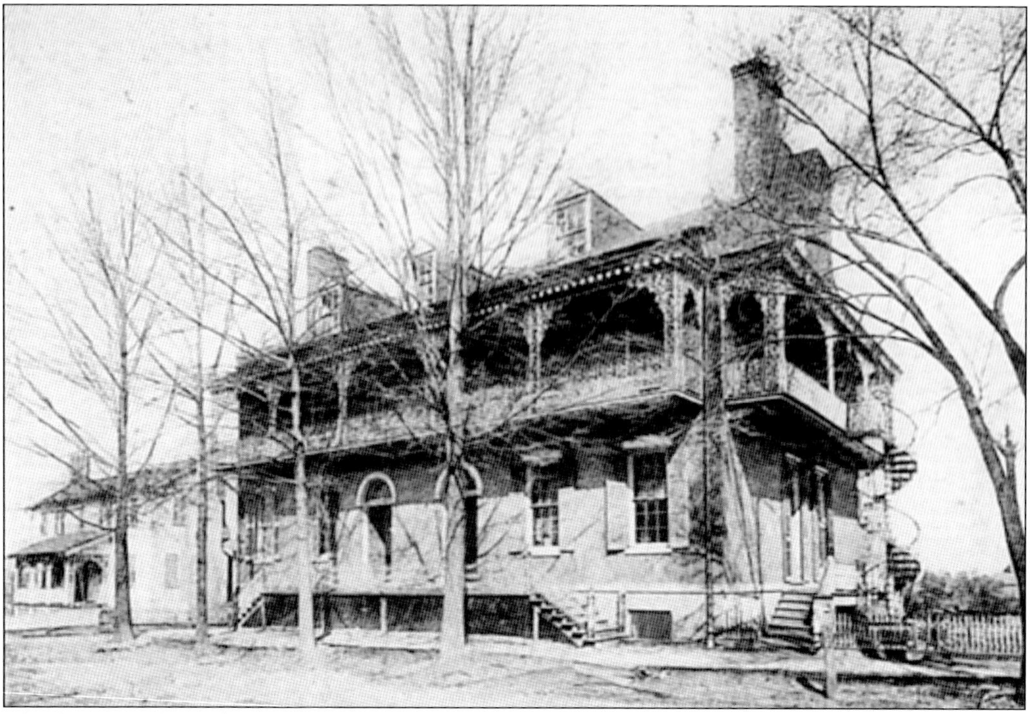

This beautiful building in Washington housed the Washington branch of the Bank of the State of Georgia. Note the spiral staircase and elaborate ironwork. The building was demolished many years ago.

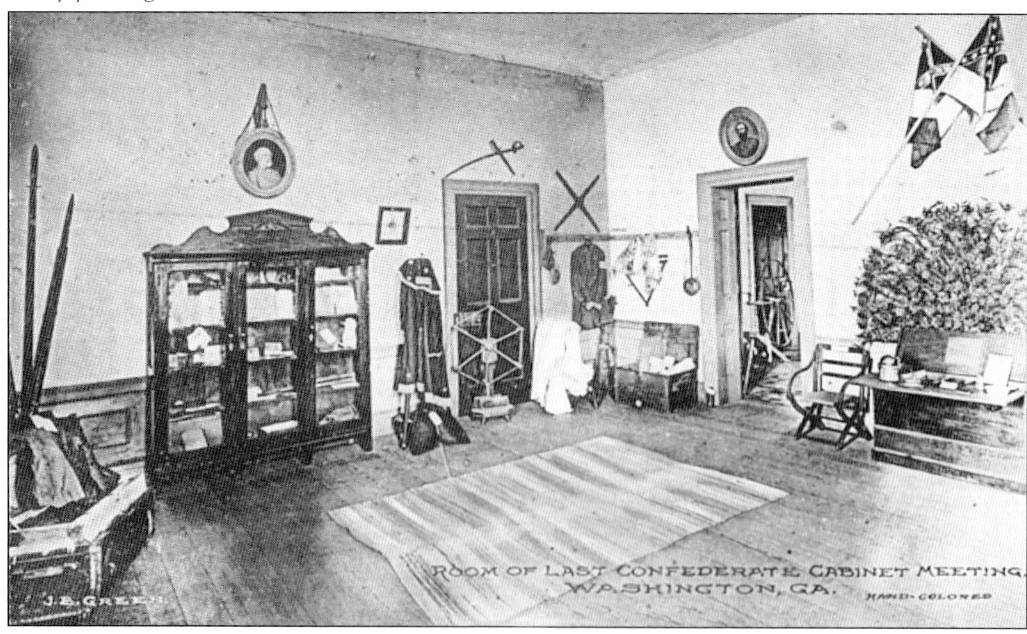

The last meeting of the Confederate cabinet was held May 4, 1865, in a room in the Bank of the State of Georgia in Washington. Confederate President Jefferson Davis and some members of his cabinet met hurriedly here while fleeing from Union soldiers after Lee had surrendered to Grant at Appamatox.

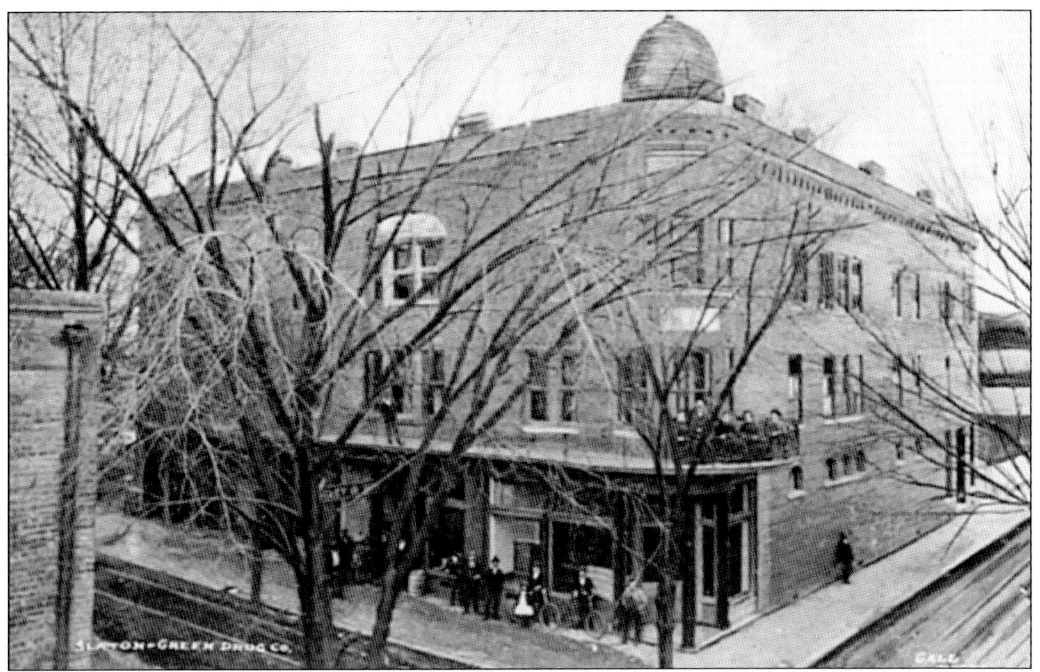

This bird's-eye view shows the Johnson Hotel and a crowd of onlookers in Washington. In 1910, W.T. Johnson owned the hotel and F.C. Omberg was its manager.

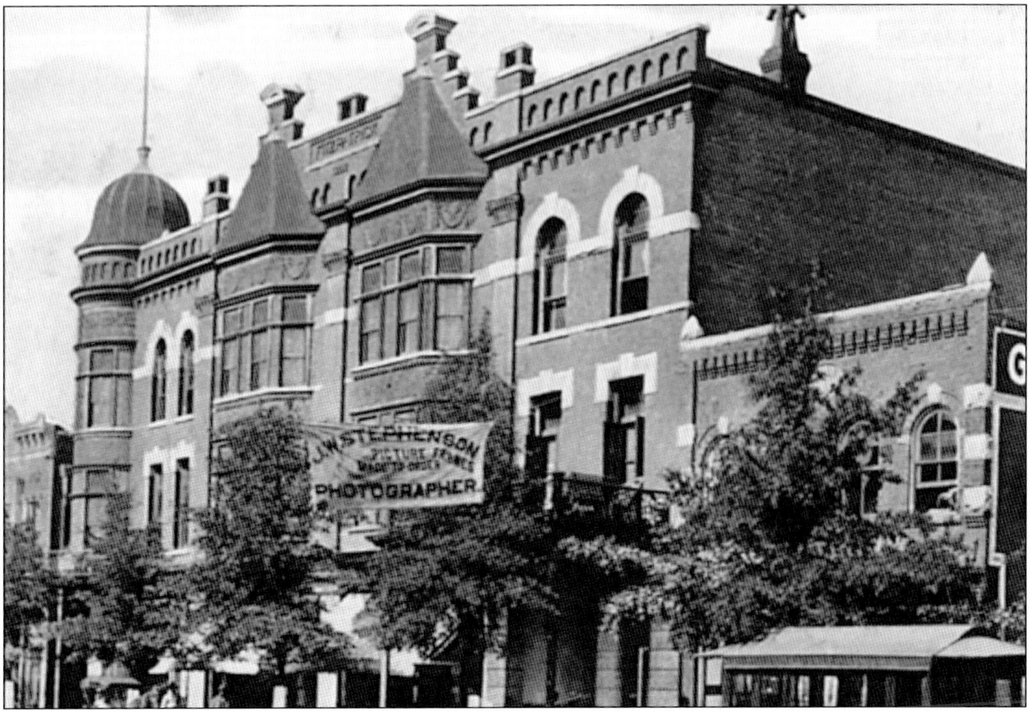

This card shows the Fitzpatrick Hotel in Washington, complete with an ad for J.W. Stephenson, photographer.

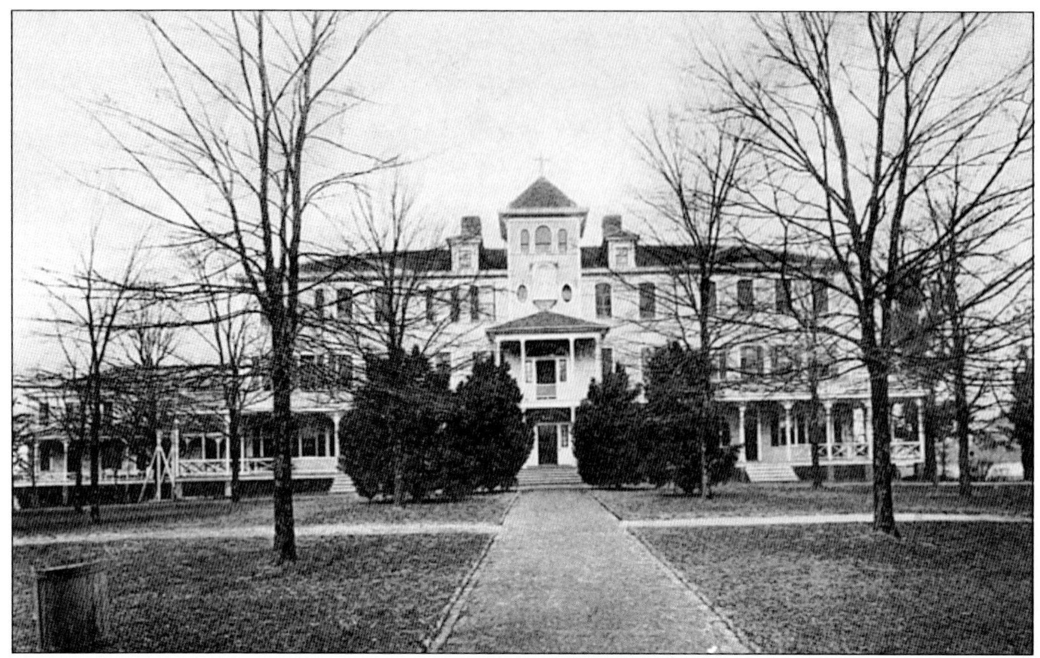

St. Joseph's Academy of Washington is featured in this *c.* 1909 post card. Although the sender put the address where the message is supposed to go and vice versa, the card was delivered anyway.

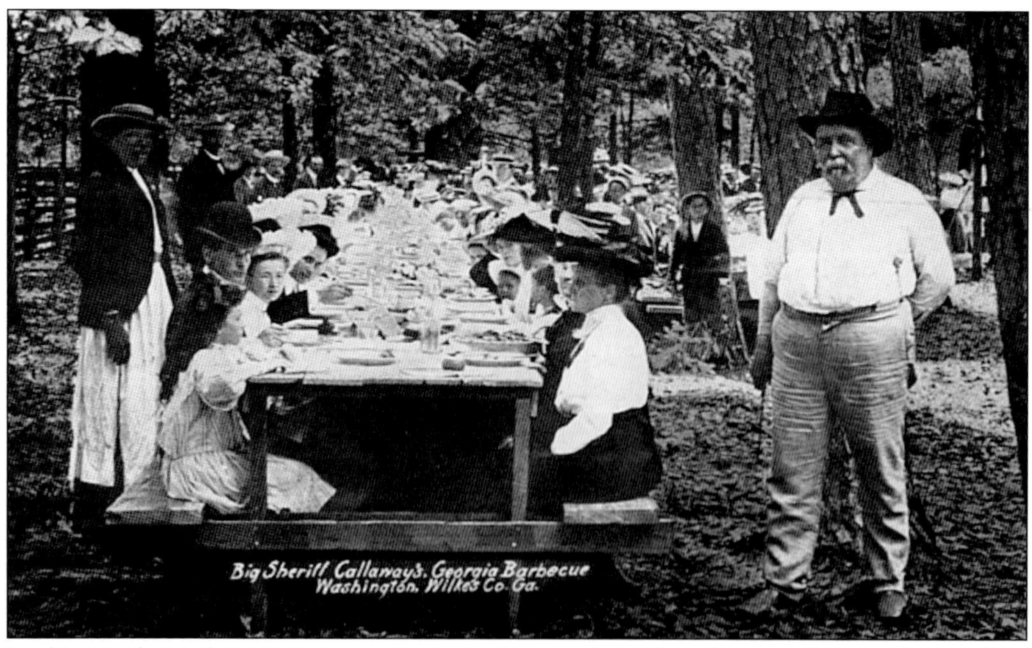

Looking at the girth of the man on the right, it's easy to see how he earned the nickname "Big Sheriff Callaway." He is shown here at a barbecue in Washington.

Four

Habersham and Stephens Counties

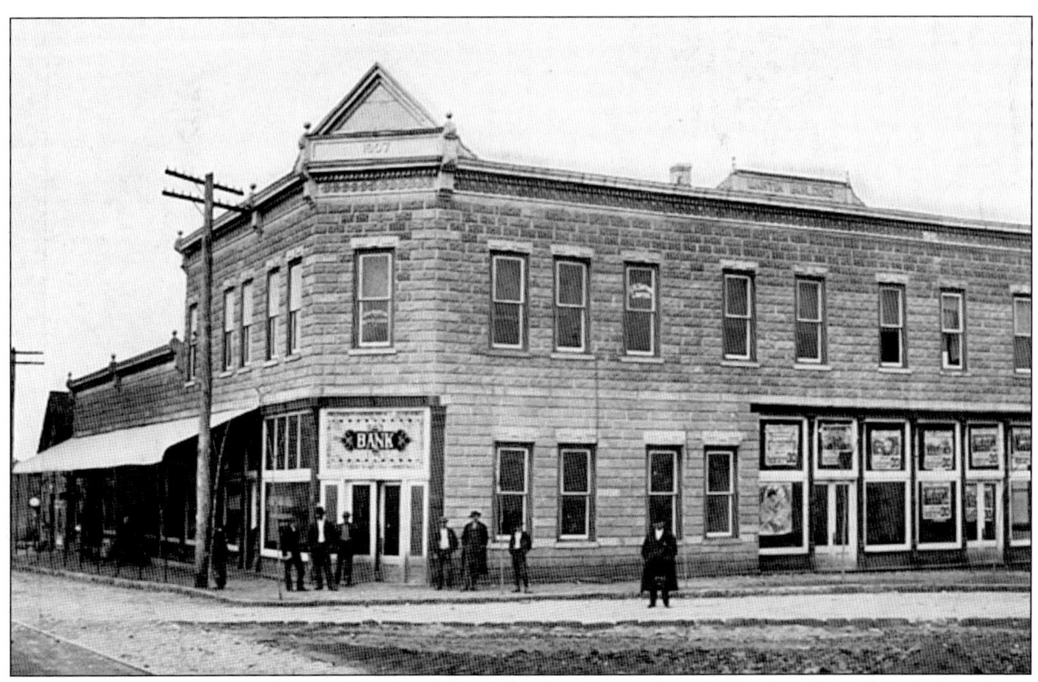

This post card shows the Martin Building (built in 1907) in Clarksville. The Habersham Bank occupied the corner section of the first floor and lawyers, real estate agents, and others had offices upstairs. In 1910 the president of the bank was E.P. West and the cashier was W.R. Asbury.

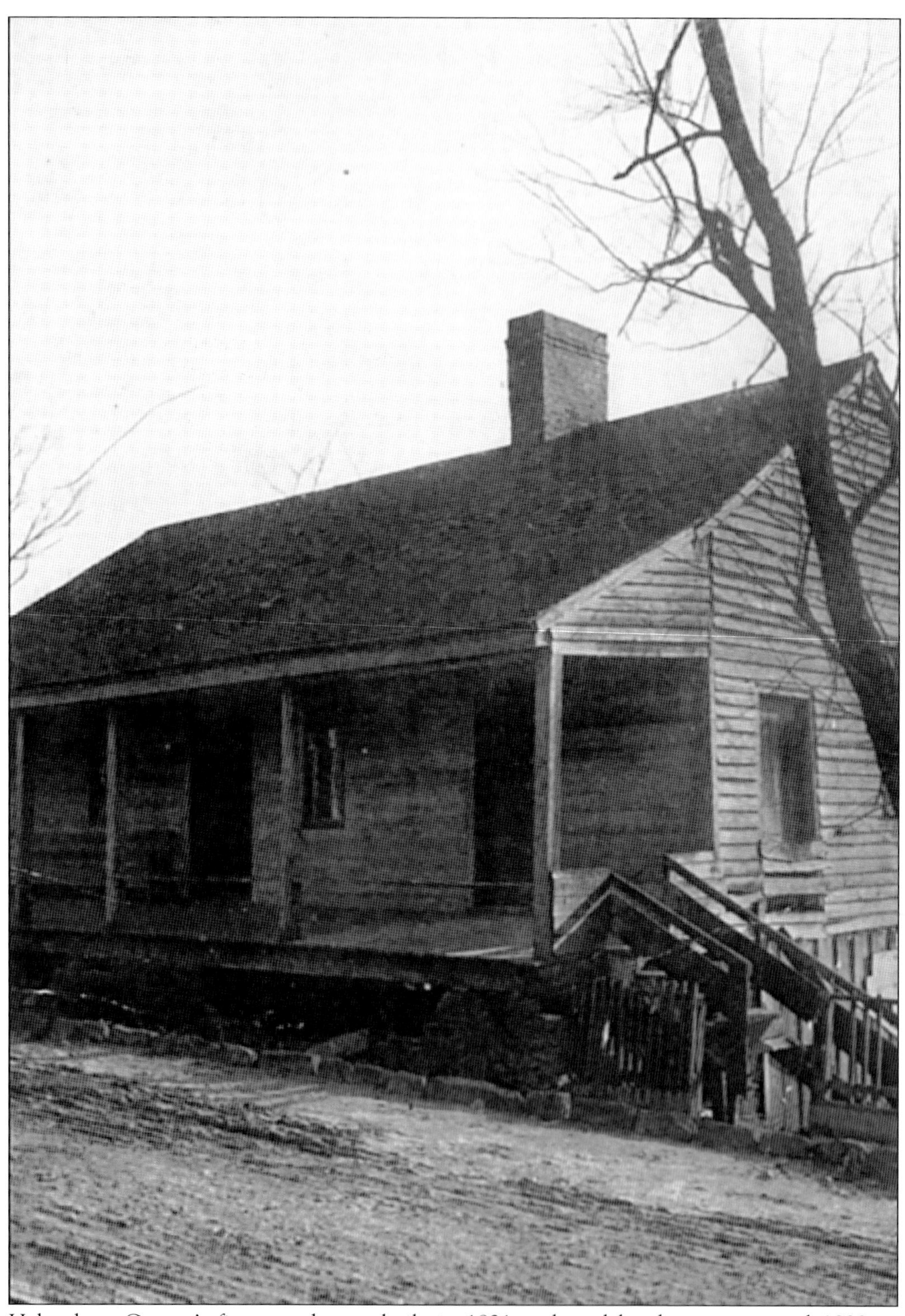

Habersham County's first courthouse, built in 1821 and used by the county until 1832, is pictured in this *c.* 1913 card.

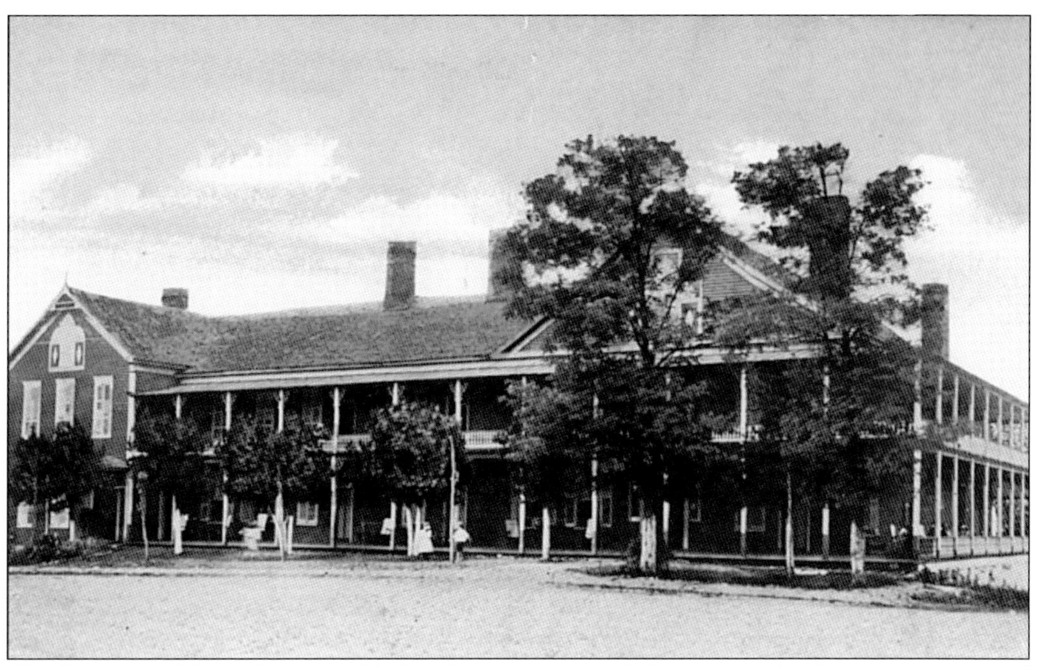

The Mountain View Hotel in Clarksville was previously known as the Spencer House and Spencer Hotel.

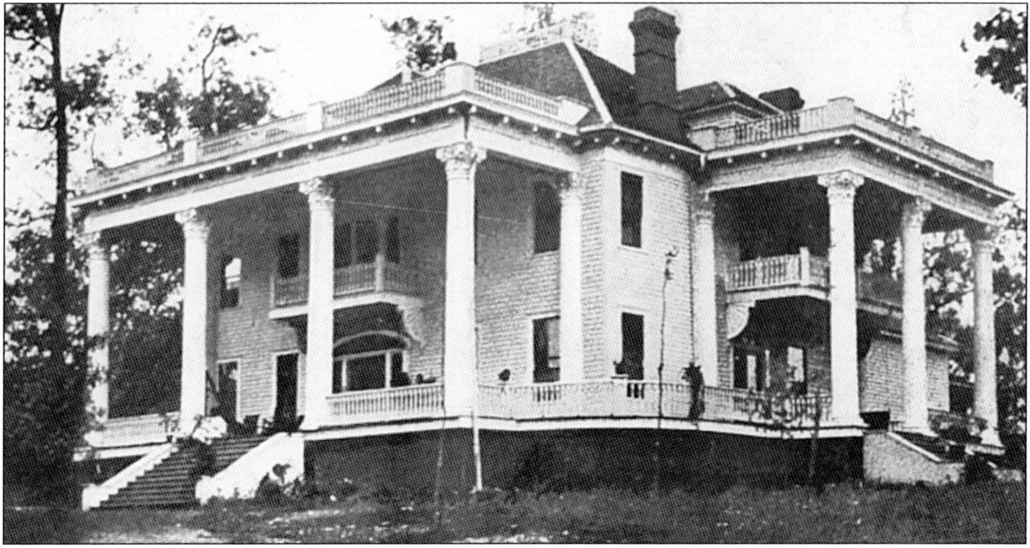

The home of W.R. Asbury was evidently a showpiece of Clarksville, as it was featured in this post card.

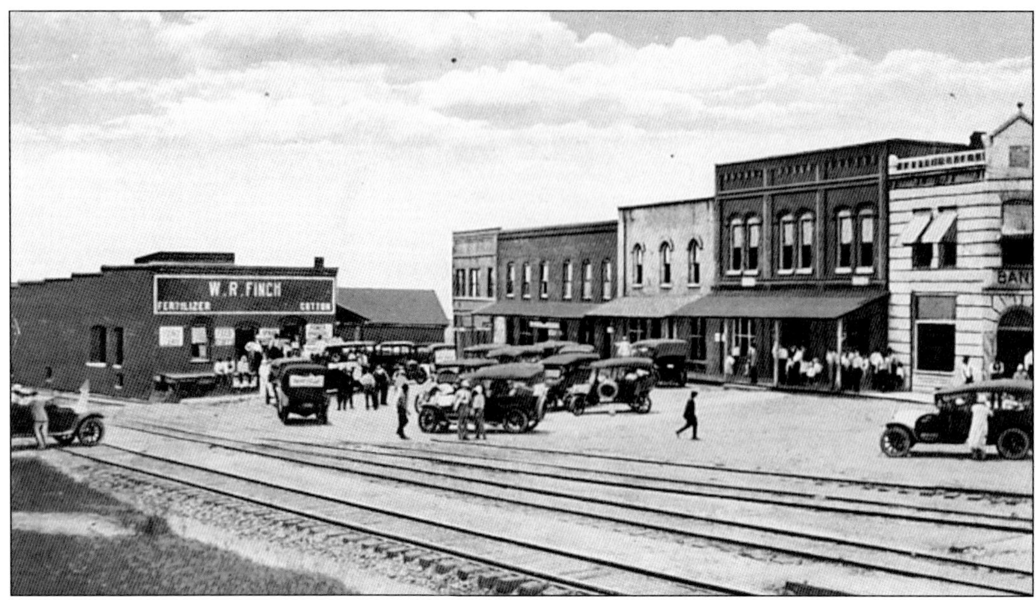

Horses are absent and cars are many in this view of Main Street in Cornelia.

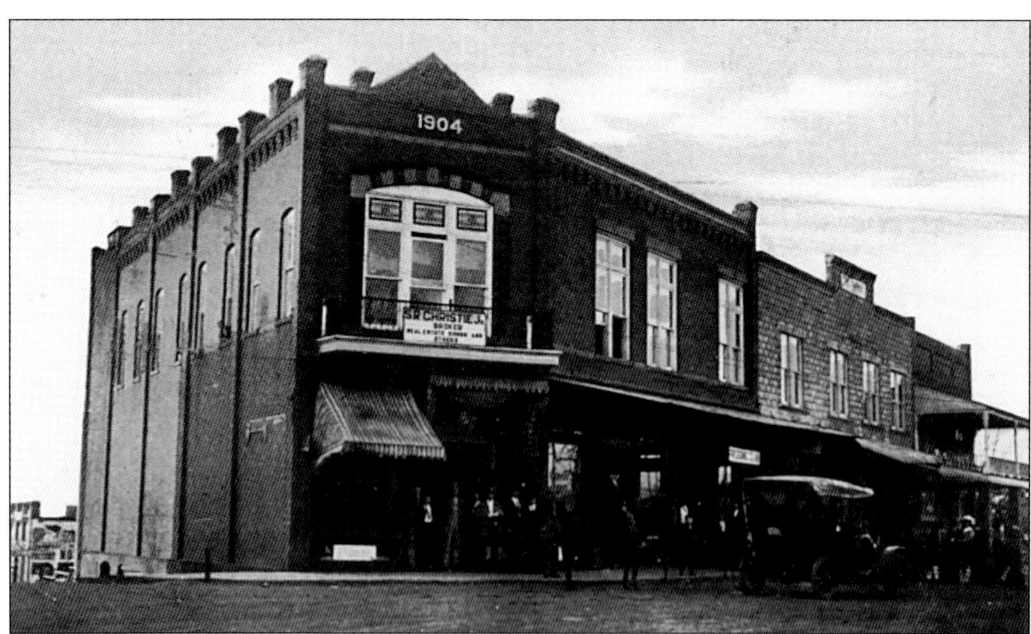

Judging by his prominent sign, S.R. Christie, broker and real estate agent, maintained a large presence in the business block of Cornelia.

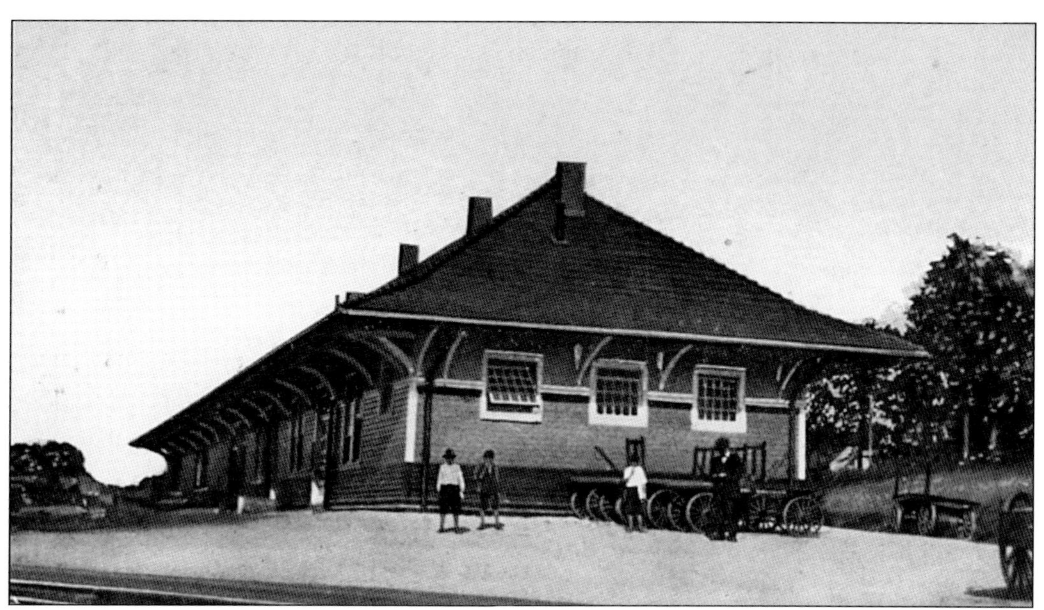

Evidently, the sender of this post card of the Southern Railway Station in Cornelia was feeling a little lonely. On the back of the card, she wrote, "Hey you. I'm looking for that letter. Hurry up and write. Better come up Sunday. Lessie."

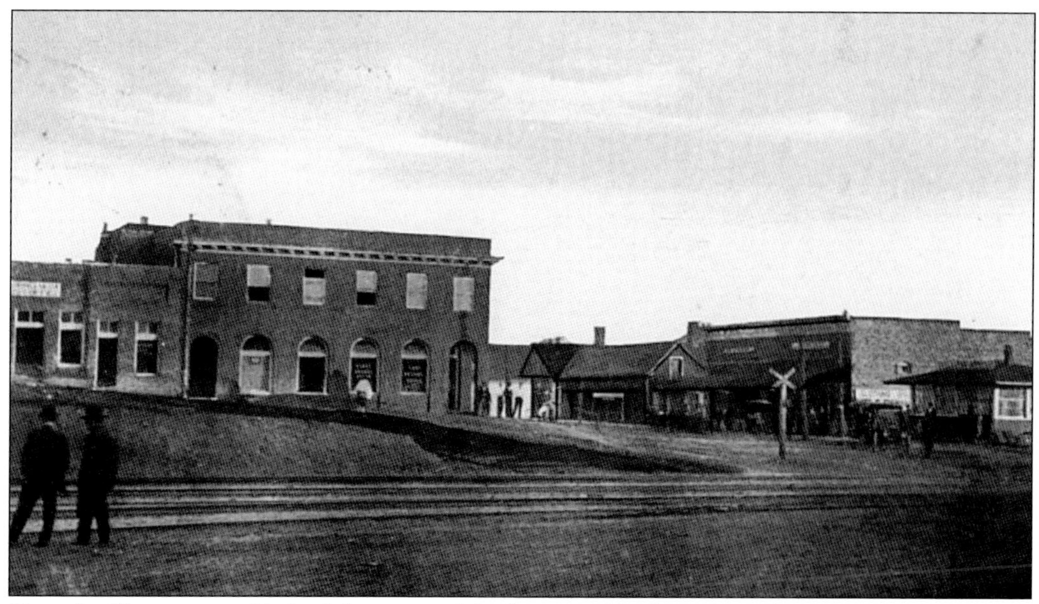

Cornelia Pharmacy published this view of the business block in Cornelia.

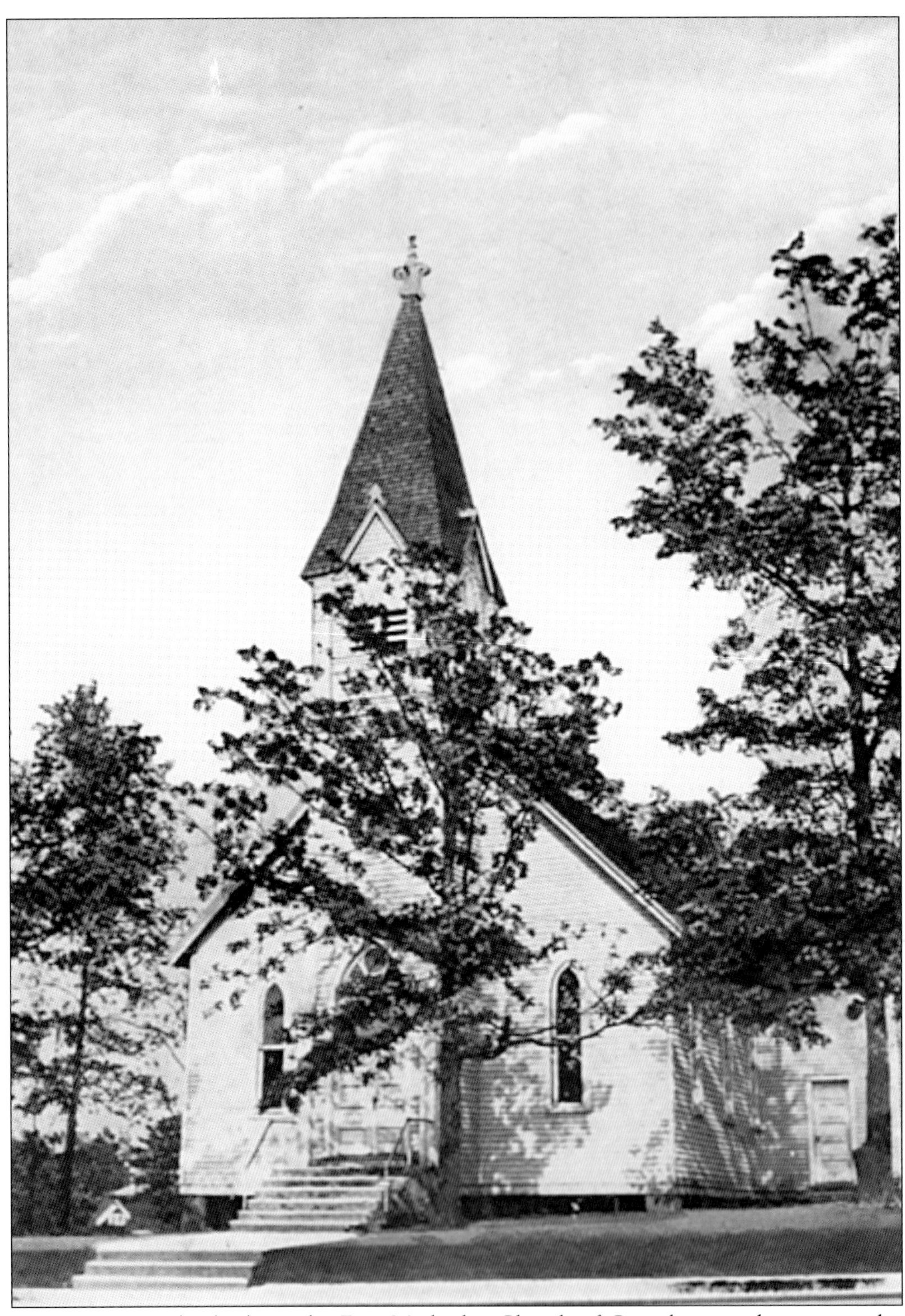

The prominent clouds above the First Methodist Church of Cornelia give this post card a majestic look.

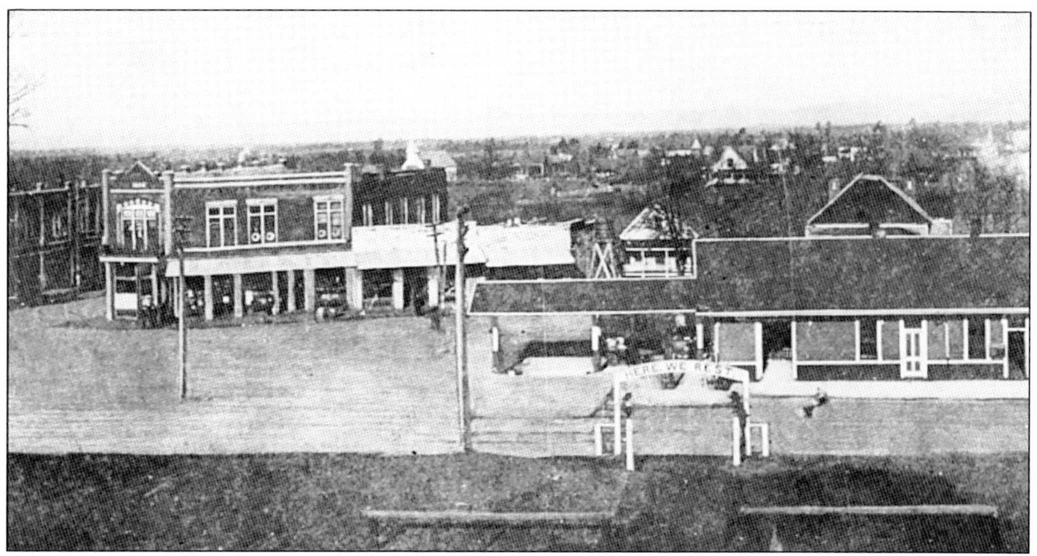

In this bird's-eye view of the business block of Cornelia, one can see the sign that greeted travelers with the words "Here We Rest."

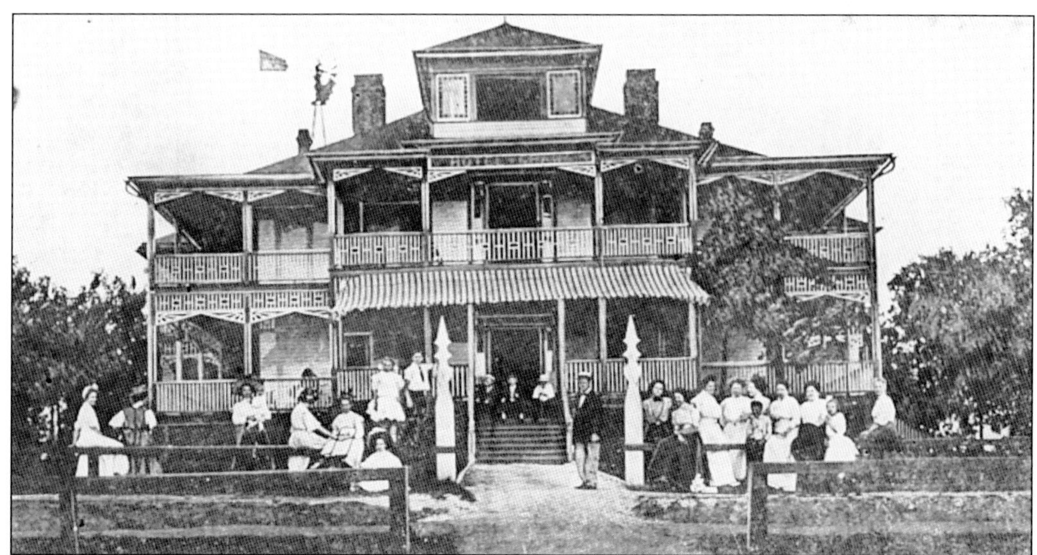
The Cornelia Drug Store published this view of the Grant House and Hotel in Cornelia.

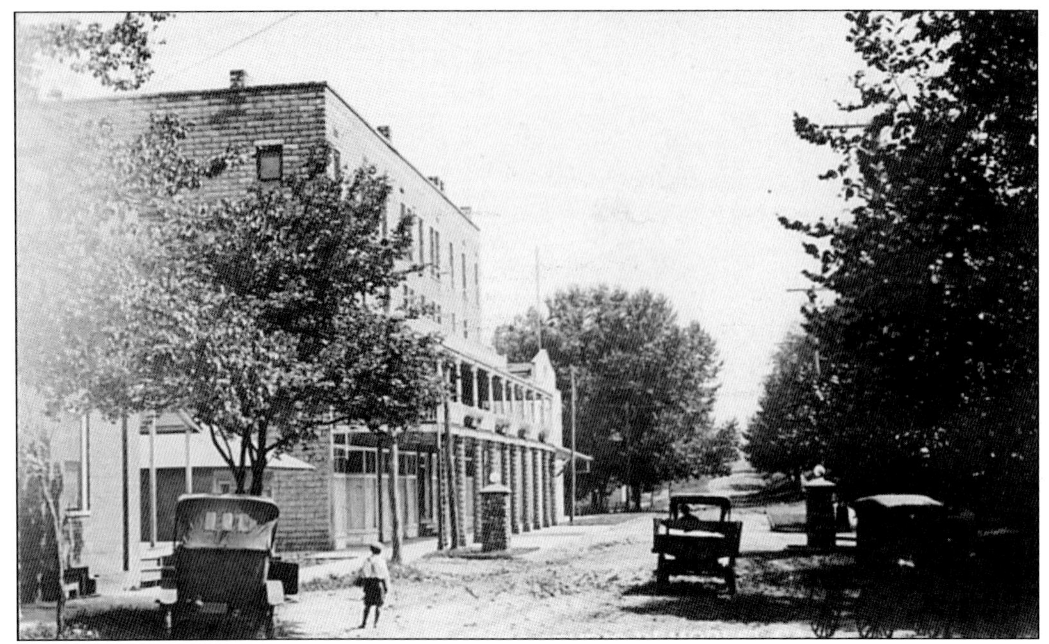

A photographer from Fisher's Studio in Demorest snapped this shot of a street scene in Demorest about 1912.

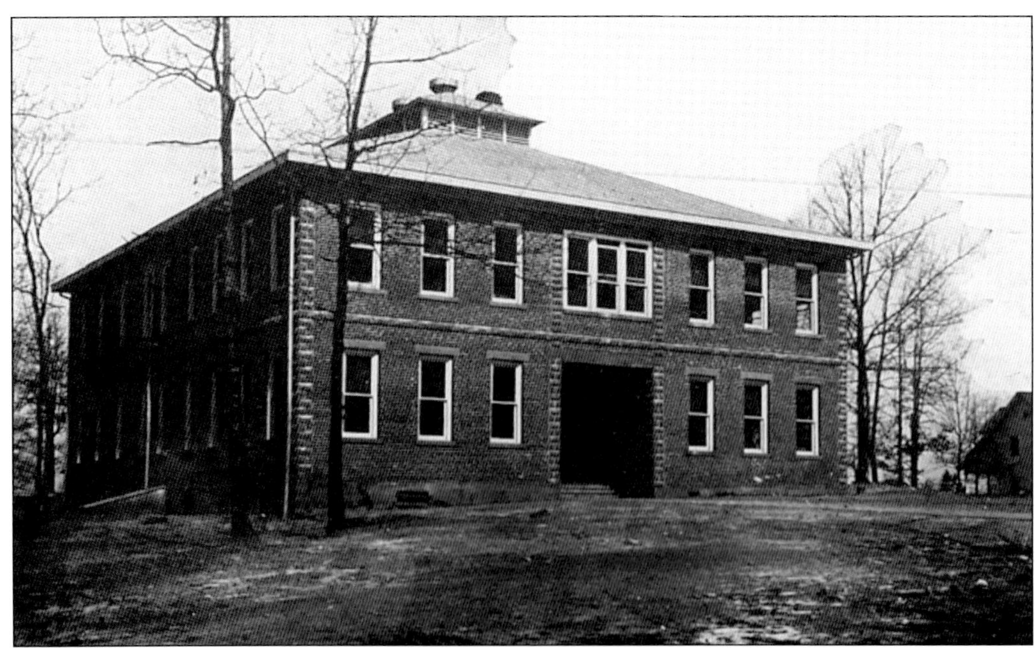

This is the Demorest Public School building.

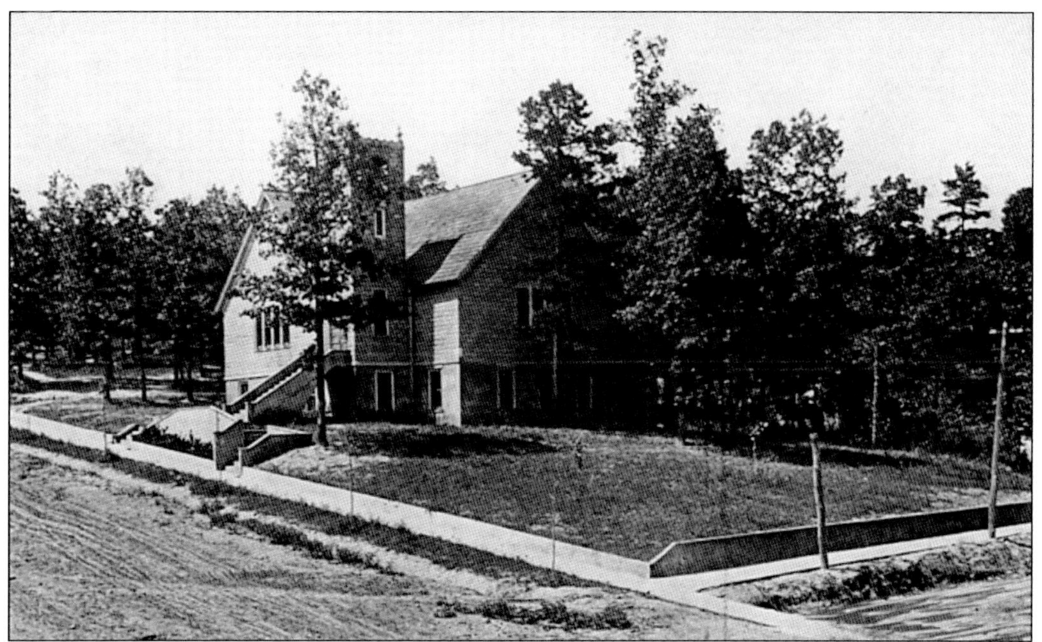

The Union Congregational Church in Demorest had a concrete sidewalk but an unpaved street at the time this photograph was taken.

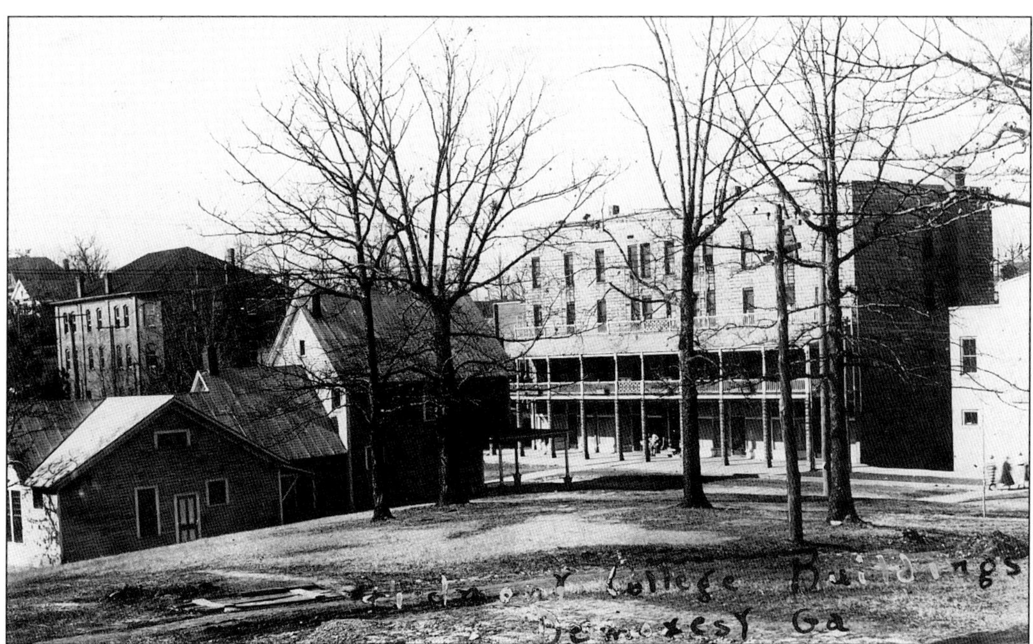

A hand-letter inscription on the front of this *c.* 1912 real-photo card reads "Piedmont College Buildings, Demorest, GA."

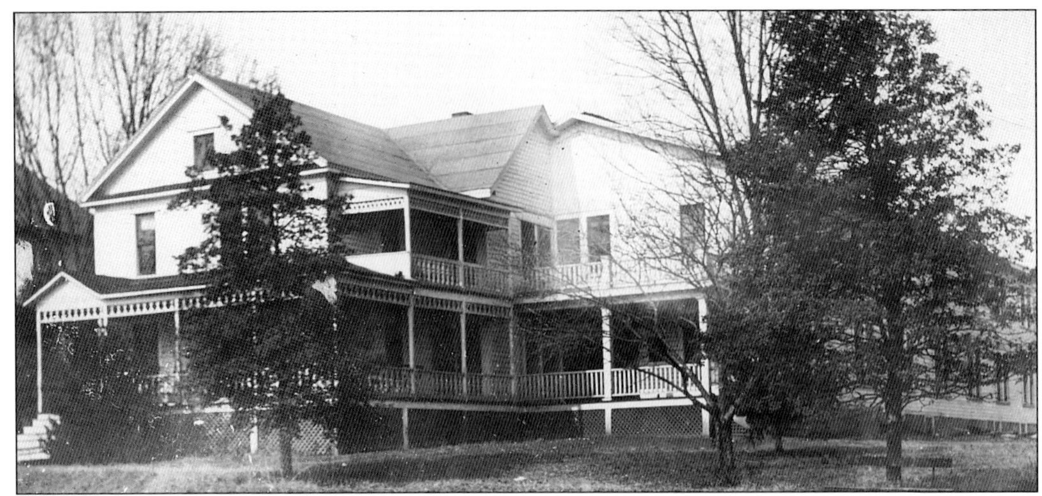

Another *c*. 1912 real-photo post card with a hand-lettered inscription shows Campbell Hall at Piedmont College.

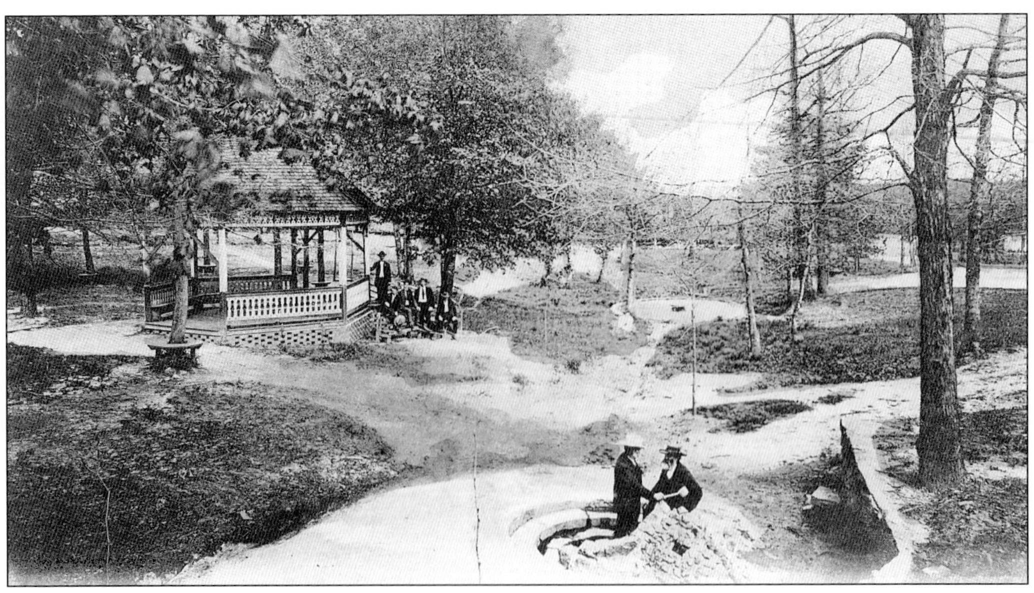

This view shows Spring Park and some visitors at Demorest.

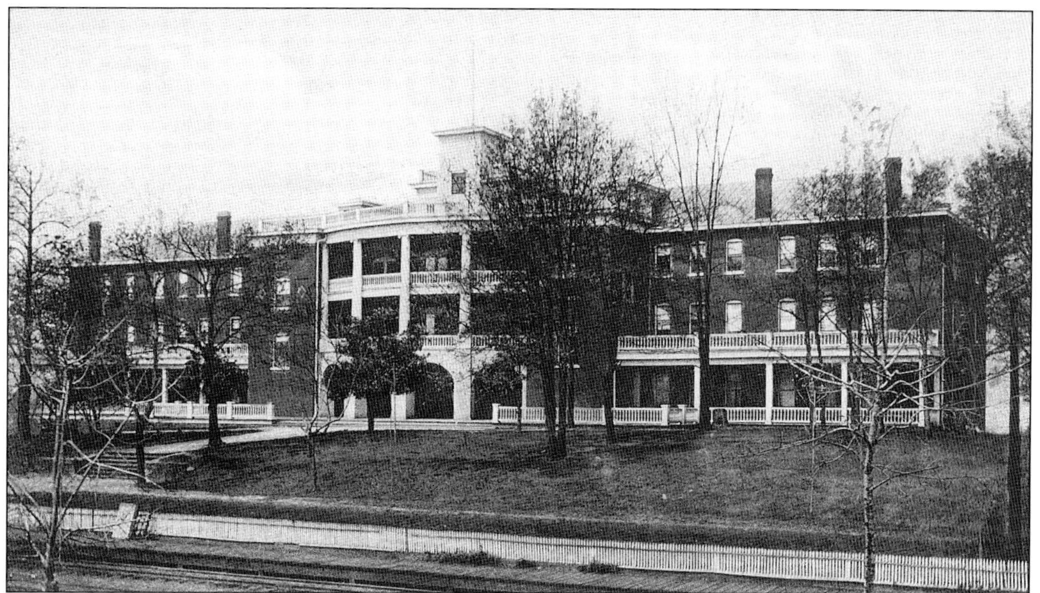

This post card published by the American News Company shows the Monterey Hotel in Mt. Airy.

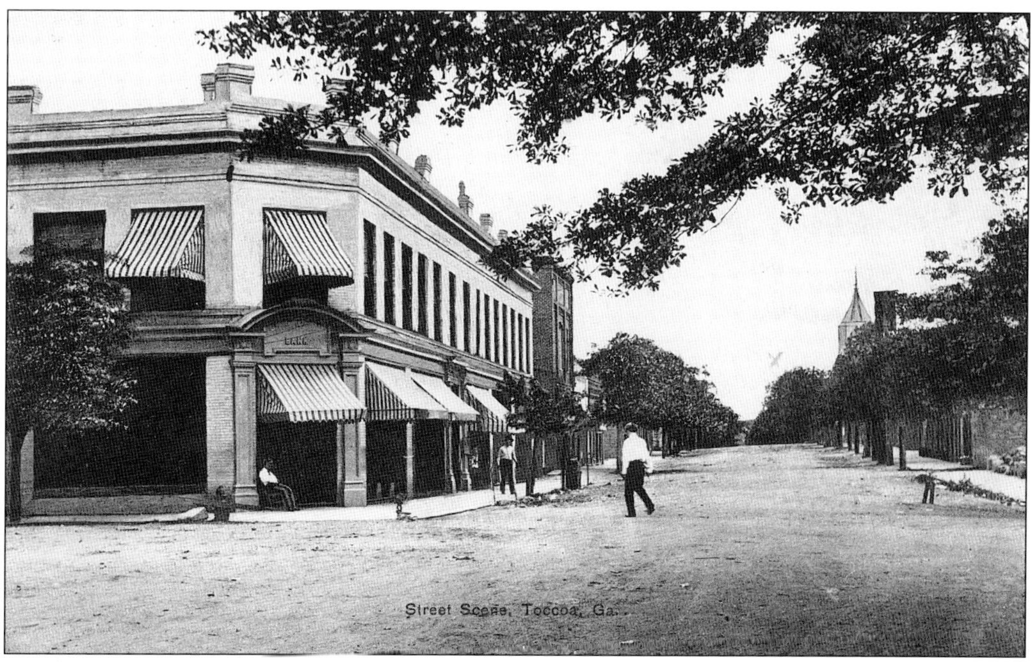

The bank was located in the building with the striped awnings in this street scene of Toccoa.

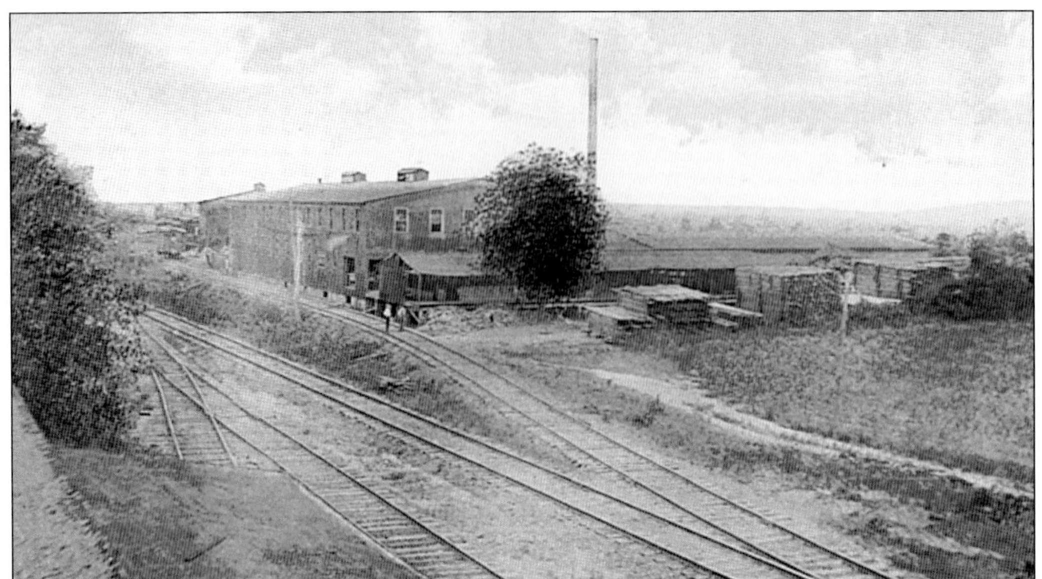

On the back of this card published by the Toccoa Board of Trade featuring the Toccoa Furniture Company are instructions for anyone seeking information on Toccoa or Stephens County to contact "Claude Bond, Secretary, Toccoa."

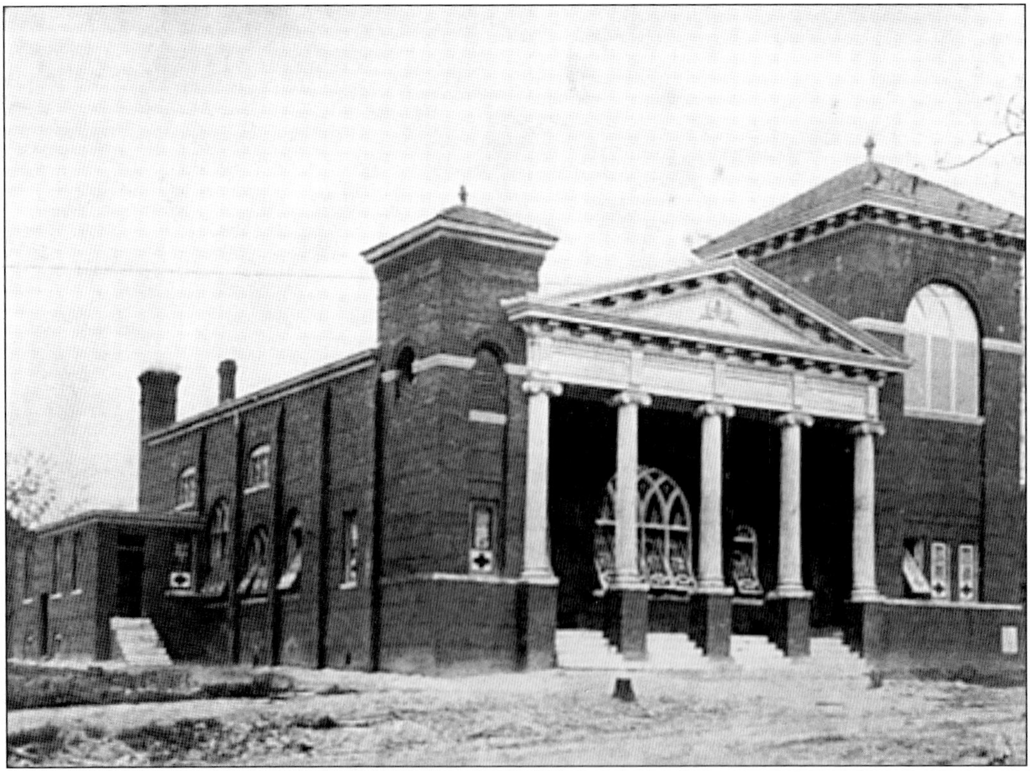

The Toccoa Pharmacy published this post card of the First Baptist Church of Toccoa.

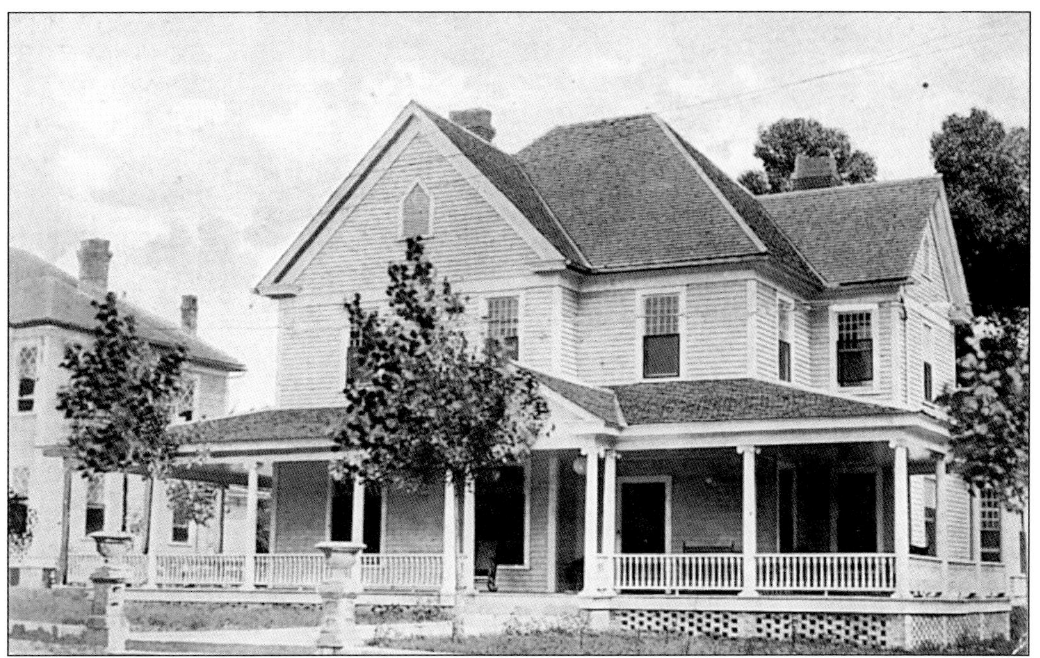

Another card published by the Toccoa Board of Trade features the home of Dr. J.H. Terrell. As before, the card directs people seeking information to contact Mr. Claude Bond.

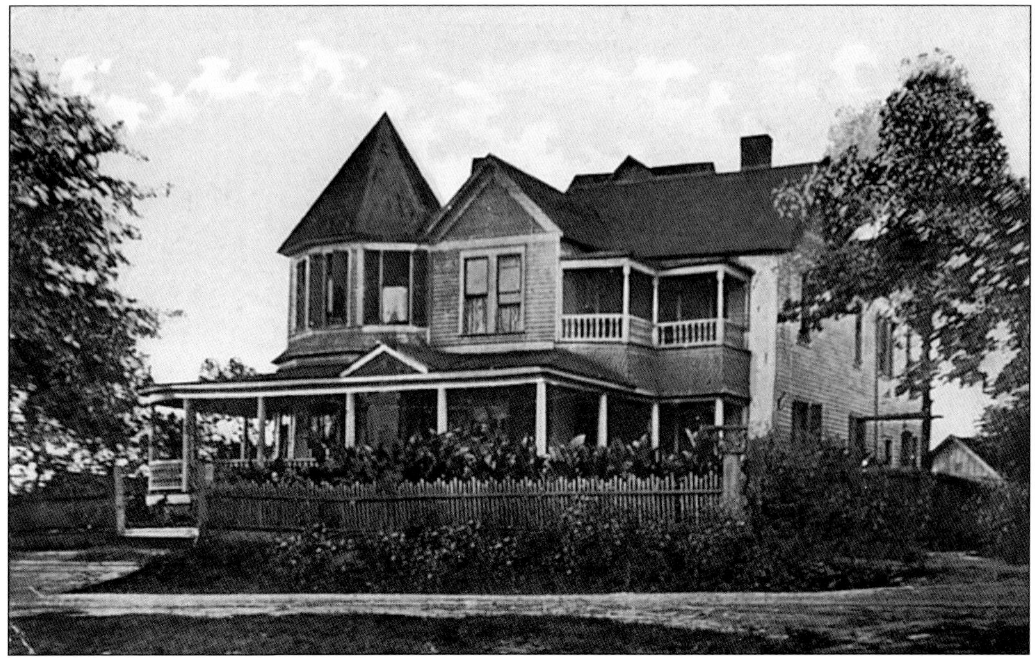

This is the residence of F.J. Hunter at Toccoa. The message on this card reads, "Hellow Carl. Tell Mrs. Werber, Carmen and Dorothy I said hellow. I have been to St. Simons since I have been away. How is all of your folks? Tell James and his brother I said hellow. Raymond Smith."

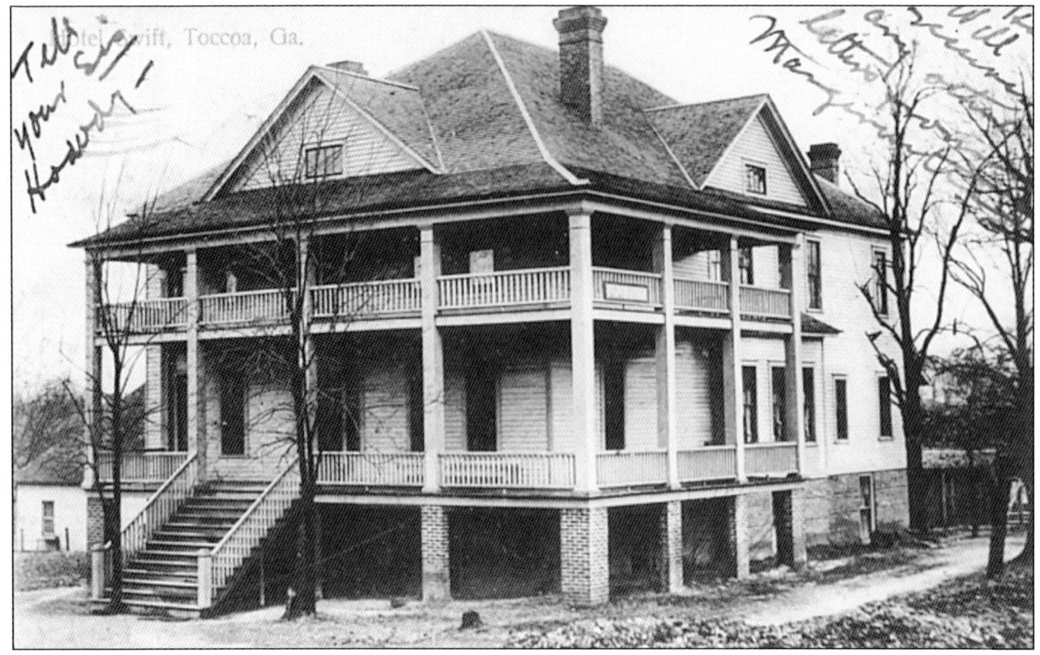

The Hotel Swift in Toccoa was the subject of this *c*. 1909 card. The hotel was run by Mrs. Ellen Swift.

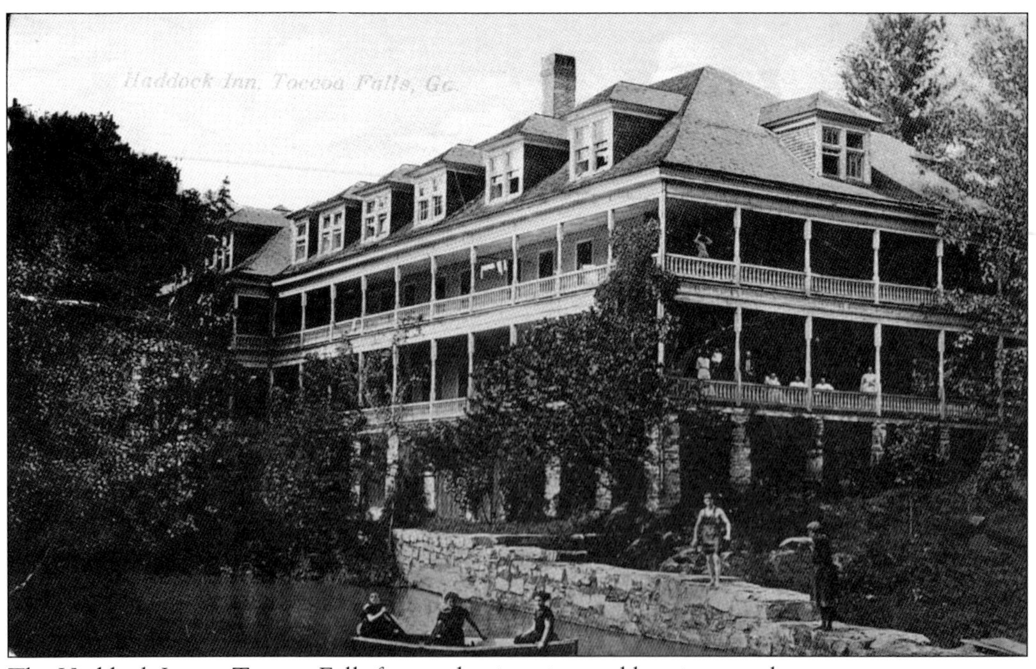

The Haddock Inn at Toccoa Falls featured swimming and boating nearby.

Five

HALL AND BARROW COUNTIES

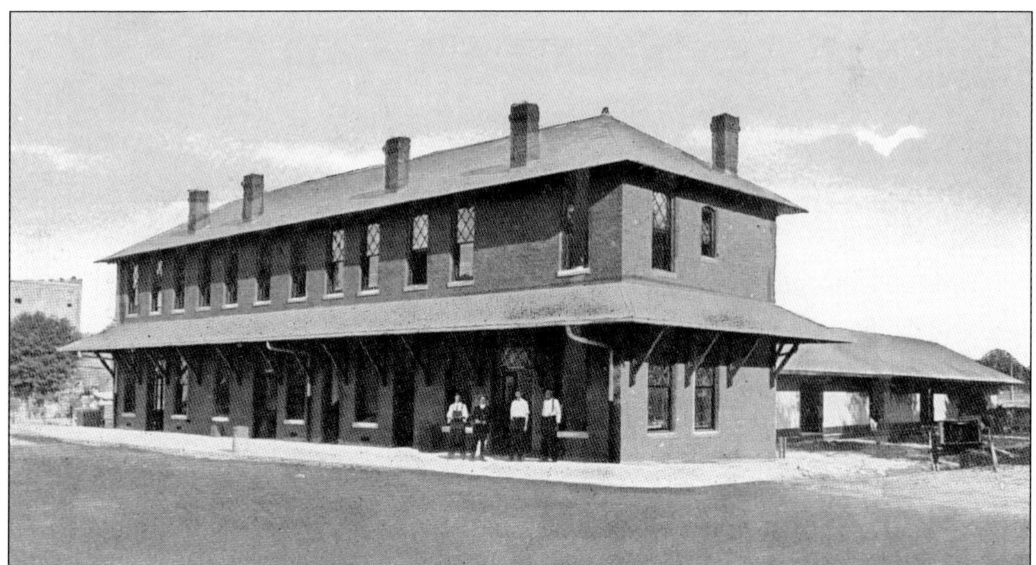

Railroad depots, train stations, and other buildings connected with railroads were favorite subjects for post card photographers. This card shows the new depot and offices of the Gainesville Midland Railroad in Gainesville.

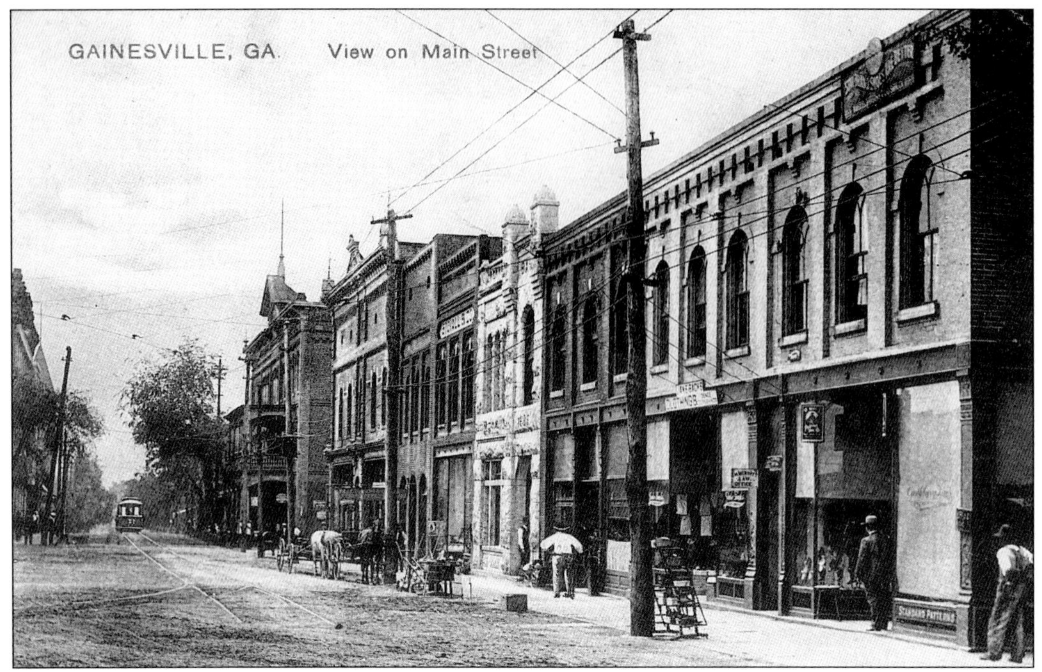

Here is a 1908 view of Main Street in Gainesville. The sender of the card was short and to the point. The back of the card reads, "What's the trouble—did you get my last letter."

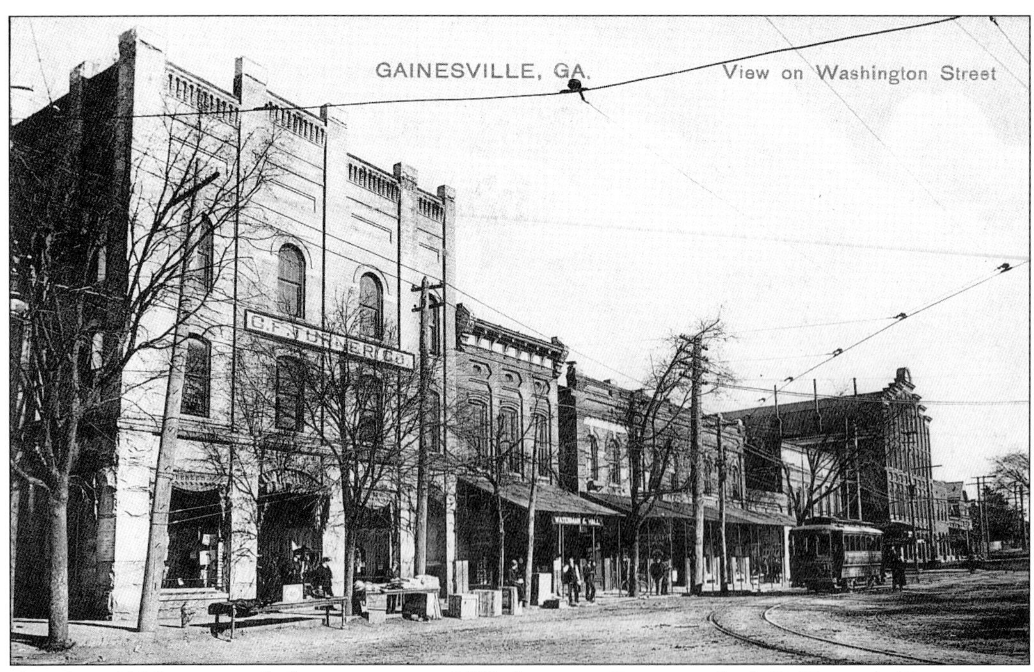

Another 1908 post card shows a view of Washington Street with G.F. Turner's Department Store on the corner.

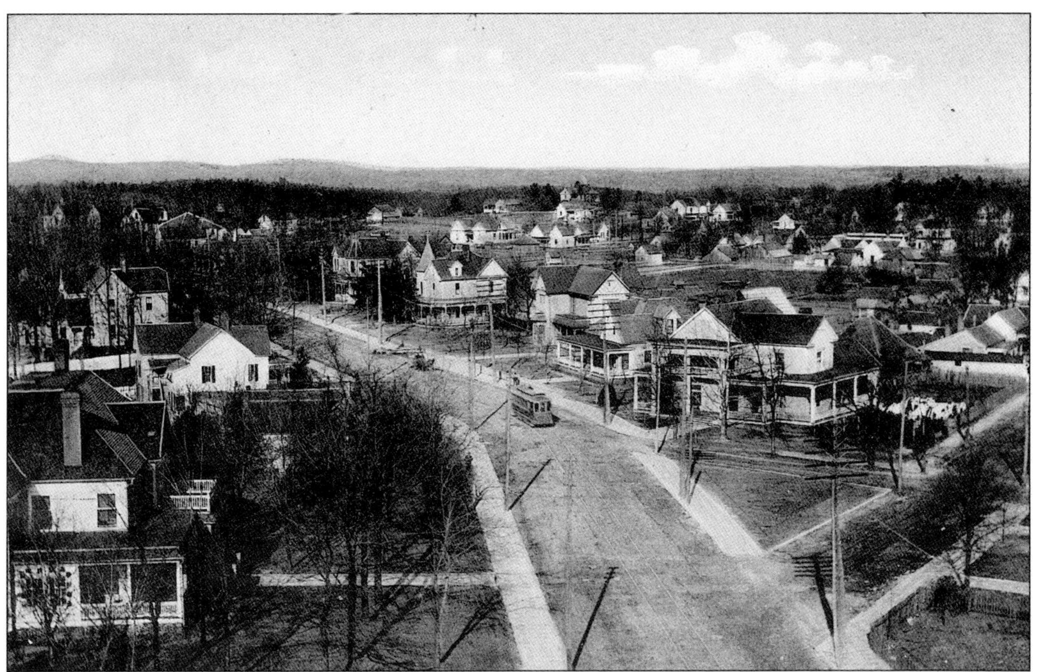

This 1908 post card shows a bird's-eye view of Gainesville's Green Street.

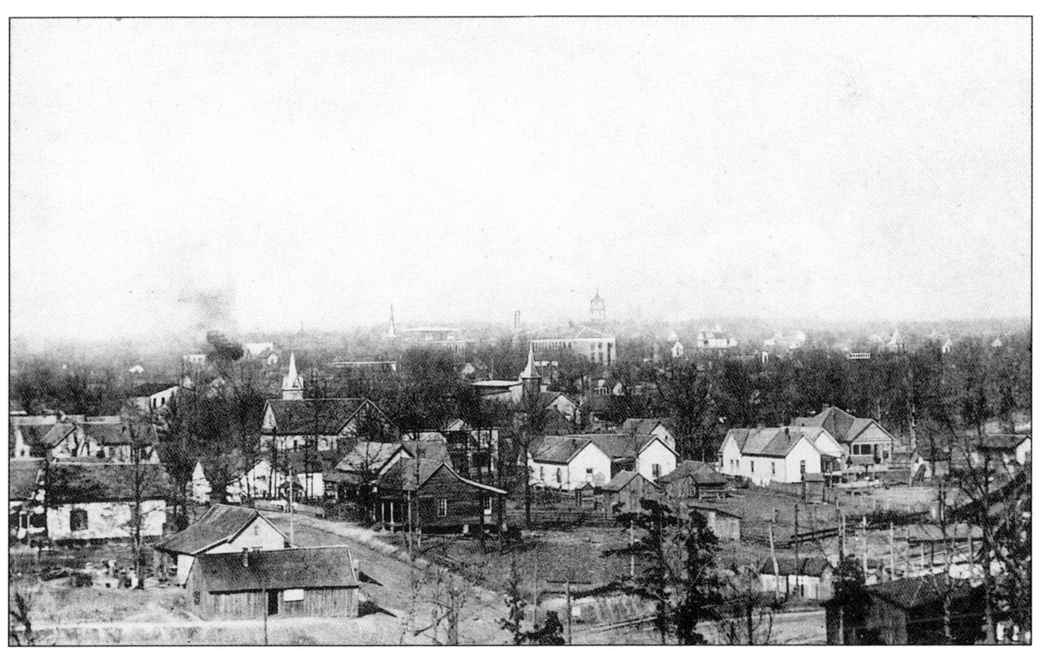

Another bird's-eye view of Gainesville shows a slightly different aspect of the town.

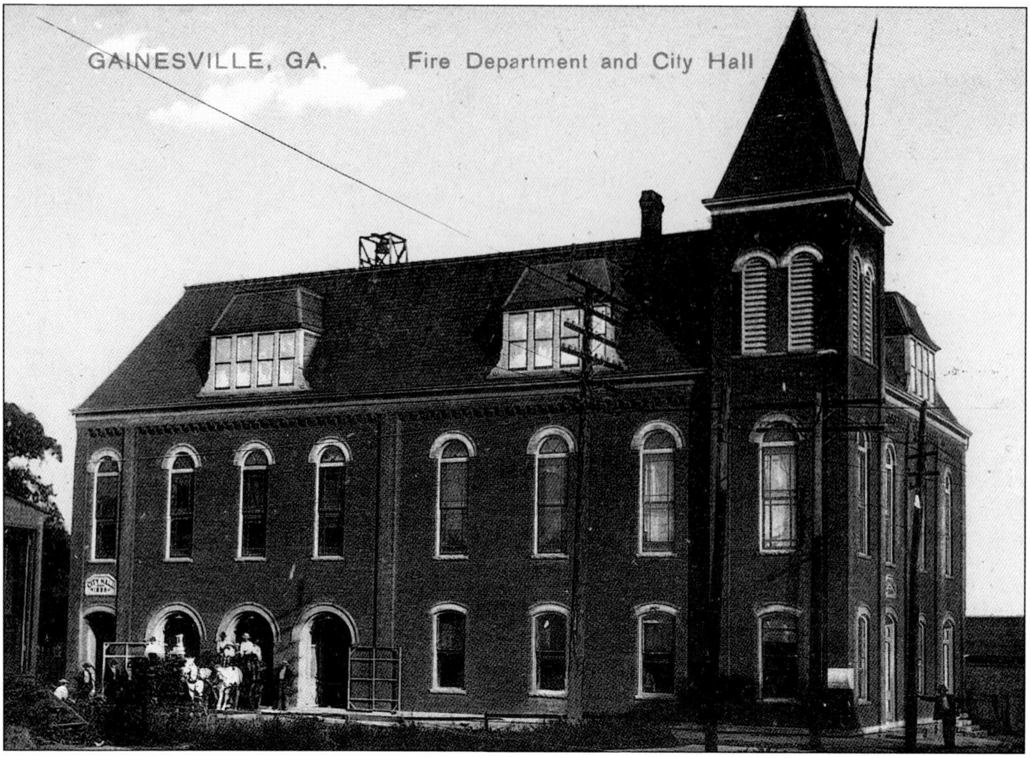

This post card shows the fire department and city hall building in Gainesville, complete with horse-drawn firefighting equipment.

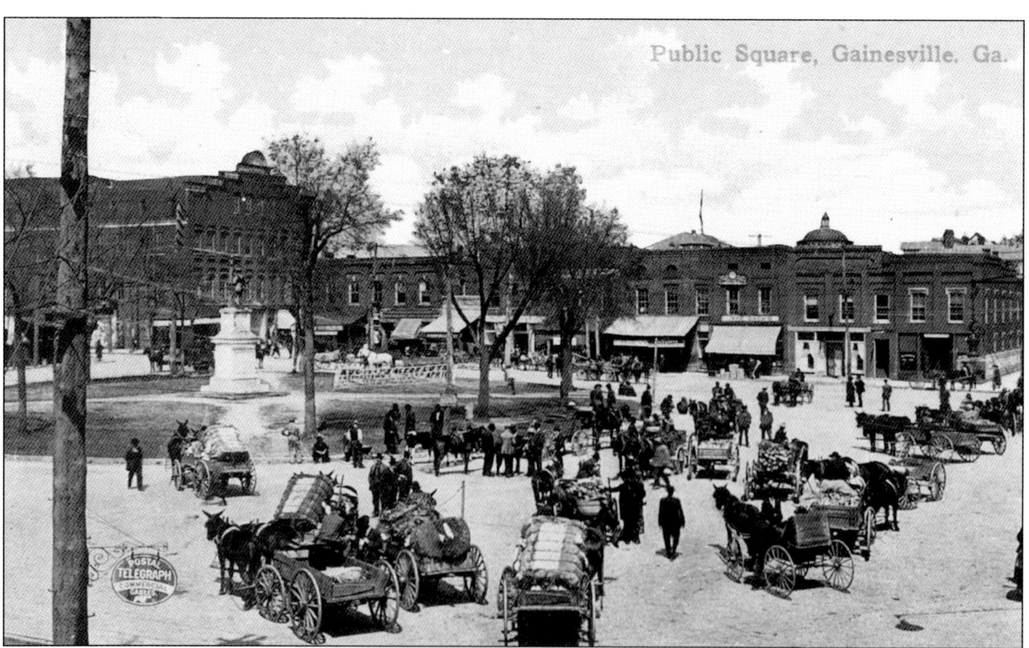

The Gainesville area had its share of cotton farmers. In this view of the public square, farmers bring their crop to market, as they did in countless other Southern towns.

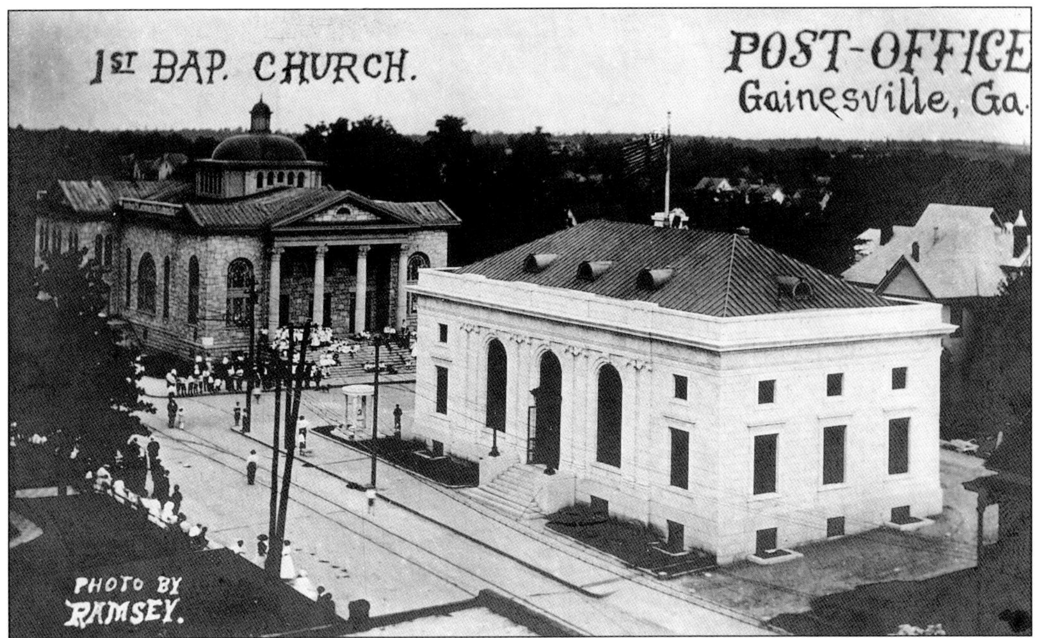

A real-photo post card by "Ramsey" shows the First Baptist Church and the post office in Gainesville.

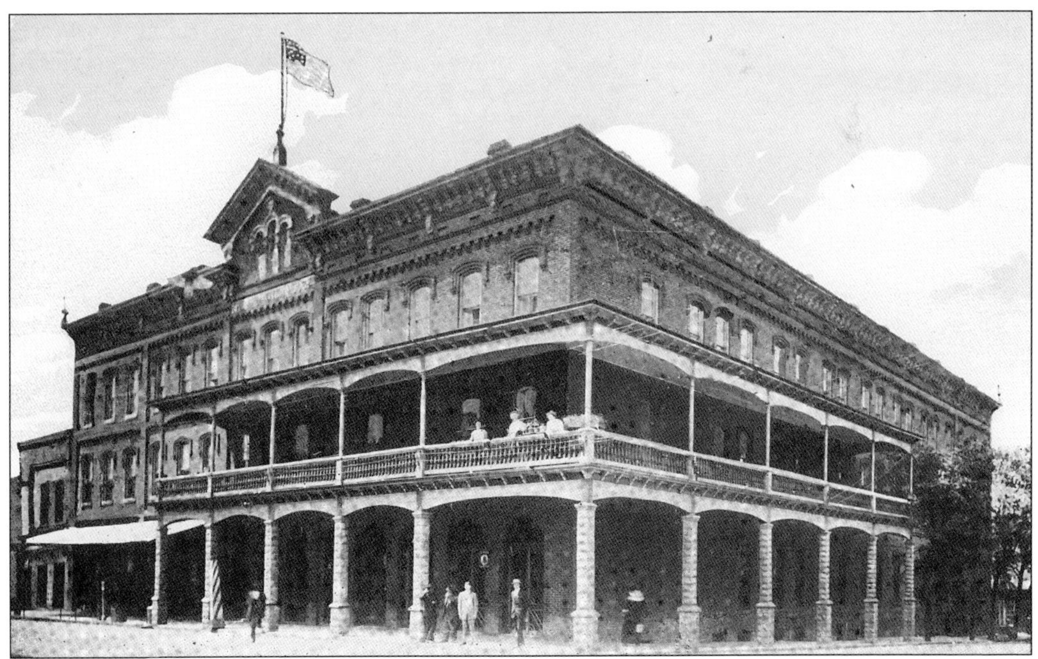
The Hotel Arlington on Main Street proudly flies the flag as guests relax on the second-story balcony.

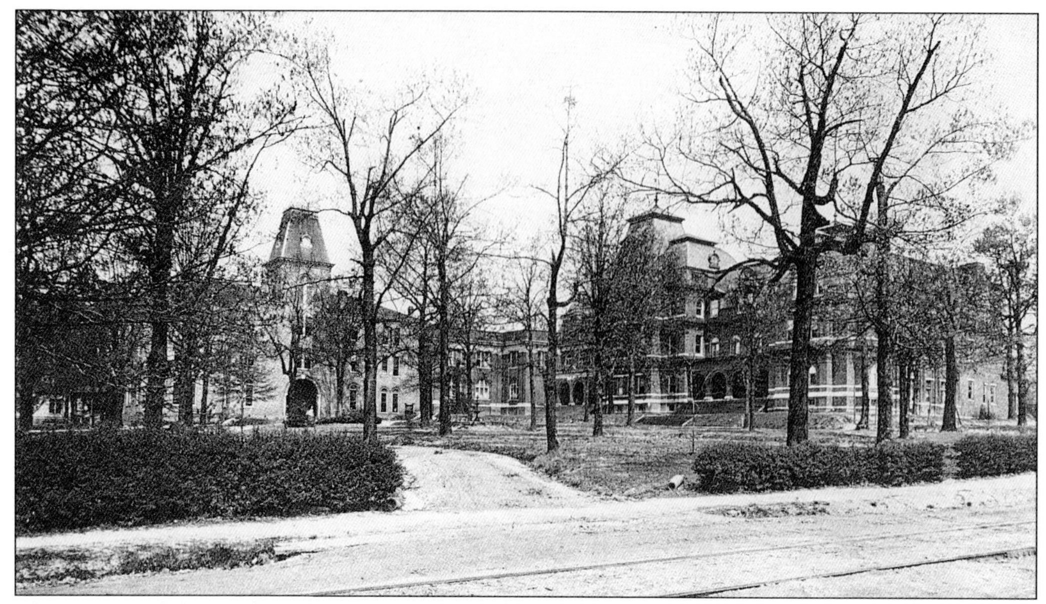

This post card shows the main part of the campus of Brenau College in Gainesville.

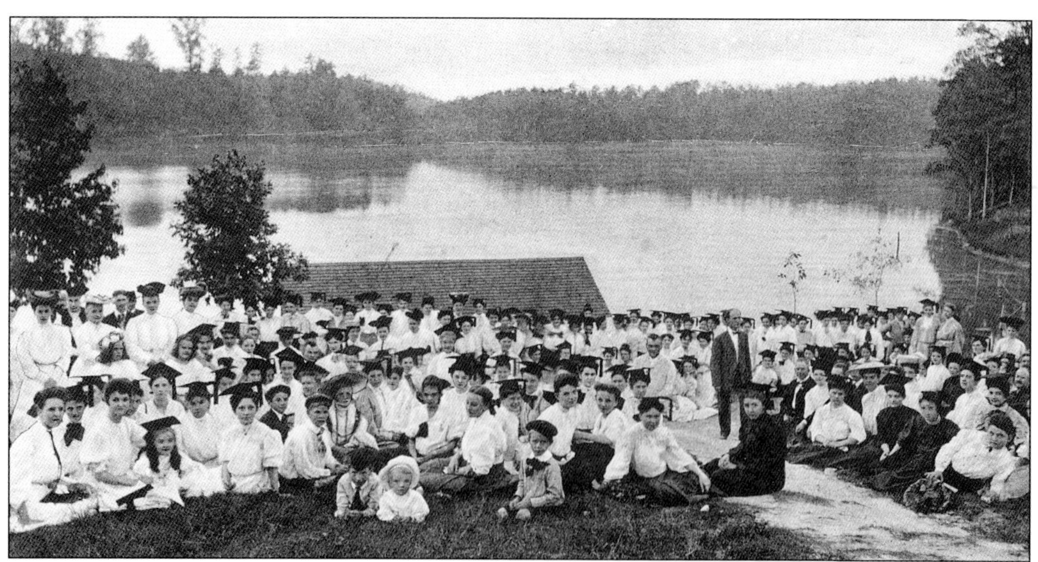

An outing of Brenau College students at Chattahoochee Park in Gainesville was captured in this post card.

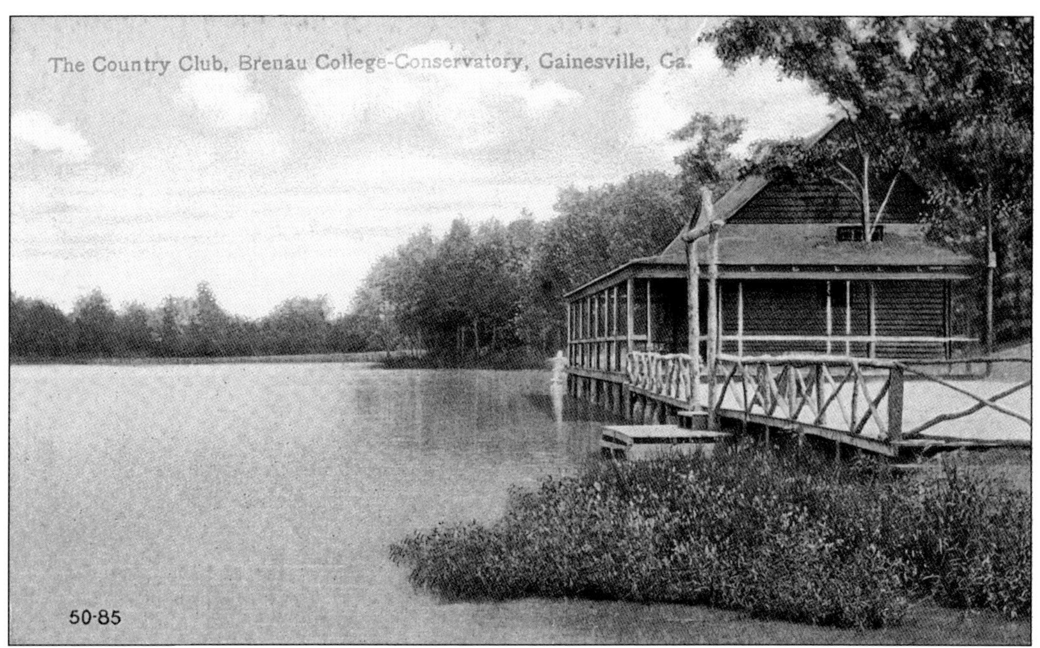

The Country Club at the Brenau College Conservatory at Gainesville shows a rustic charm in this card.

Students enjoy the Club House at Brenau College in Gainesville in this *c.* 1908 post card.

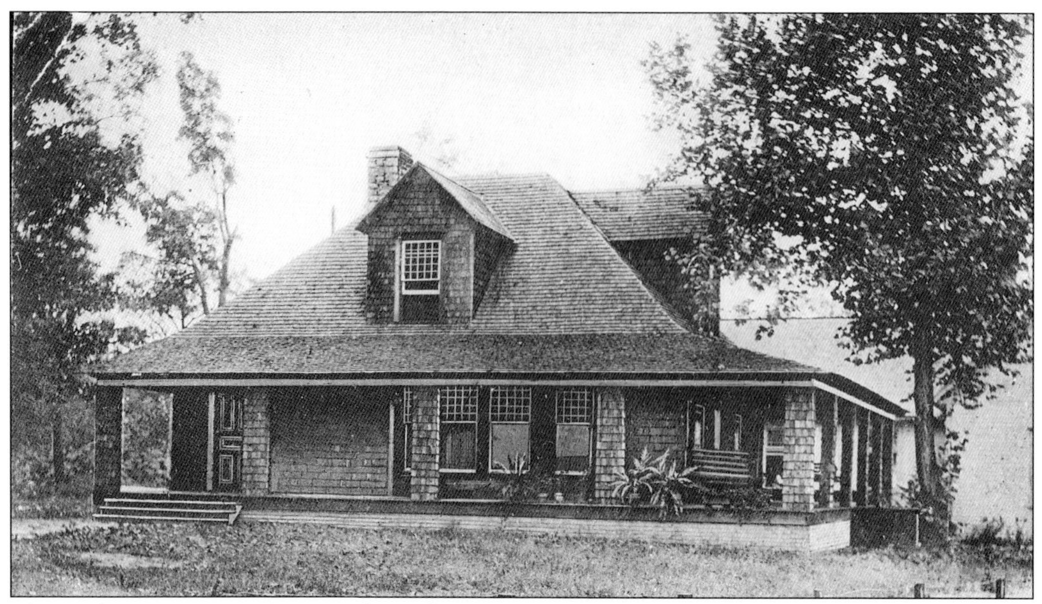

This is the Beta Sigma Omicron bungalow at Brenau College in Gainesville.

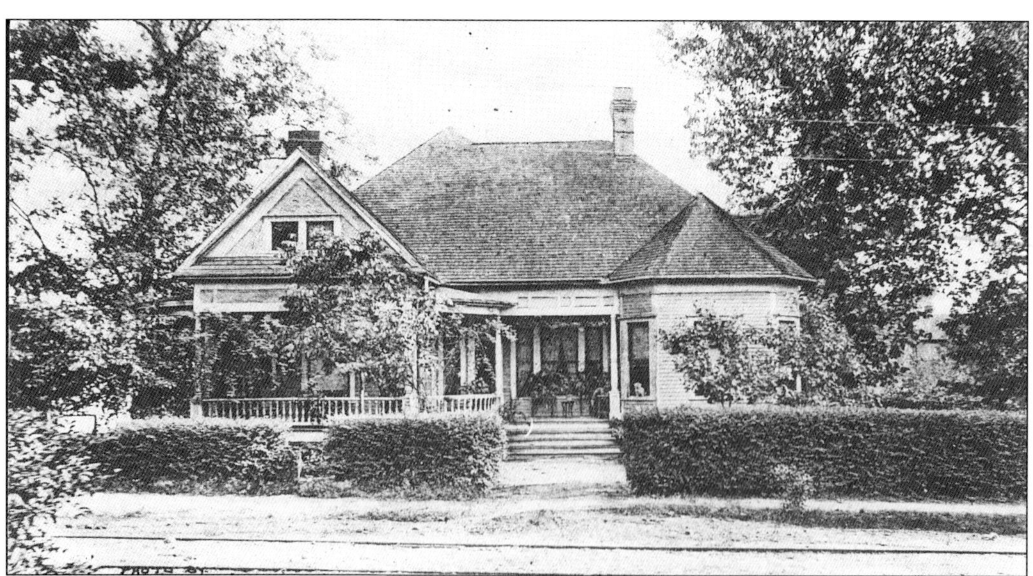

This is the Sigma Phi Epsilon house at Brenau College in Gainesville. The sender of this card had urgent personal business to attend to. She wrote: "Got here alright and having a fine time. Please look in our middle dresser drawer and bring my white girdle & be sure to bring my blue skirt. Maude."

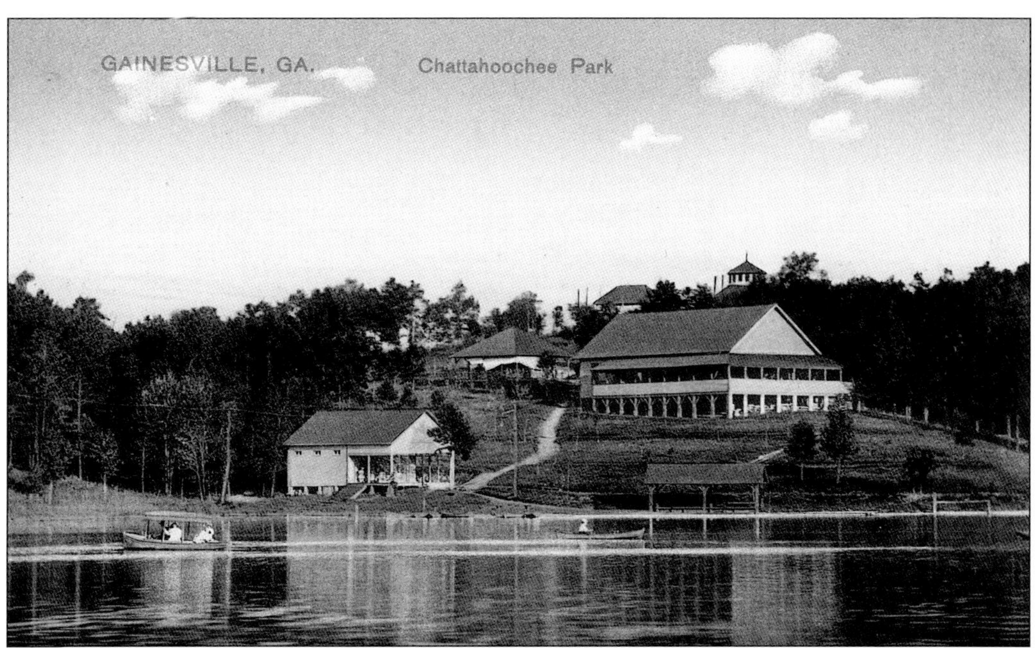

Canoers and boaters enjoy the waters of Chattahoochee Park at Gainesville in this picturesque post card view.

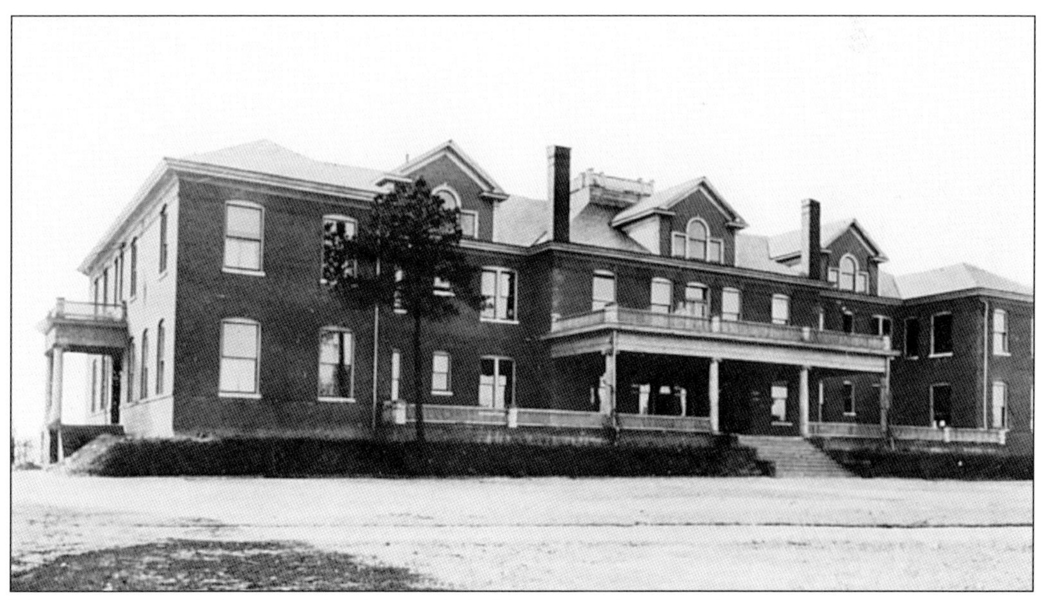
This is the main building of the Riverside Military Academy in Gainesville.

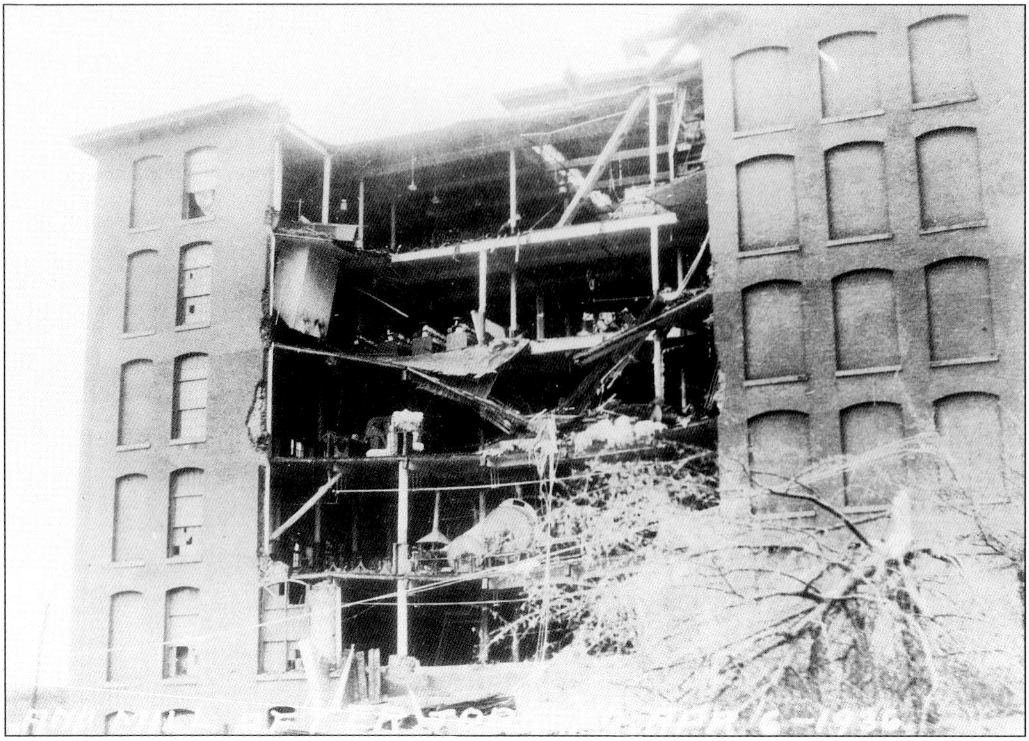

A devastating tornado destroyed much of Gainesville on April 6, 1936, killing more than 130 people.

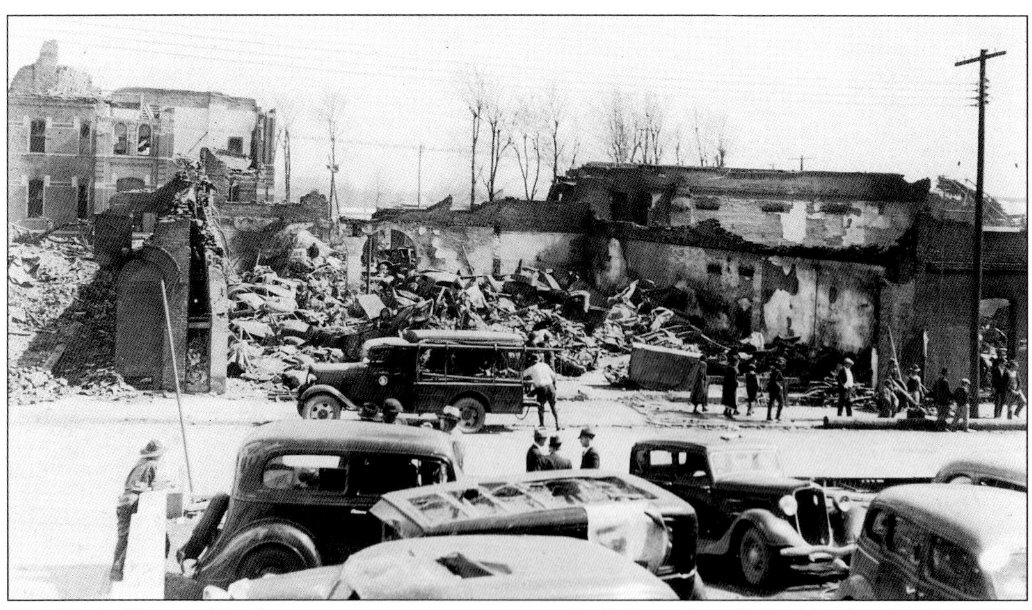

The Pruitt-Barrett Hardware store was among many buildings demolished in the April 6, 1936 tornado in Gainesville.

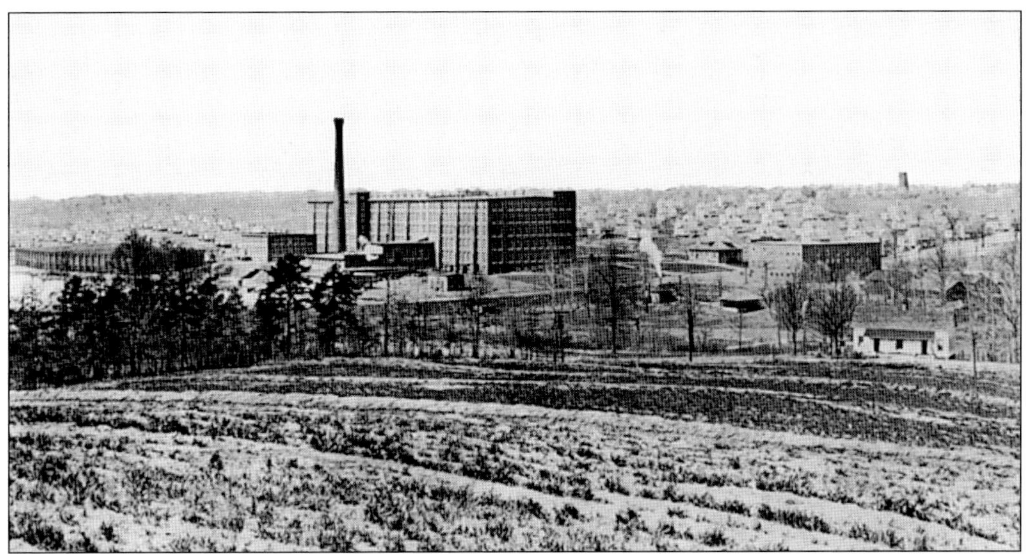

This bird's-eye view of the Pacolet Manufacturing Company in New Holland shows both the large manufacturing plant and the surrounding farmland.

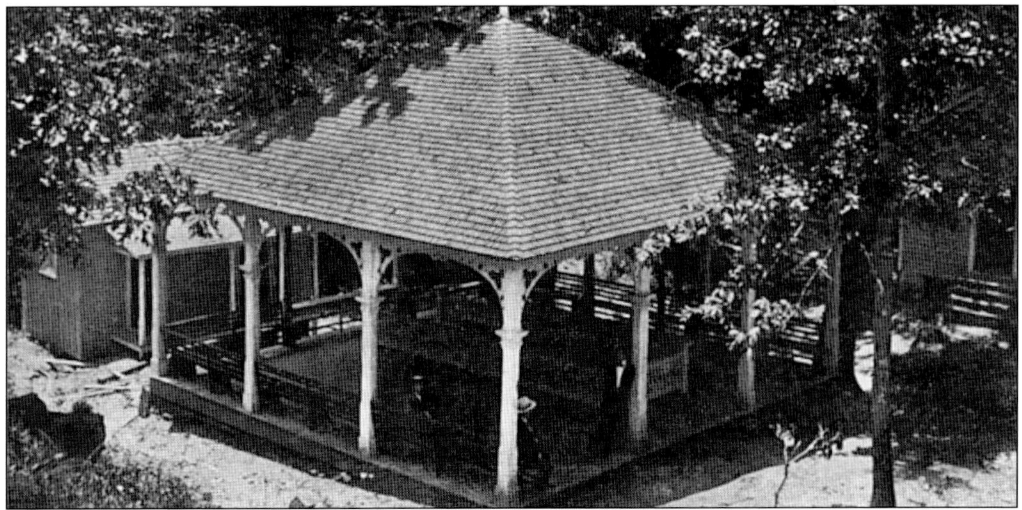

This c. 1906 post card shows a couple of gentlemen enjoying the beauty of White Sulphur Springs in Hall County. There was also a White Sulphur Springs in Meriwether County, which was better known than this Hall County site.

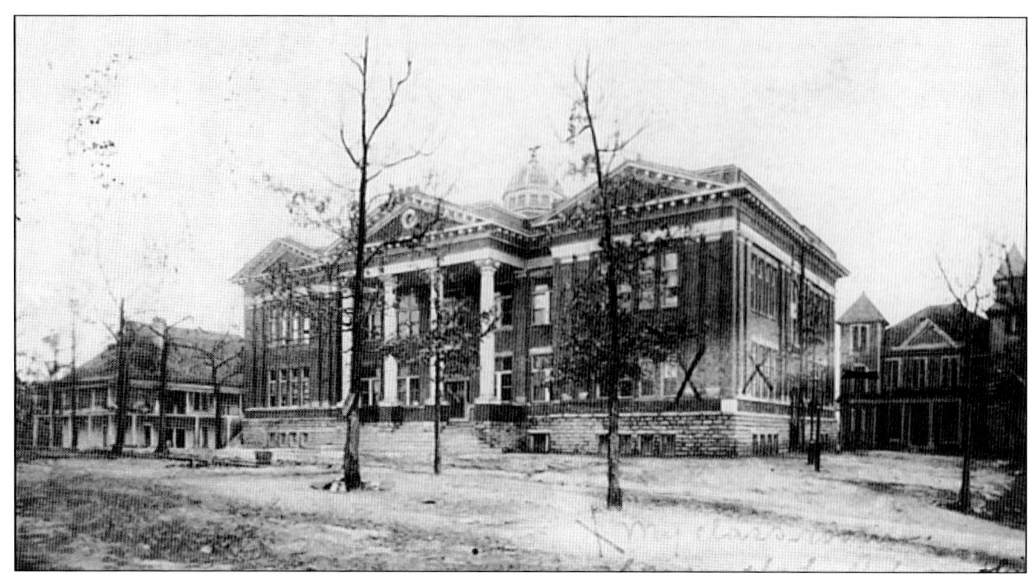

This post card shows the girls' and boys' dormitory at the Perry Rainey Institute in Auburn.

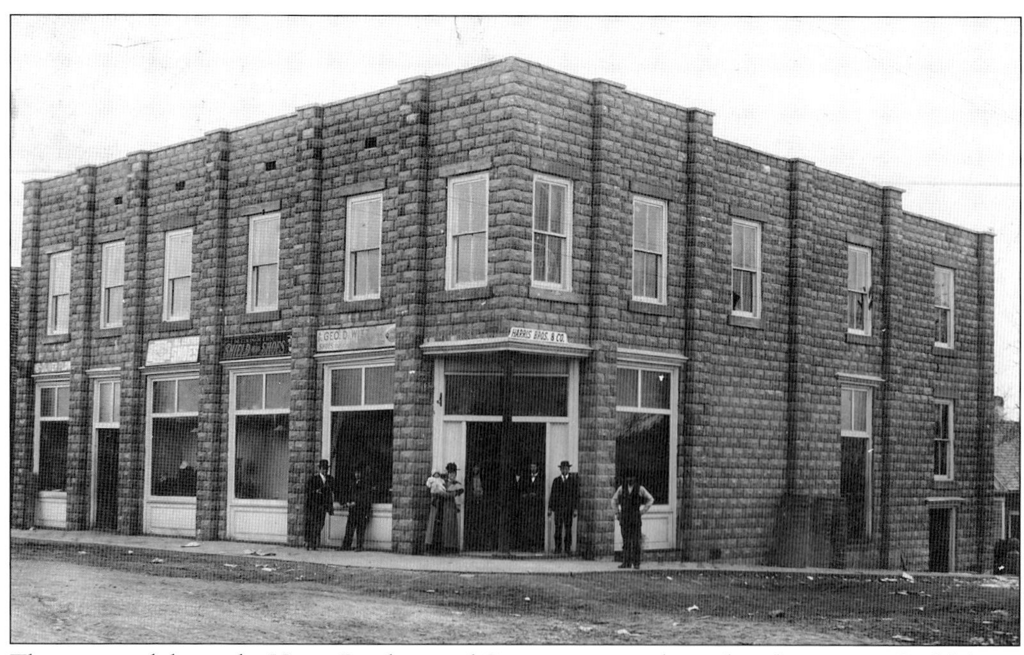

This post card shows the Harris Brothers and Company general merchandise store in Bethlehem, as well as some customers of the store.

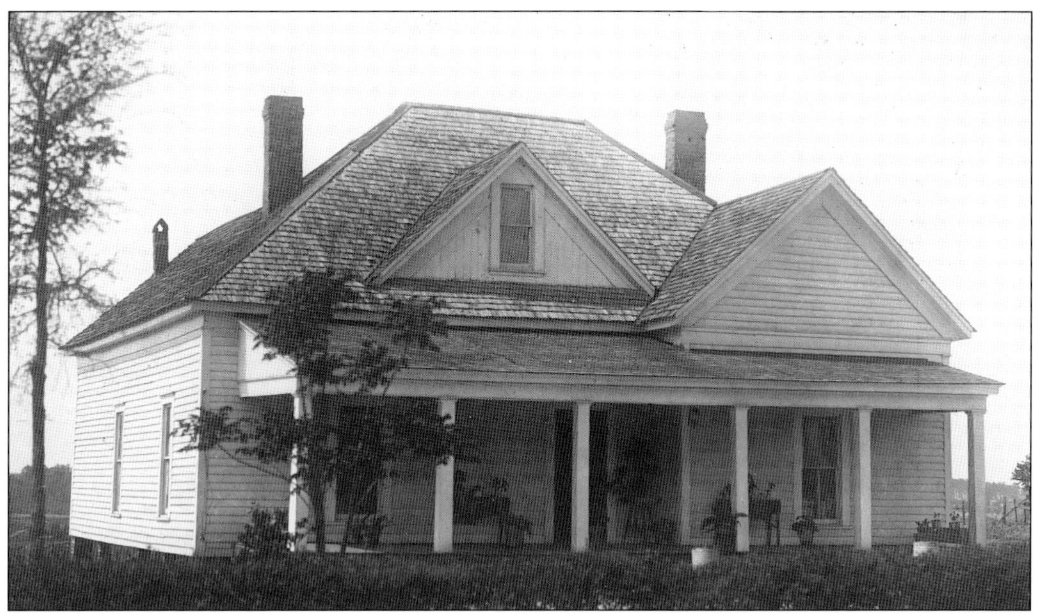

This real-photo post card shows the home of H.A. Hardy in Statham about 1907.

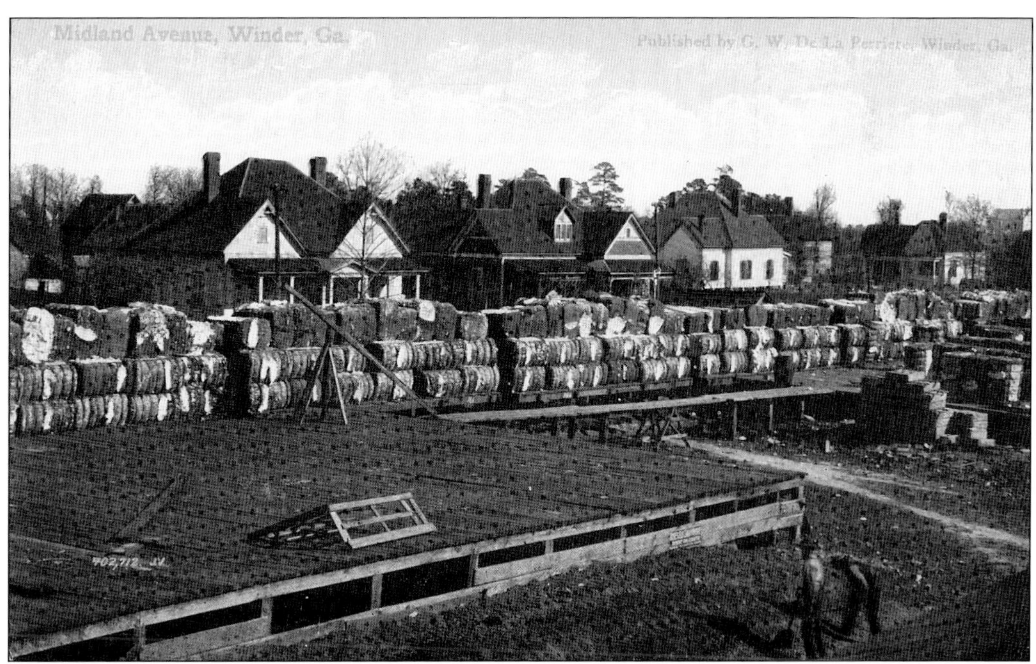

This hand-colored post card, published by G.W. De La Pierre of Winder, shows Midland Avenue in Winder, as well as dozens of bales of cotton.

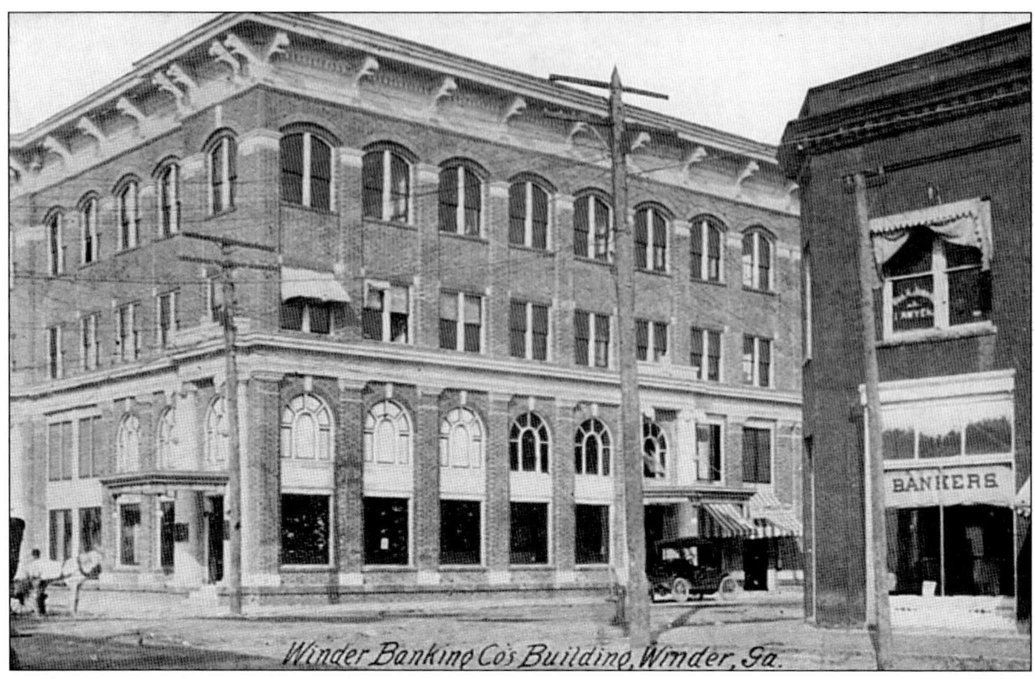

In this view of the Winder Banking Company, note the second-story offices of Geo. A. Johns, lawyer. In 1910, the president of the bank was T.A. Maynard.

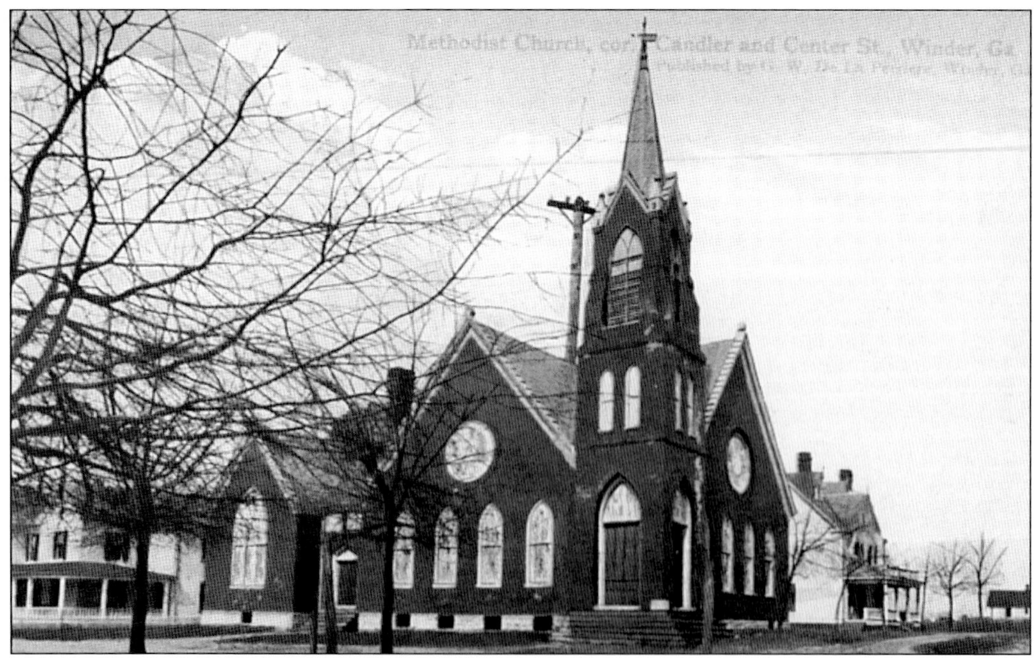

The Methodist church at the corner of Candler and Center Streets in Winder was evidently photographed in winter, judging by the lack of foliage on the trees.

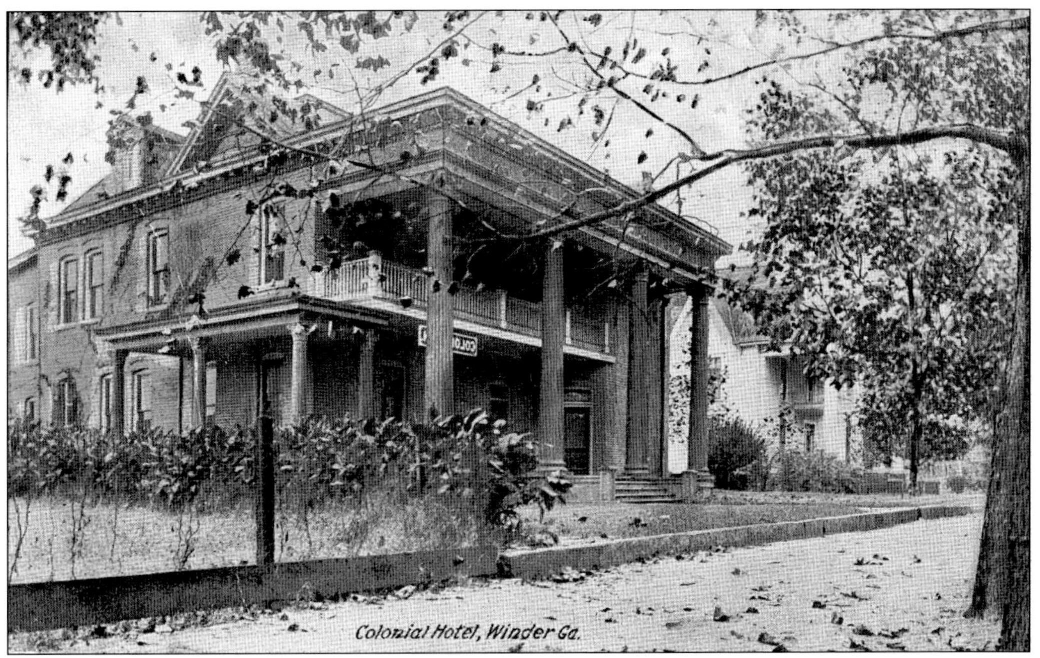

This post card shows the Colonial Hotel in Winder.

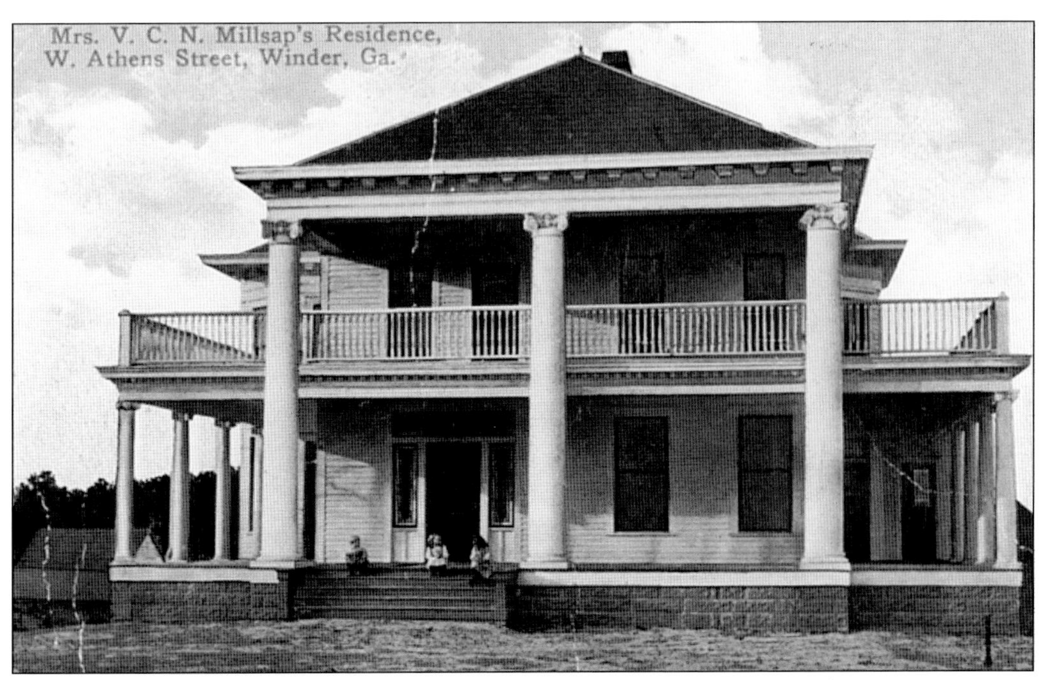

Three children sit on the front step of Mrs. V.C.N. Millsap's house in Winder.

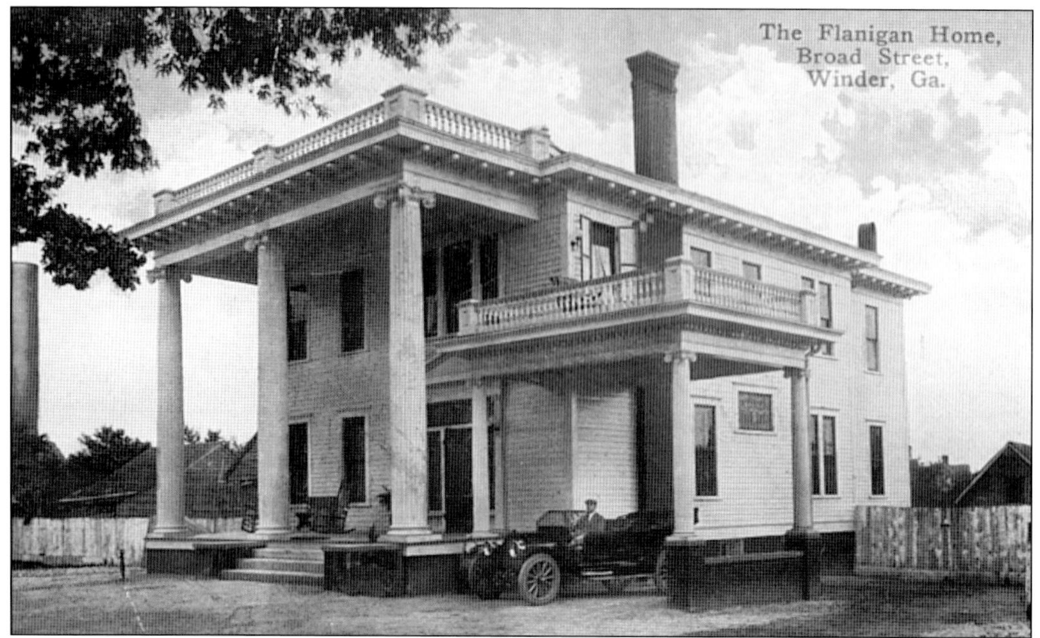

Alongside the Flanigan home in Winder is what appears to be a new automobile and a proud driver. Note the second-floor balcony, complete with padded chair for comfort.

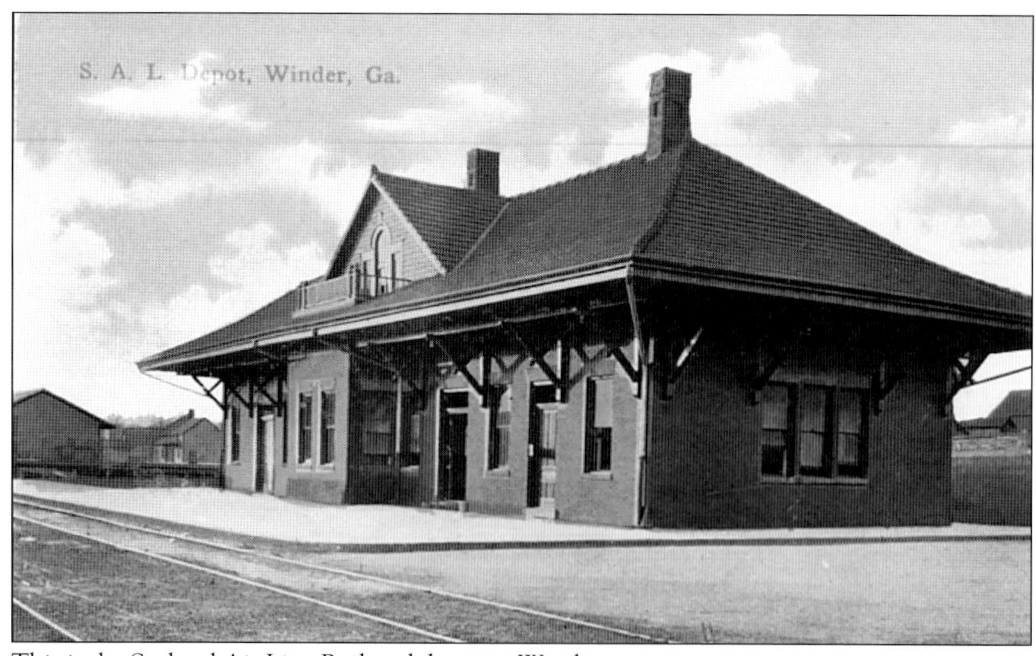

This is the Seabord Air Line Railroad depot in Winder.

Six

Jackson County

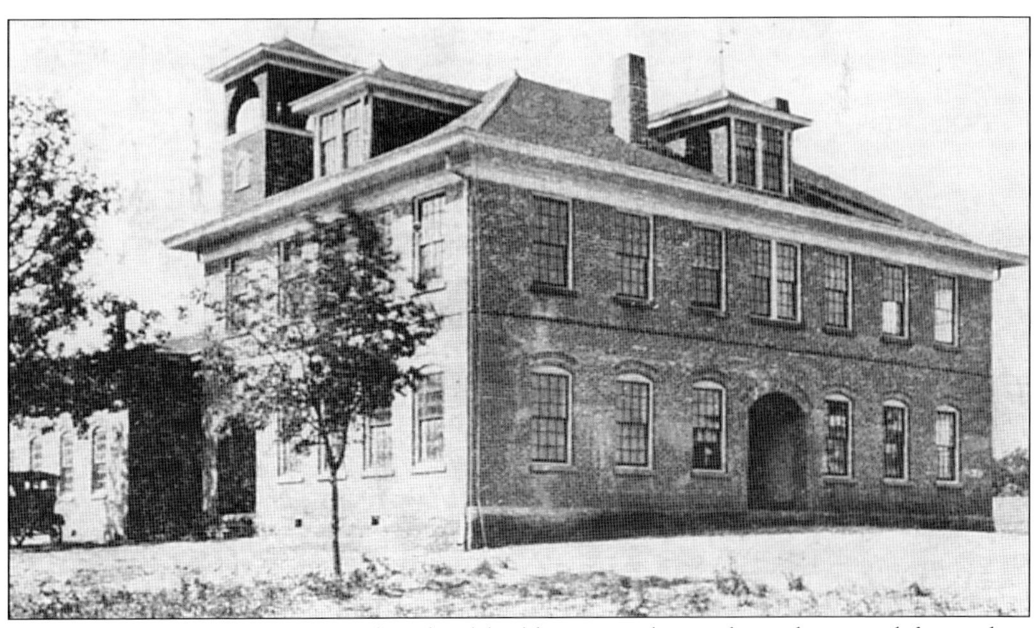

Shown here is the Braselton High School building. Braselton achieved national fame when Athens native Kim Basinger bought most of the town in 1991.

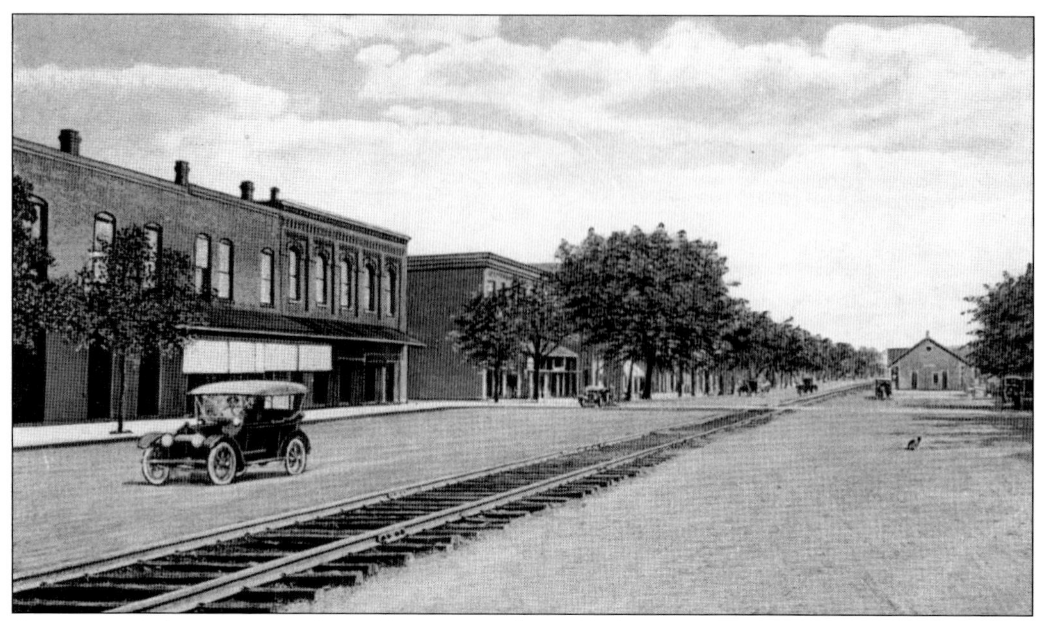

An uncrowded street scene shows Commerce about 1912.

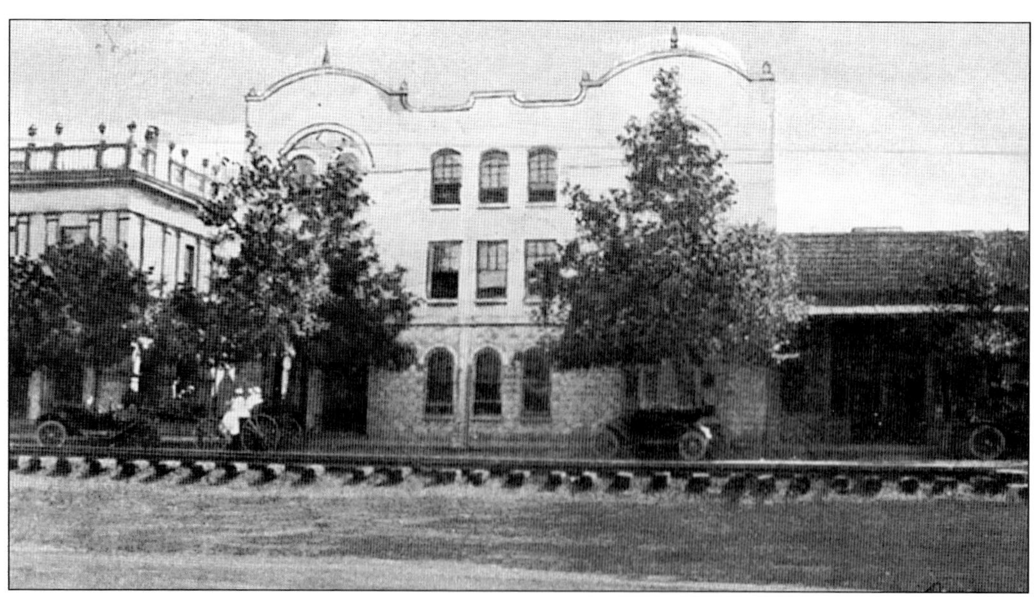

The sender of this post card featuring the Central Hotel wrote, "Hope you are enjoying life to the uttermost these days. My, wish I could see you. Guess you are getting about ready to leave the hospital. Write sometimes."

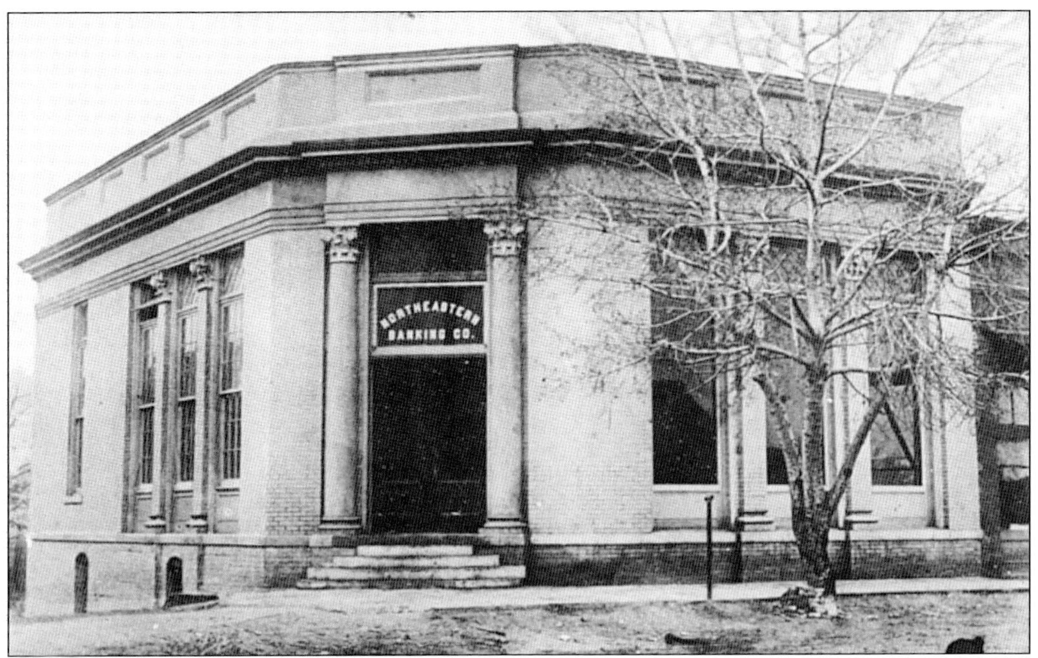

The Northeastern Banking Company's office in Commerce is shown in this *c.* 1908 post card. The president of the bank was Lamartine G. Hardman.

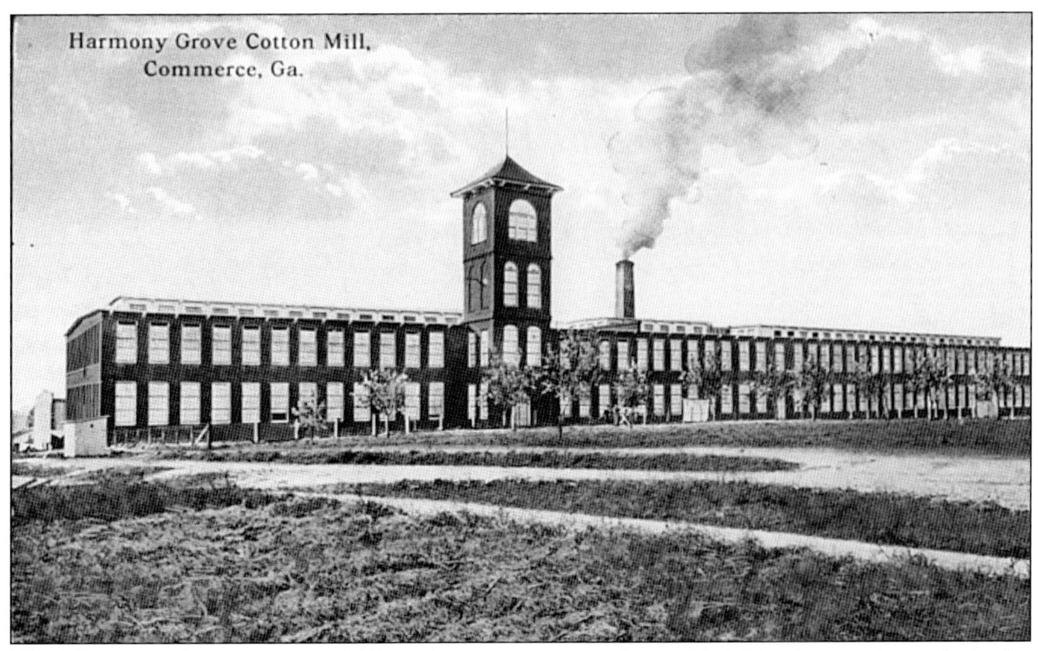

The Harmony Grove Cotton Mill in Commerce, complete with billowing smokestack, is the focus of this card.

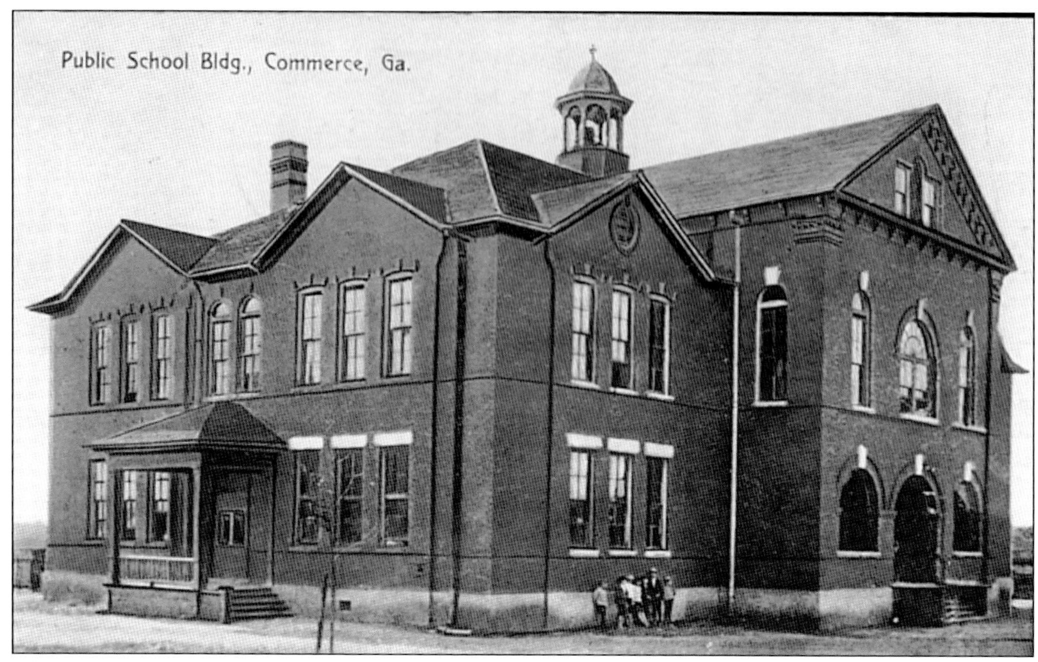

This card shows the public school building in Commerce.

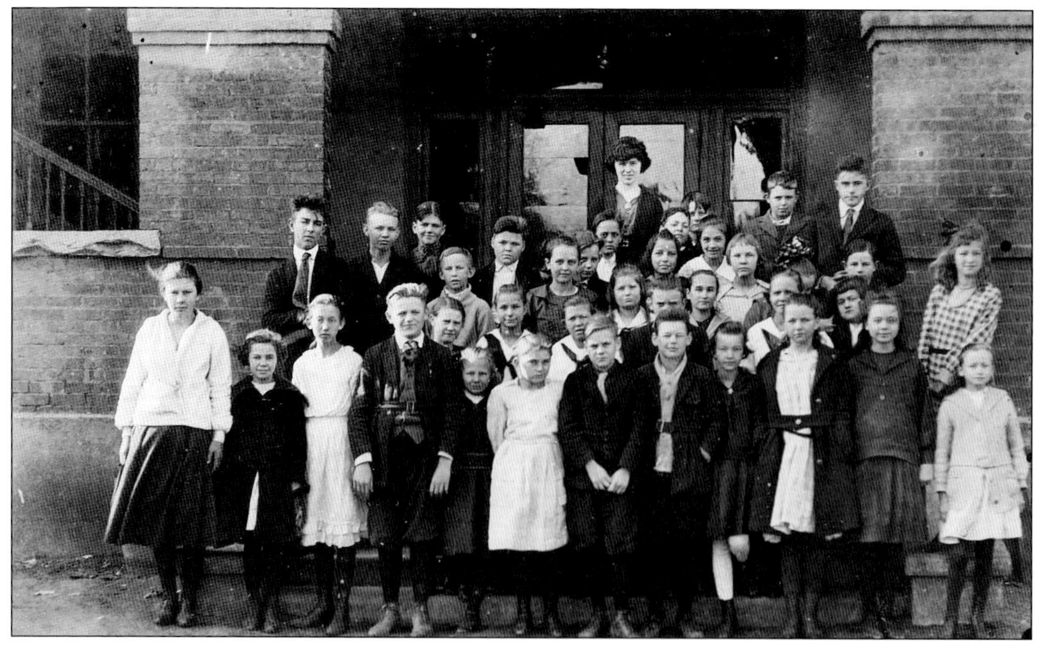

The 1920 sixth-grade class at the Commerce school had this photograph taken in November of that year.

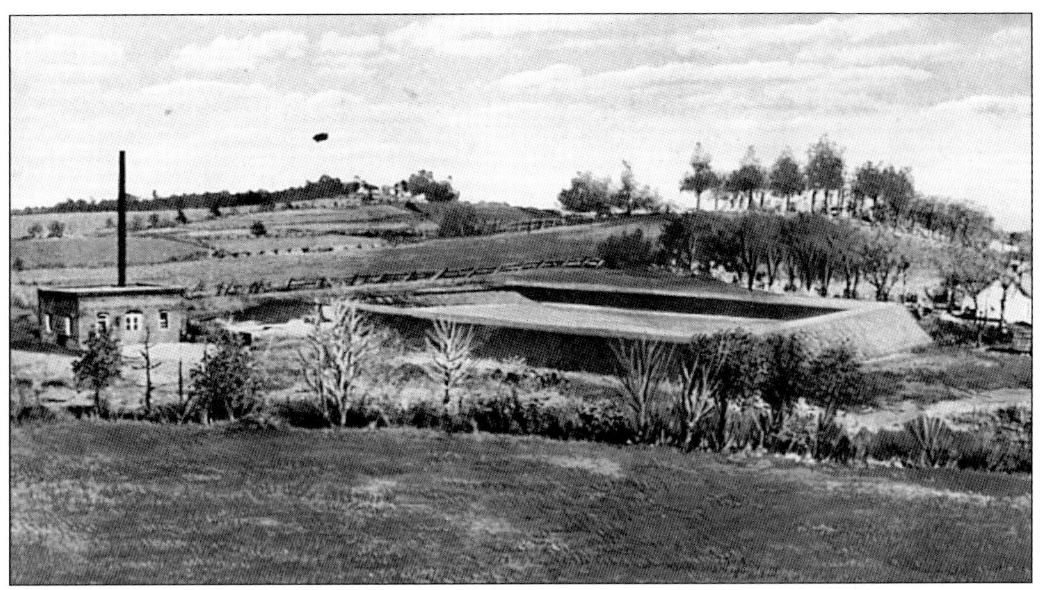

The municipal waterworks at Commerce was the subject of this post card.

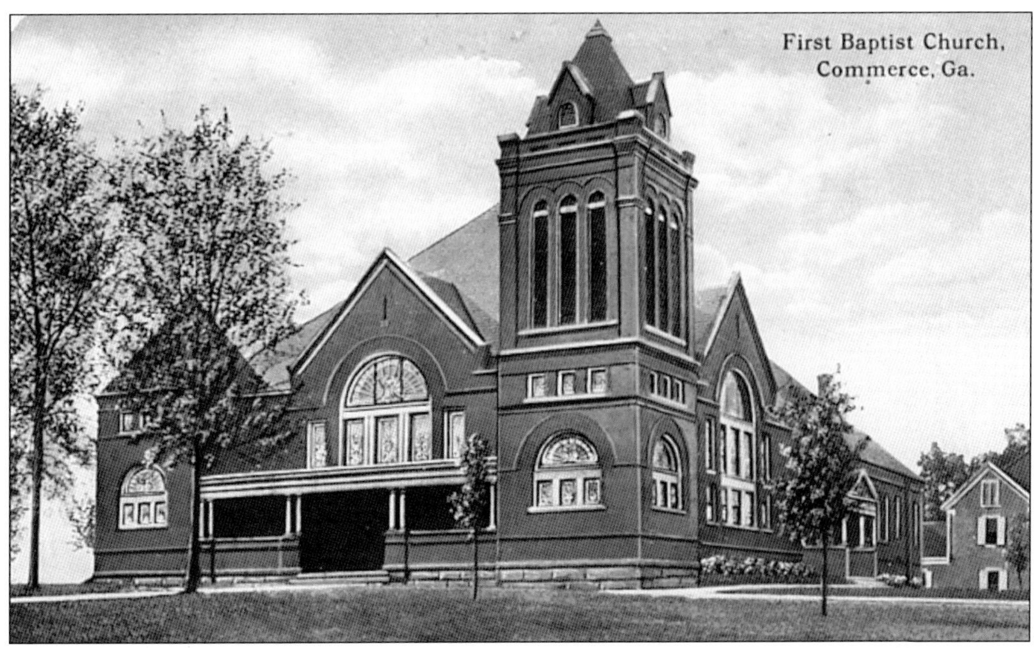

The sender of this post card of the First Baptist Church in Commerce wrote, "Hello! How are everybody at the college? You bet I am having a good time. Don't know when I will be back with you. I want to make me a few dresses—I may come about the 16. Have you heard from Miss Franklin? Wish that I could see all of you. I am expecting to hear from you real soon. Love, Gladys."

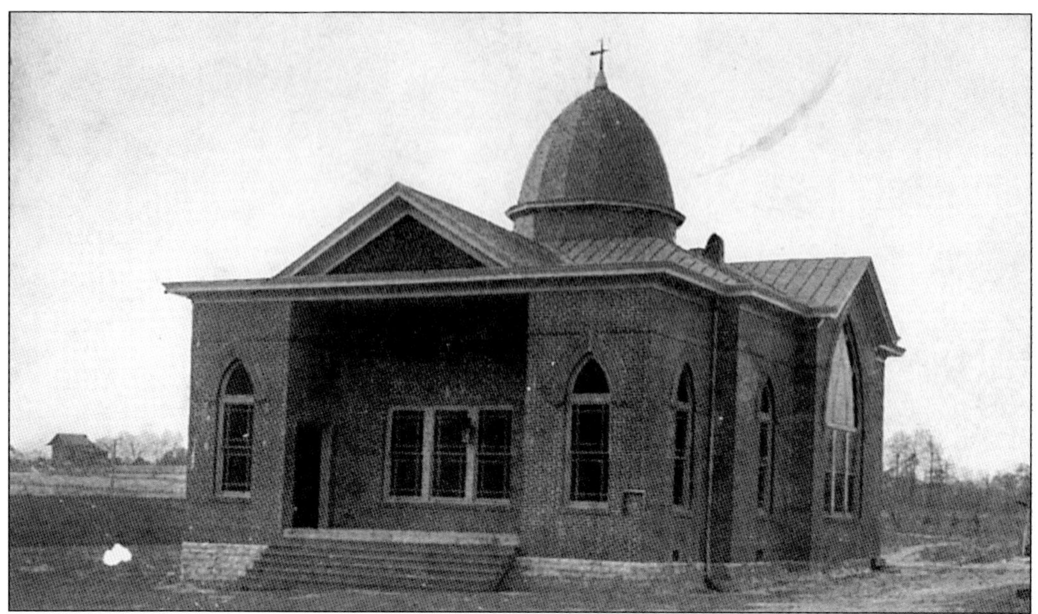

This card showing the Baptist church in Hoschton was mailed to Athens. The message reads, "Dear Miss Bird, I have been having a real good time this summer but I am in the house now with mamma and little Margaret Lee. She is one weak old and I am anxious for school to start. Oh how I wish you could be my teacher another year. C.M.E."

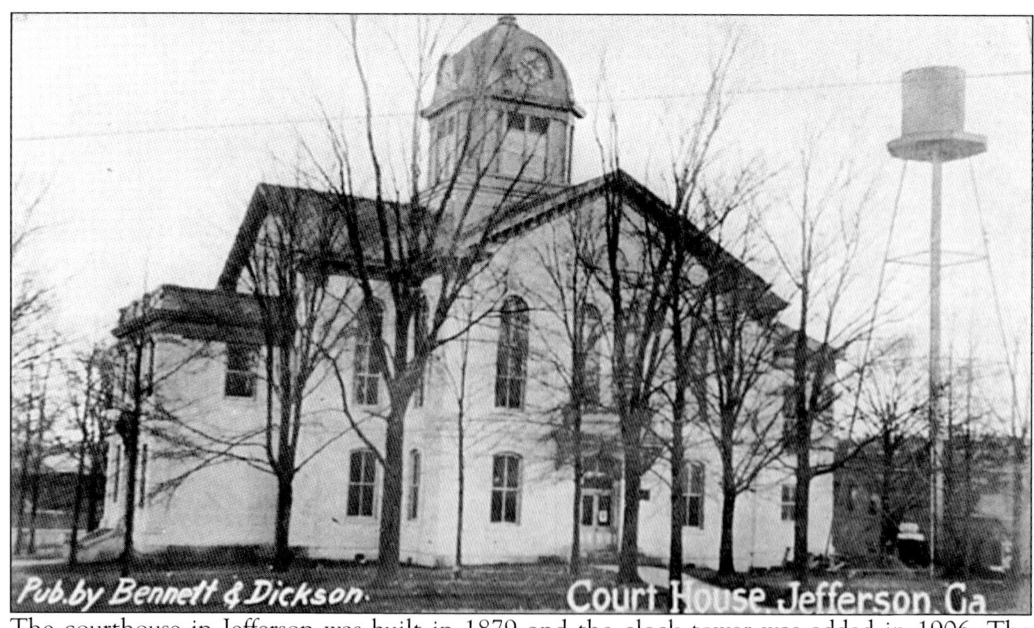

The courthouse in Jefferson was built in 1879 and the clock tower was added in 1906. The water tower is on the right.

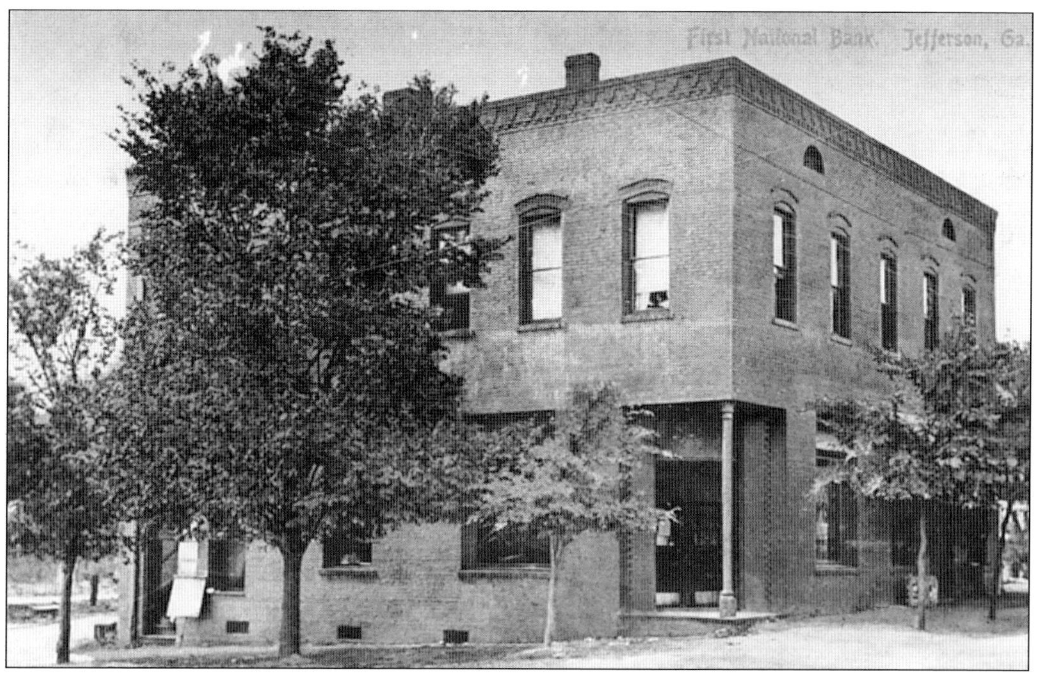

This card shows the First National Bank of Jefferson about 1908. The president was H.I. Mobley and the cashier was A.C. Appleby.

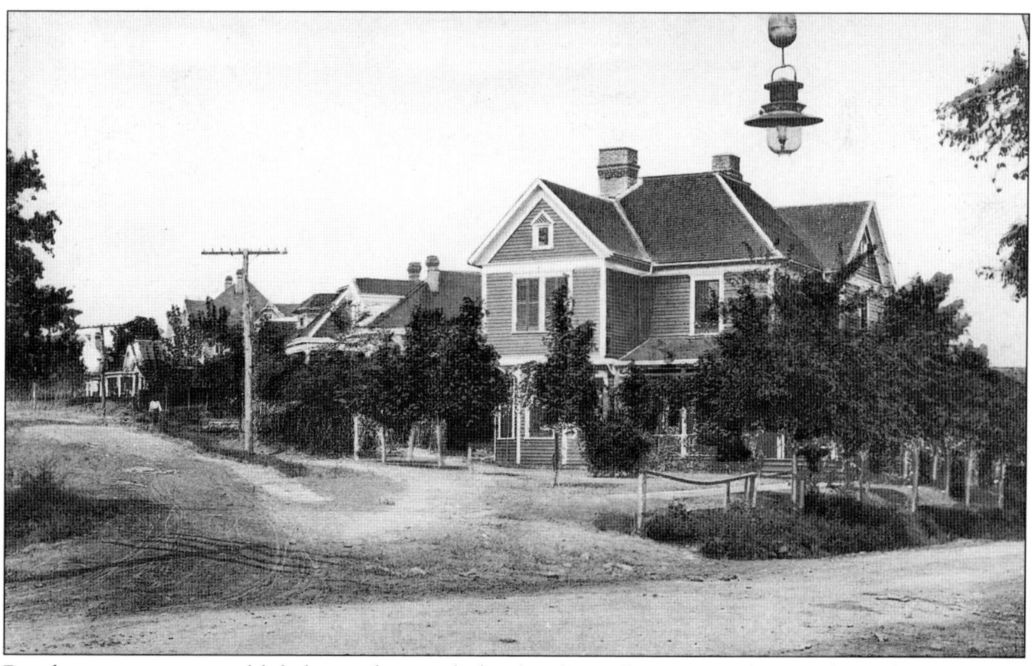

Readers can see an old-fashioned streetlight (top) in this view of a residential section on Lawrenceville Street in Jefferson.

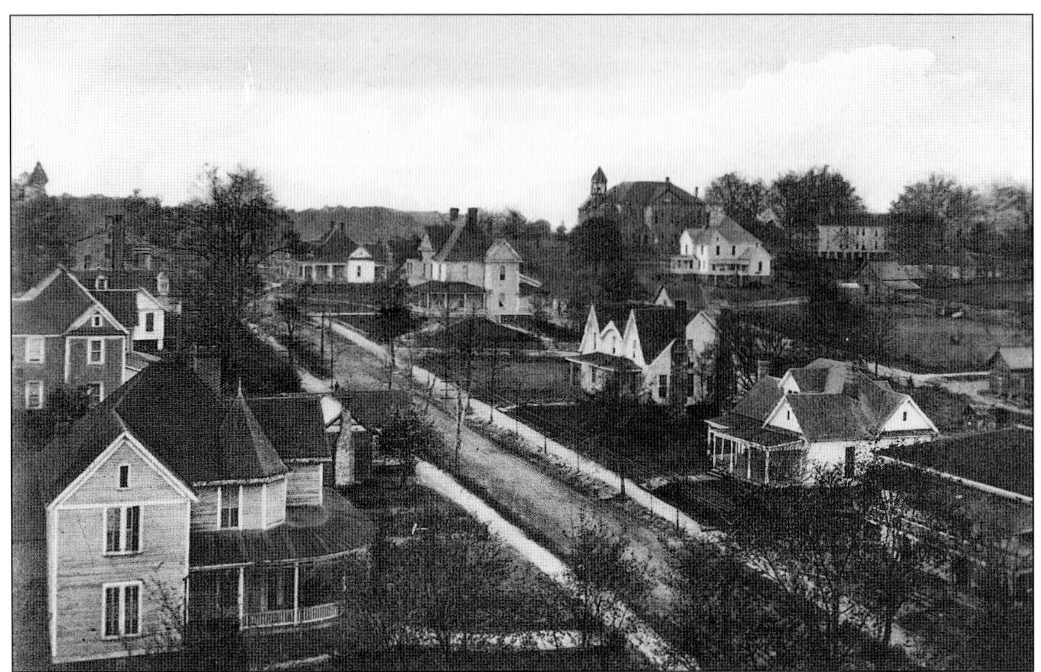

Power lines are visible, but the streets are still unpaved in this view looking north on Washington Street in Jefferson.

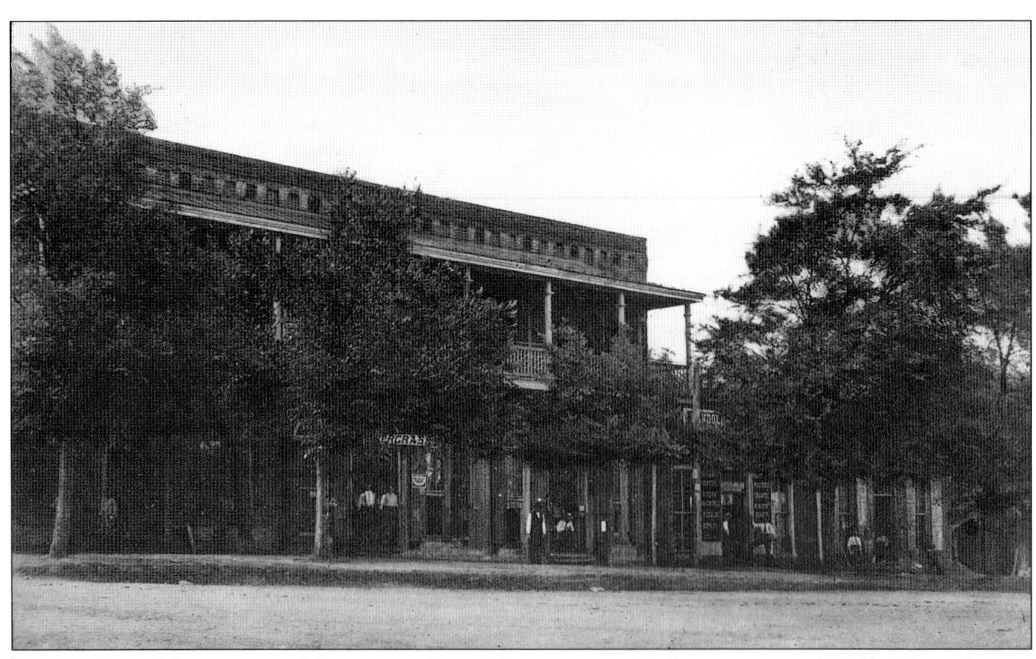

The sender of this post card featuring the public square in Jefferson wrote, "Hello Tom; I guess you will be surprised to receive a card from me. I hope you want wait so long to answer it. I saw Freddie yesterday. They are all well. Your friend, Maggie Brown."

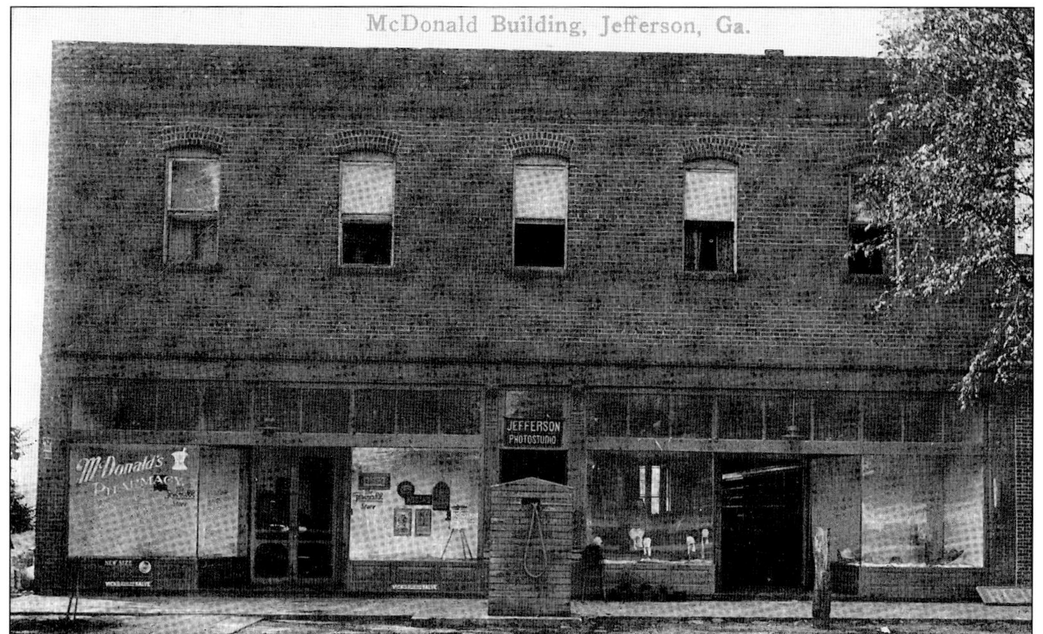

In this post card of the McDonald Building in Jefferson, note the signs for McDonald's Pharmacy and the Jefferson Photostudio, as well as the old-fashioned gas pump and hose in front.

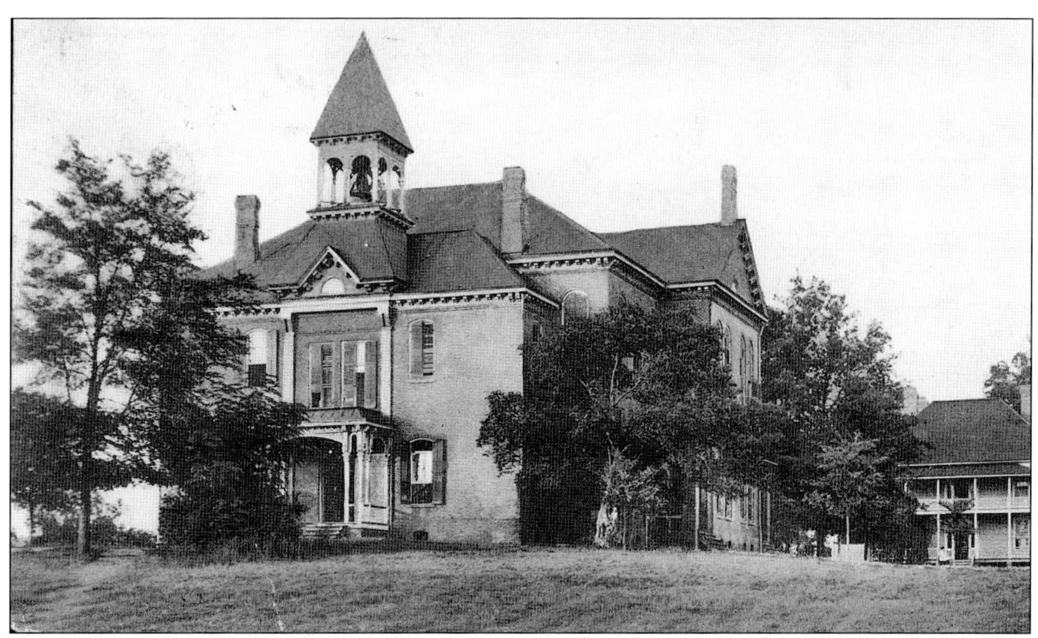

Pictured here is the Martin Institute and Dormitory in Jefferson.

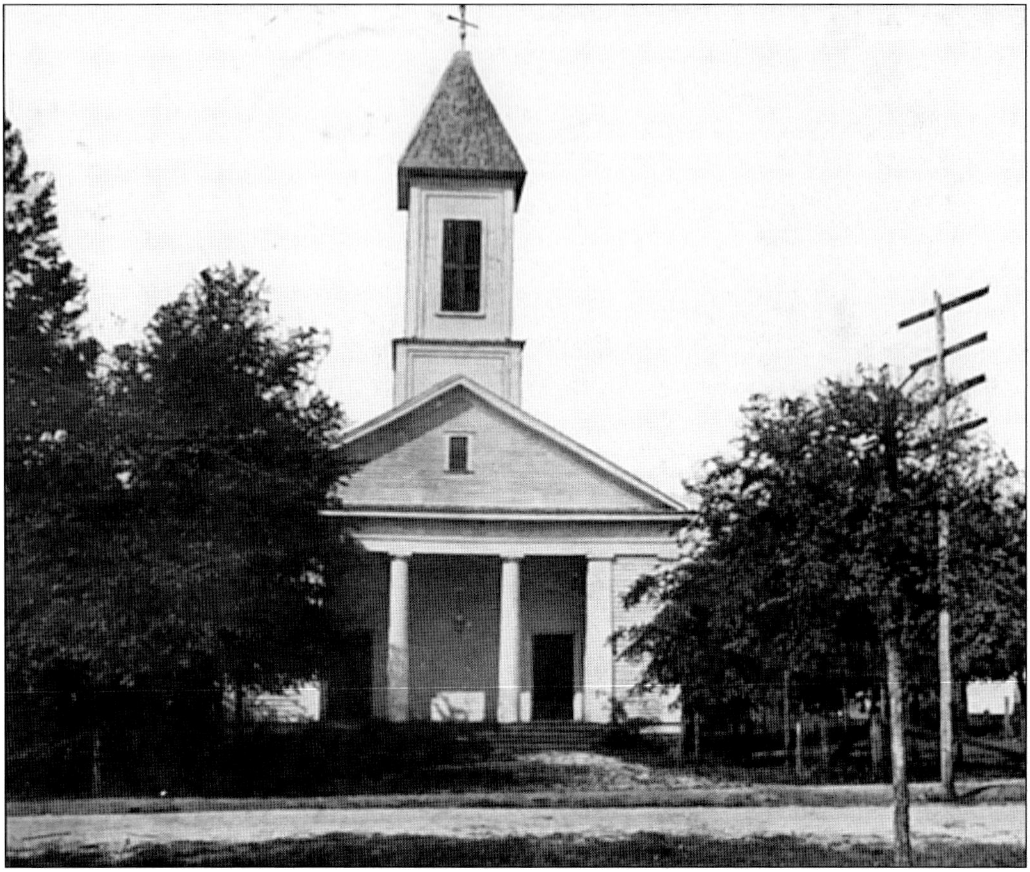

This card features the Presbyterian church in Jefferson.

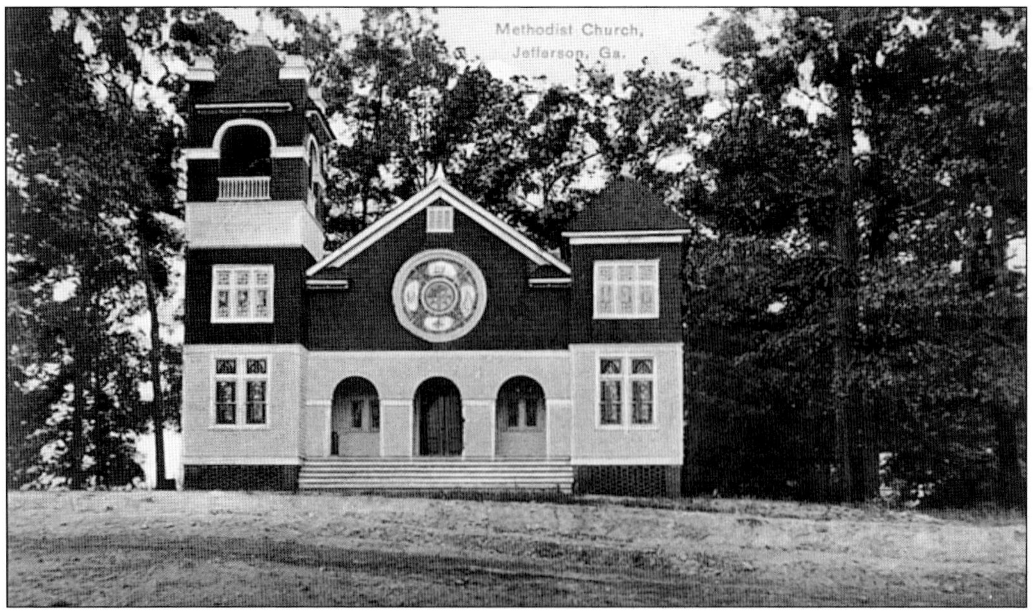

The Methodist church in Jefferson is featured in this hand-colored post card.

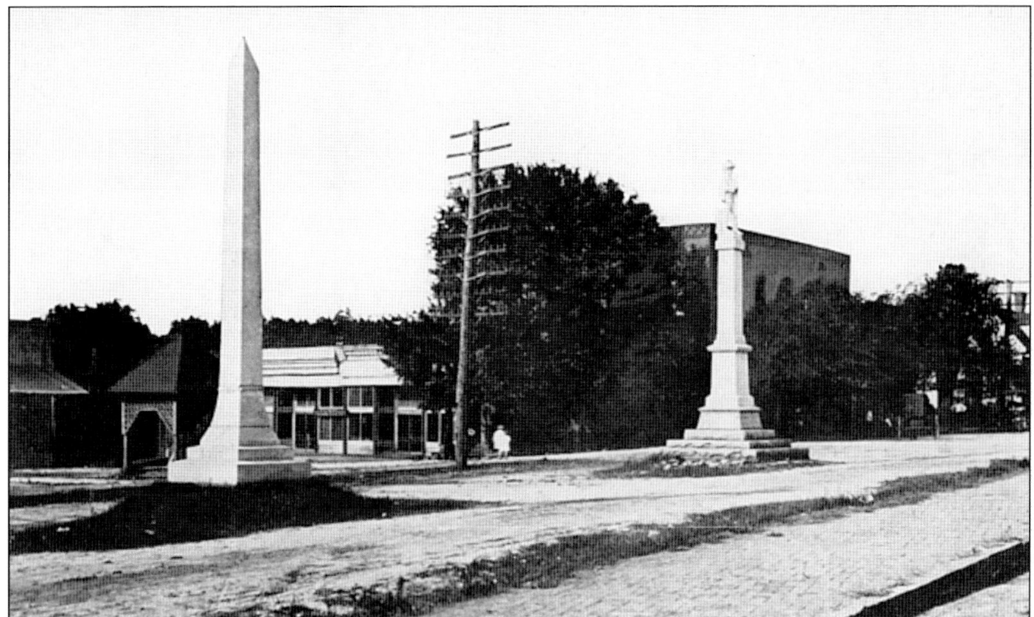

The Crawford W. Long Monument and the Confederate Monument in the public square in Jefferson are the subjects of this post card. The Confederate Monument was unveiled on Confederate Memorial Day, April 26, 1911. The Confederate soldier on the monument was accidentally toppled and broken in 1940 and was replaced with a Jerusalem cross.

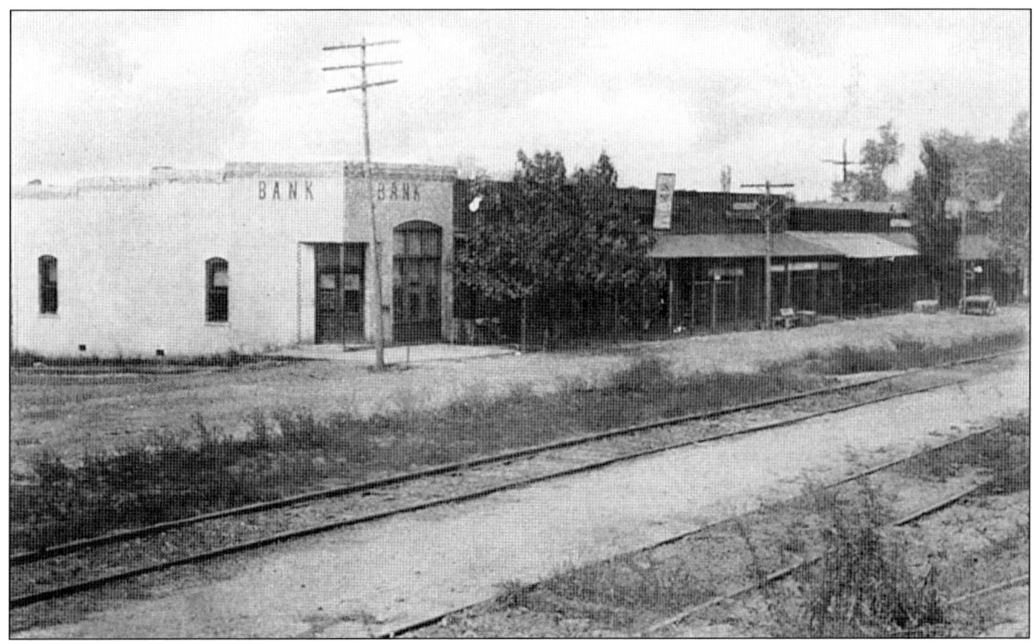

A c. 1911 view of Maysville shows the bank on the corner.

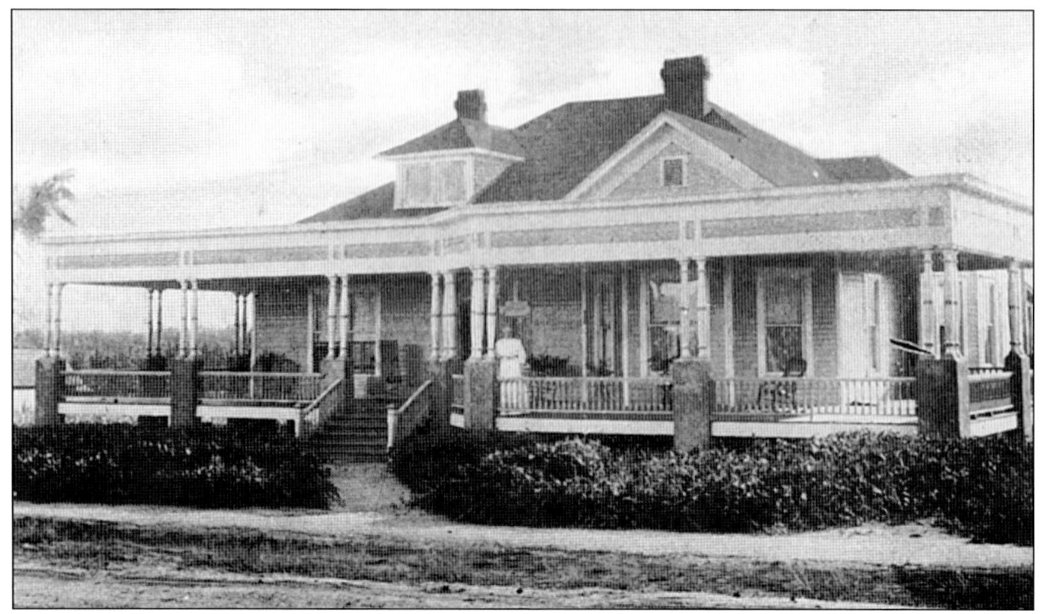

The elaborate home of Dr. W.G. Sharp, including wrap-around porch and rocking chairs, is featured in this post card of Maysville. Dr. Sharp was a dentist in Maysville.

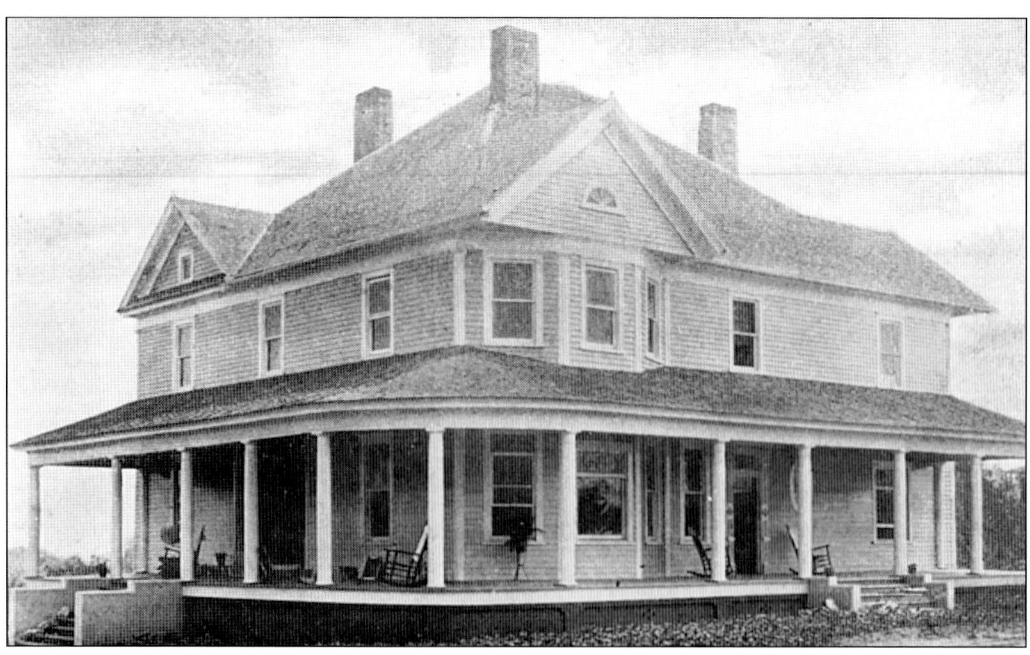

Like Dr. Sharp's home, the home of Mr. Boon Suddeth's residence in Maysville features a wrap-around porch and rockers. Mr. Suddeth operated a sawmill and lumber yard.

Seven

Lumpkin, Towns, and White Counties

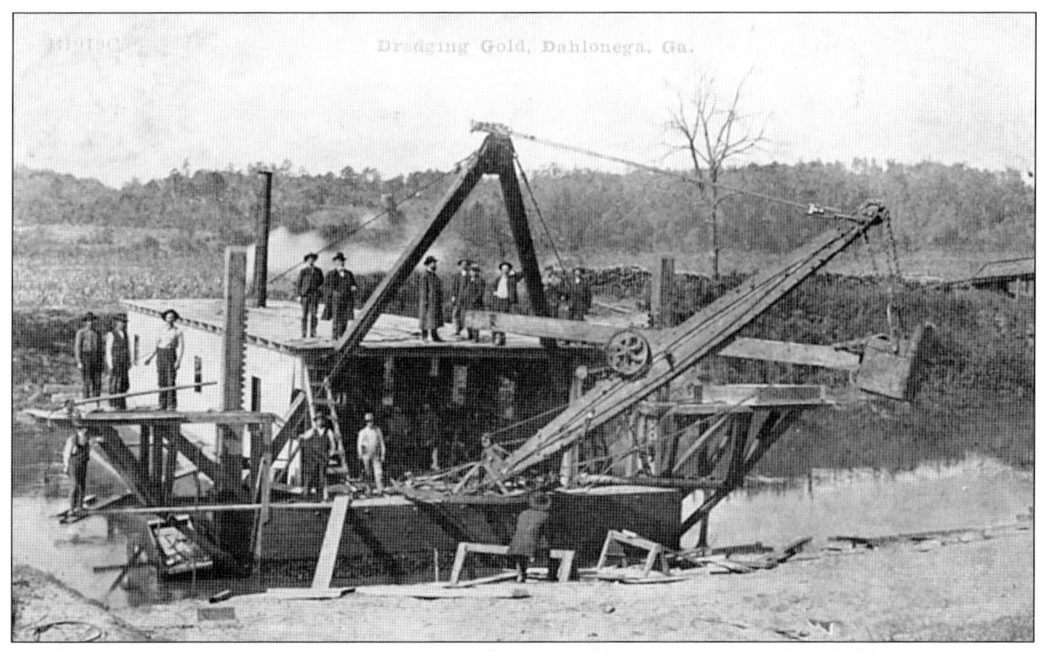

Gold miners are using a steam shovel to dredge for gold in this post card of Dahlonega.

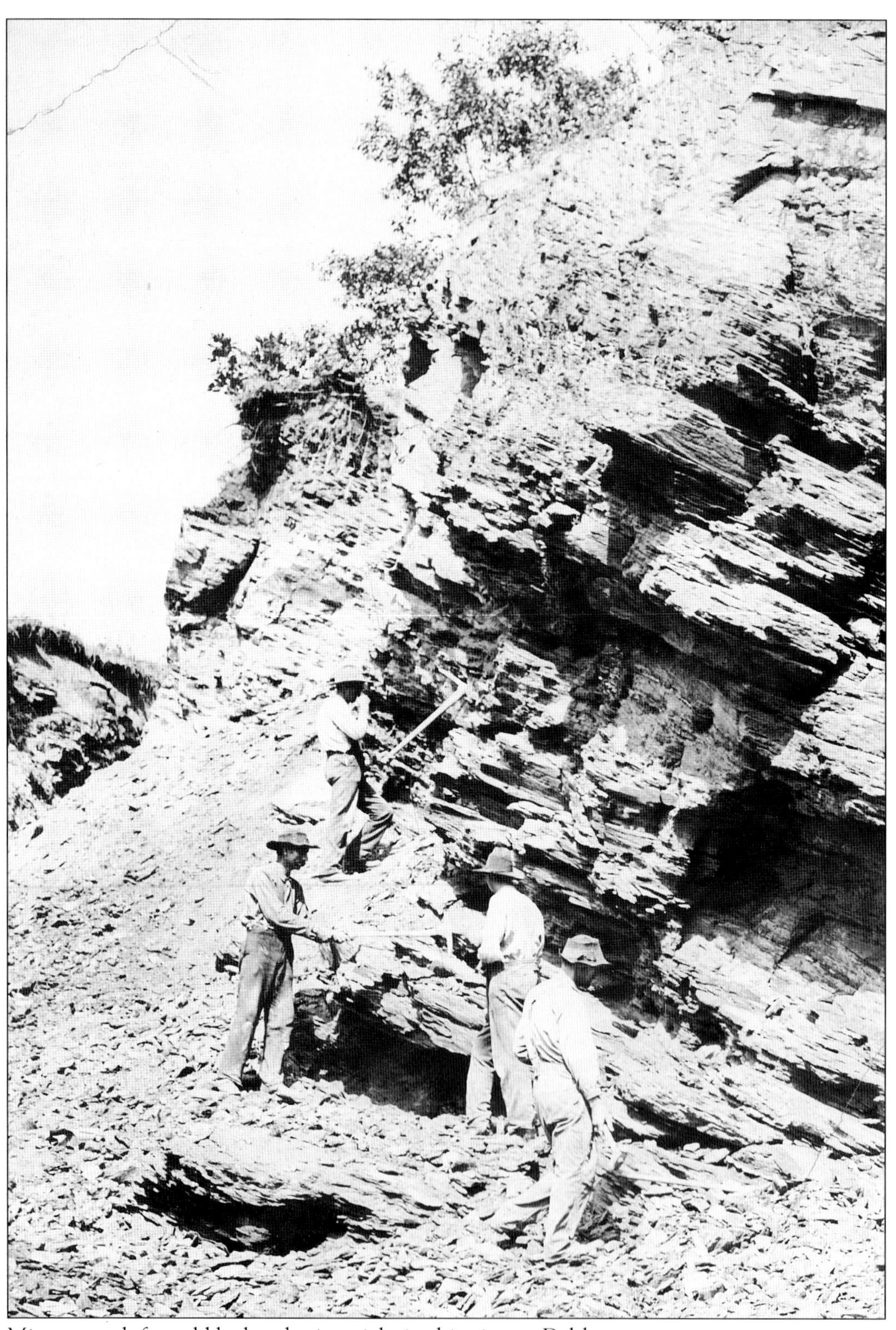

Miners search for gold by hand using picks in this view at Dahlonega.

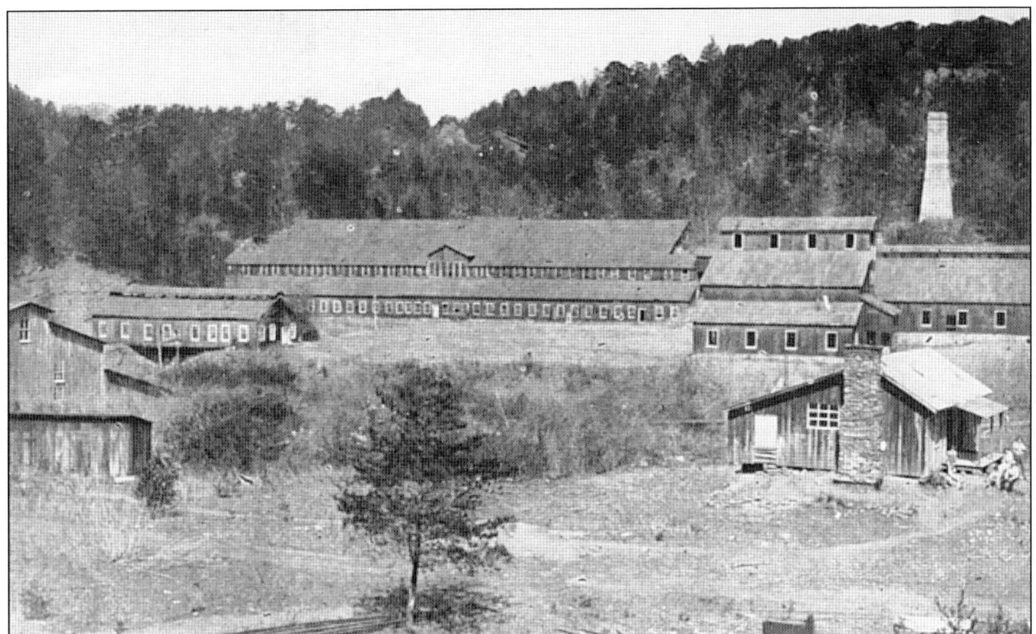

The fact that gold brought investment to Dahlonega is evident in this view of the million-dollar plant of the Consolidated Gold Mining Company of Dahlonega.

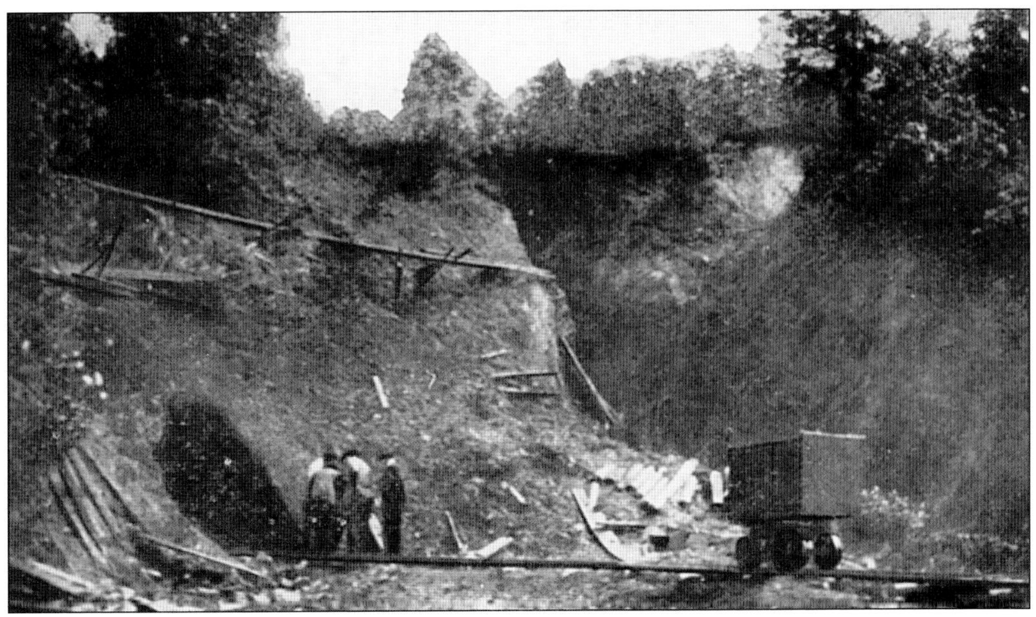

A mining scene in Dahlonega shows workers in front of a mine tunnel.

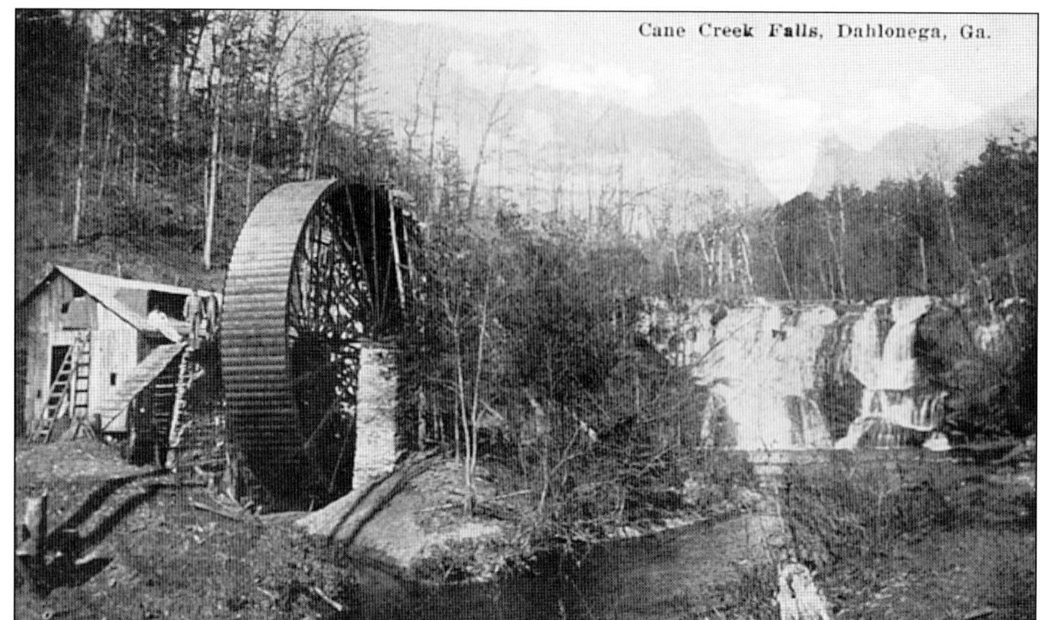

This mill, in operation at Cane Creek Falls near Dahlonega, was powered by a huge "undershot" waterwheel. Water ran under the wheel and caused it to turn, whereas with overshot wheels, water ran over the top of the wheel.

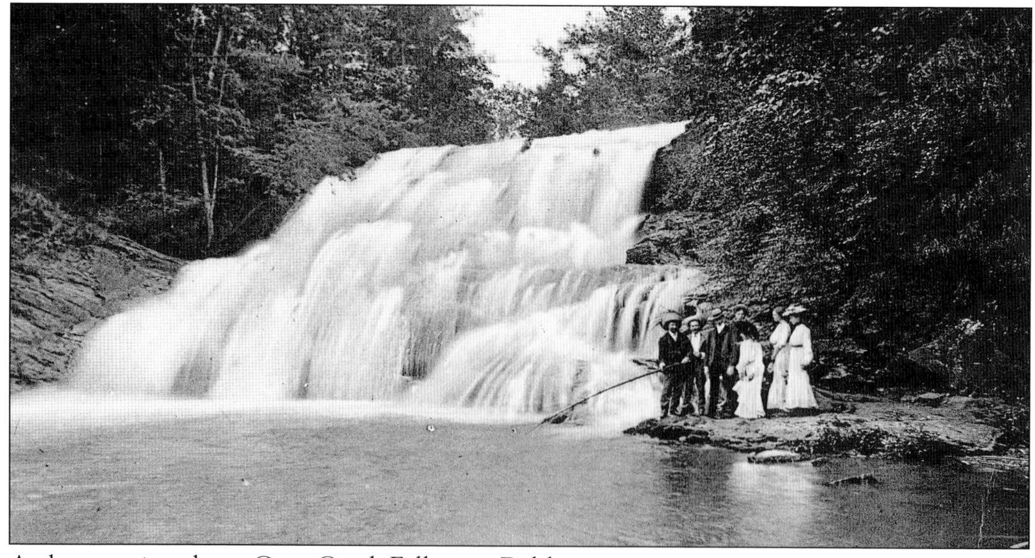

A close up view shows Cane Creek Falls near Dahlonega.

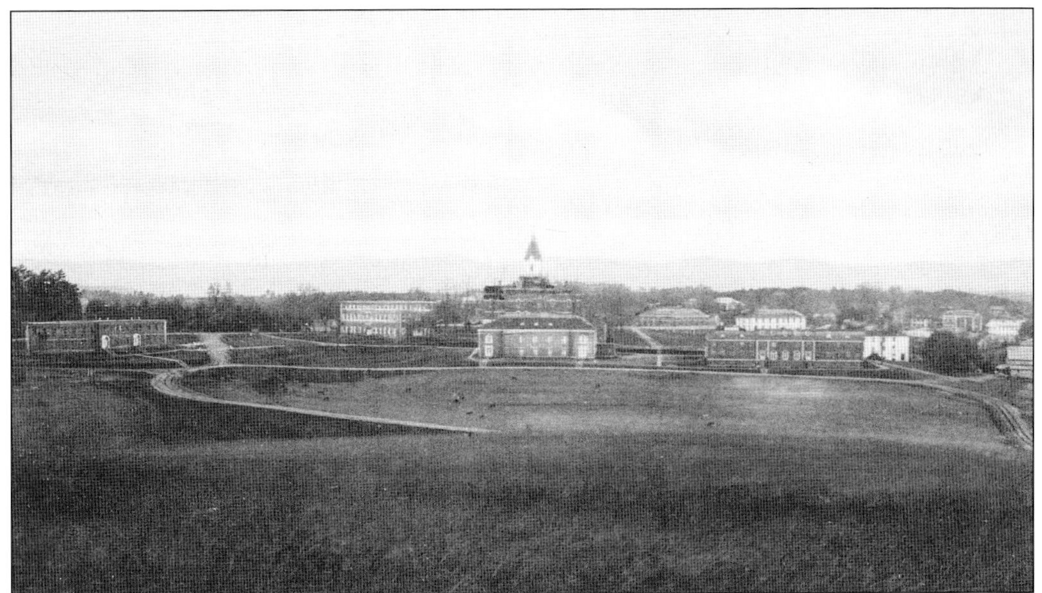
North Georgia College in Dahlonega is the subject of this post card.

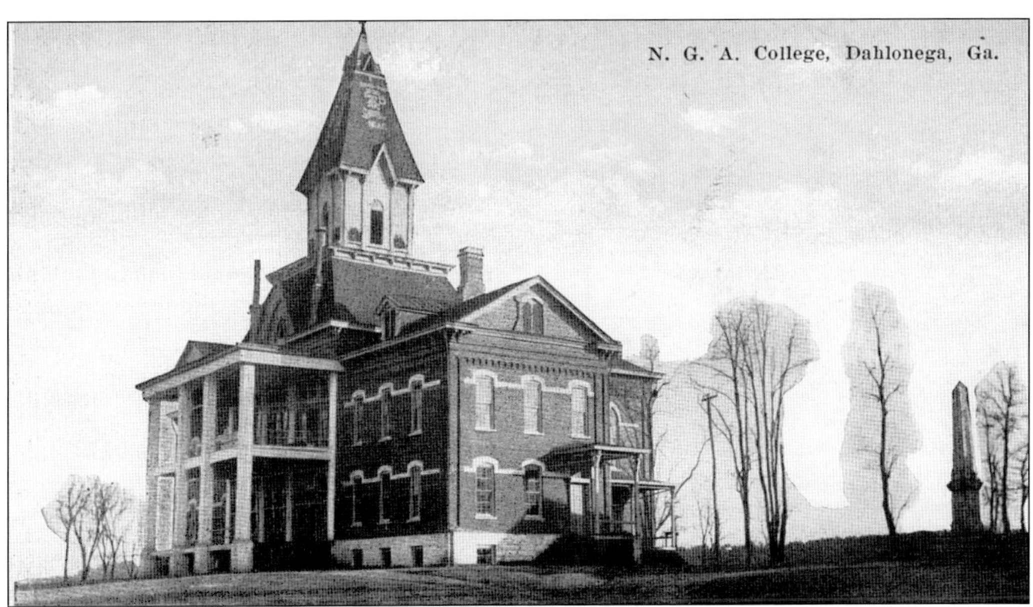

The landscape appears bleak in this view of North Georgia College at Dahlonega.

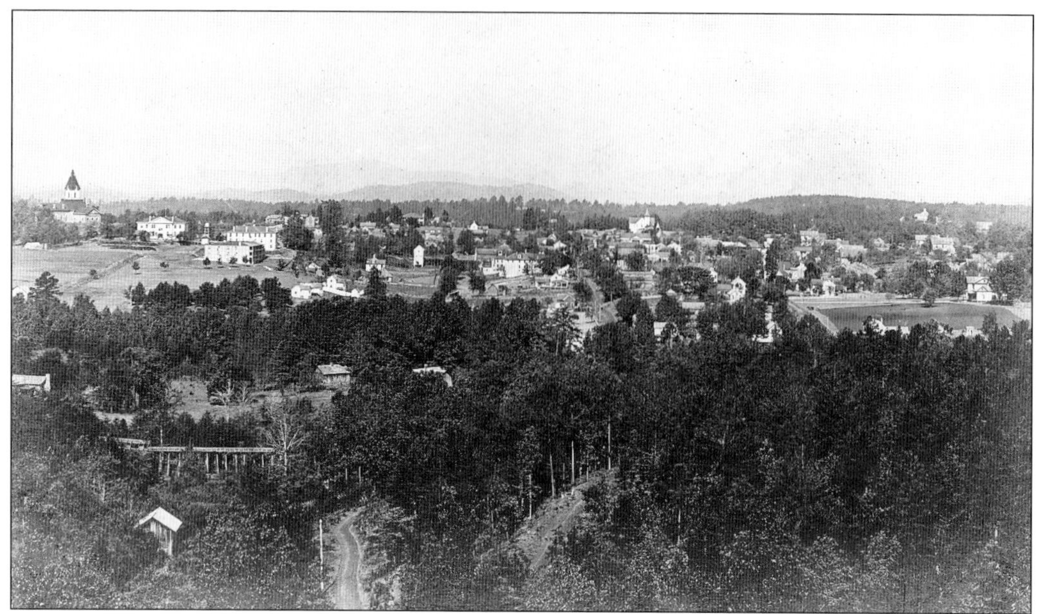

This bird's-eye photograph of Dahlonega, taken from Findley Ridge, gives a wonderful view of the town.

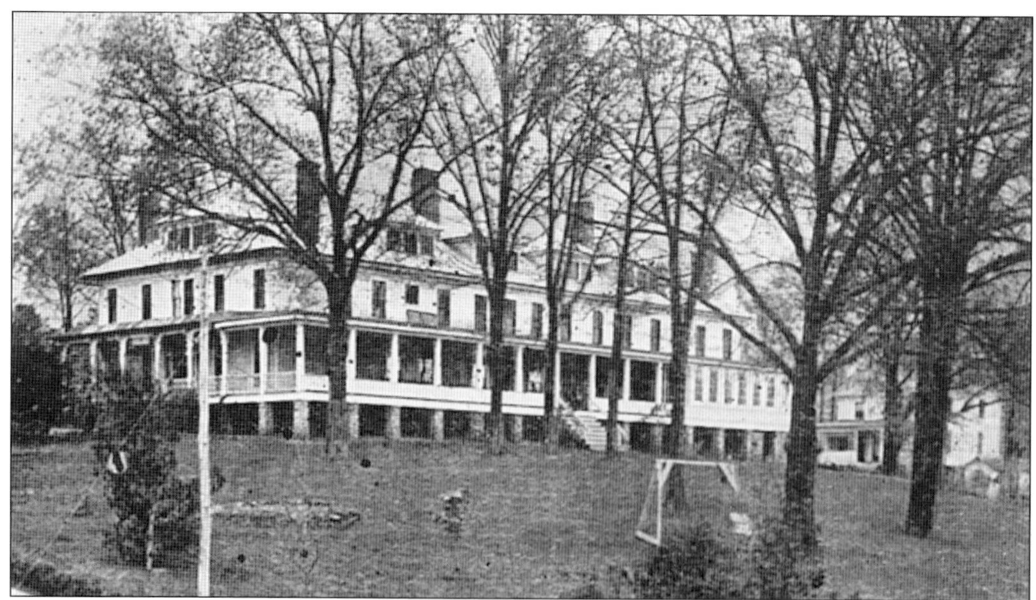

A printed advertisement on the back of this card featuring Zimmer's Mountain Lodge reads, "Zimmer's Mountain Lodge. In the heart of the Blue Ridge Mountains. Dahlonega, Georgia. Open Year Round — Steam Heat."

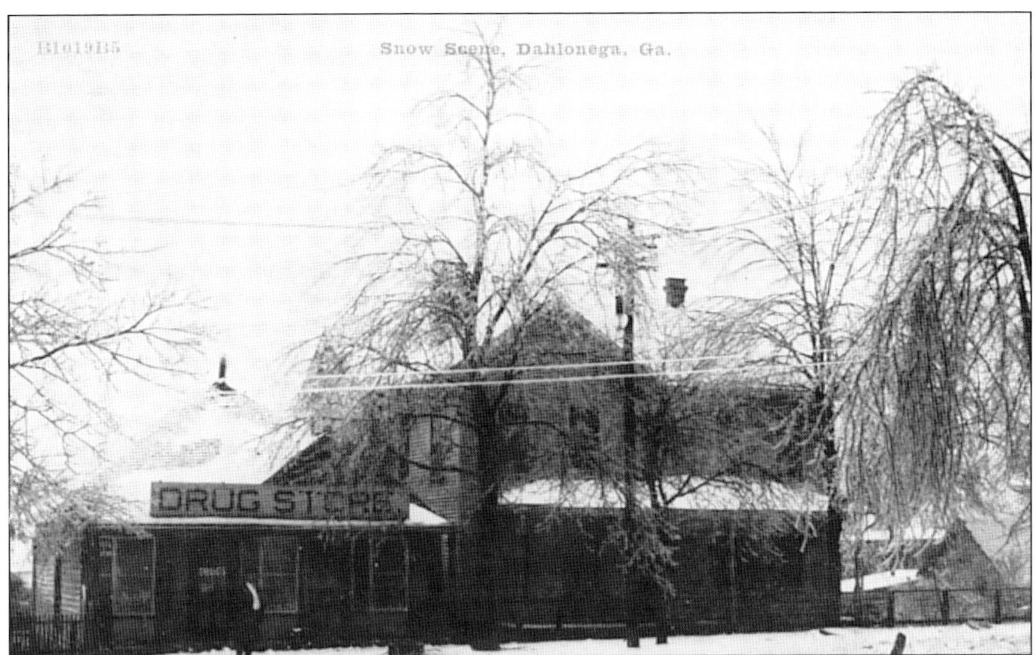

Ice and snow cause tree limbs and power lines to droop in this *c.* 1910 postcard view of Dahlonega.

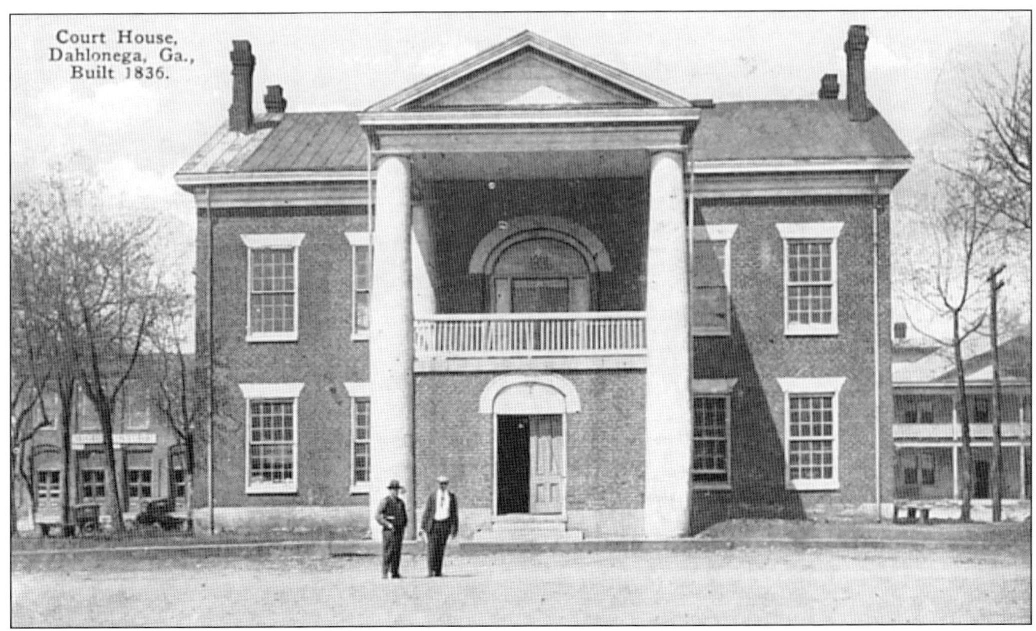

Two gentlemen managed to get their pictures included in this view of the Court House in Dahlonega. The courthouse was built in 1836 and is now used as a museum.

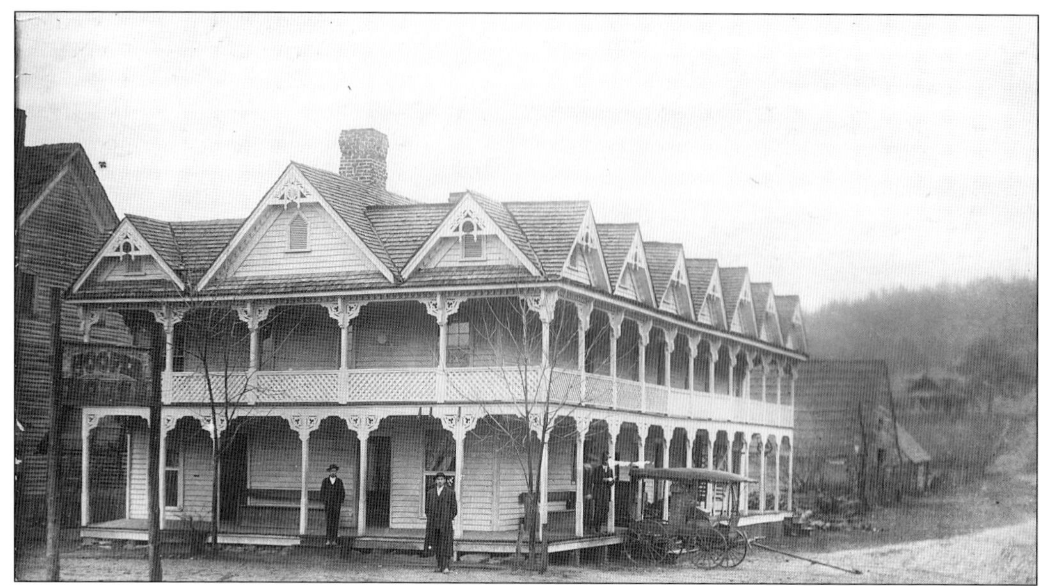

The magnificent Hooper House, a hotel at Hiawassee, was operated by Mr. J.T. Hooper.

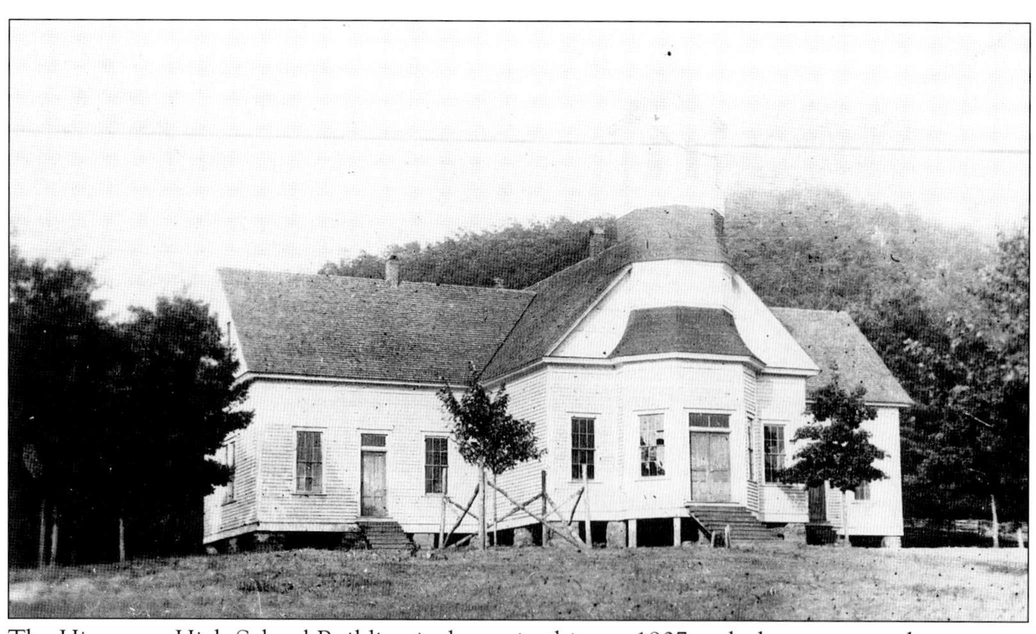

The Hiawassee High School Building is shown in this pre-1907 real-photo post card.

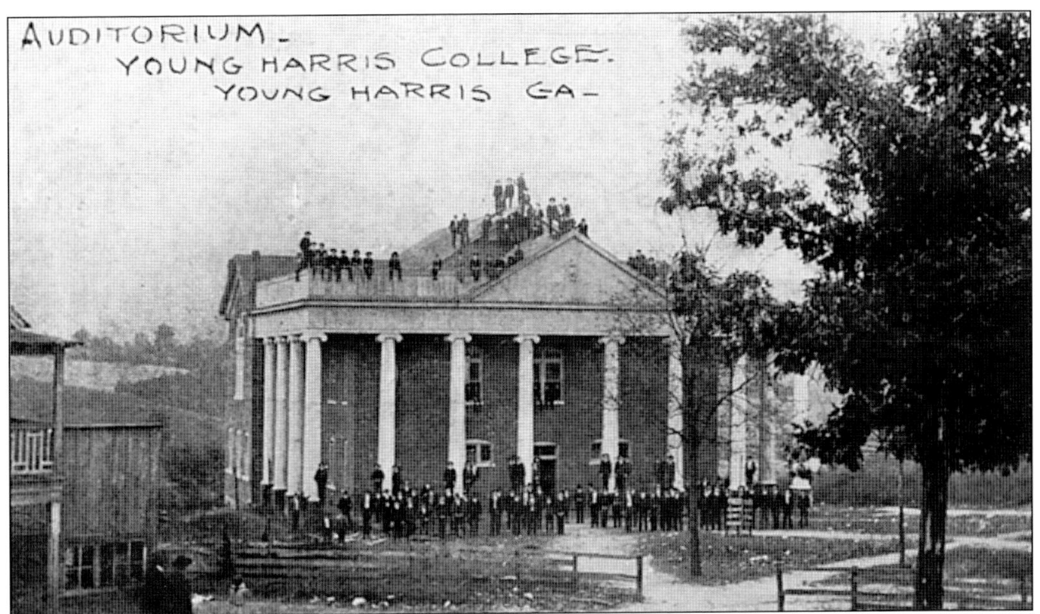

Note the numbers of people standing on the roof of the auditorium at Young Harris College in this card.

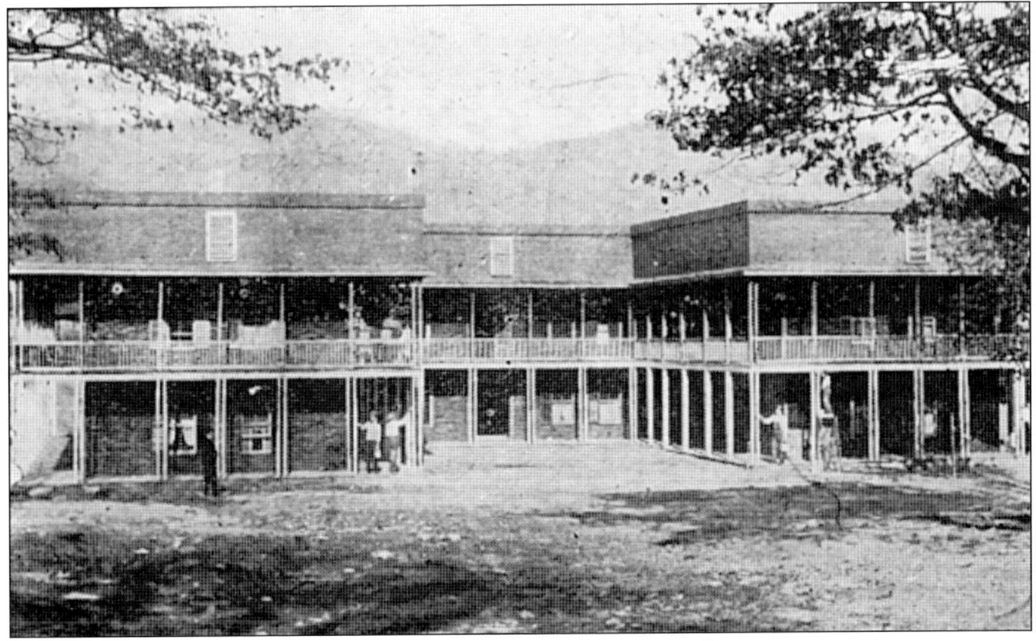
This *c*. 1910 card shows the girls' dormitory at Young Harris College.

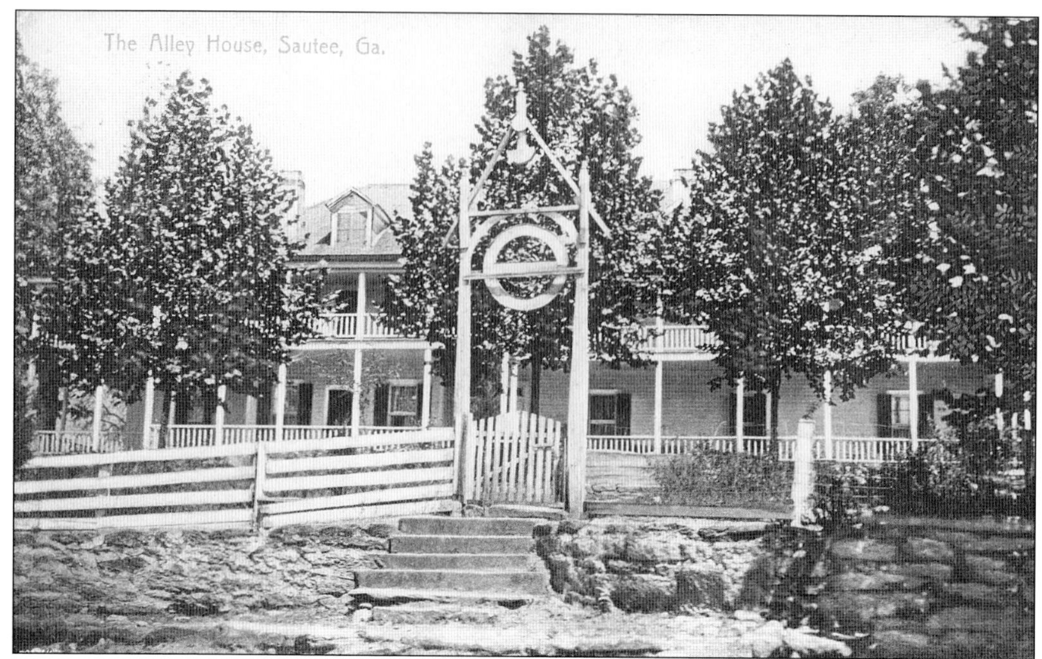

The Alley House in Sautee is featured on this card, which was mailed to New Orleans on August 17, 1910. The message contains some interesting information: "Dear Jim, This is where we are staying. How do you like the gate? It used to have on it, 'Nacoochee Hotel, Open all the Year Round.' Your Cousin, M.S."

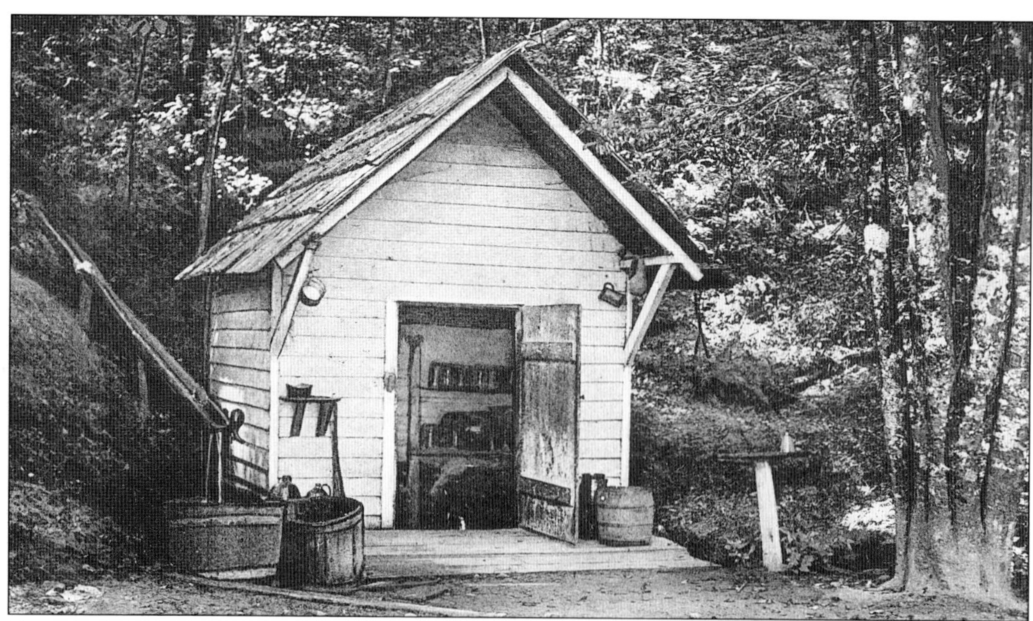

This card shows Cason's Spring in Sautee.

Eight

Morgan, Oconee, and Walton Counties

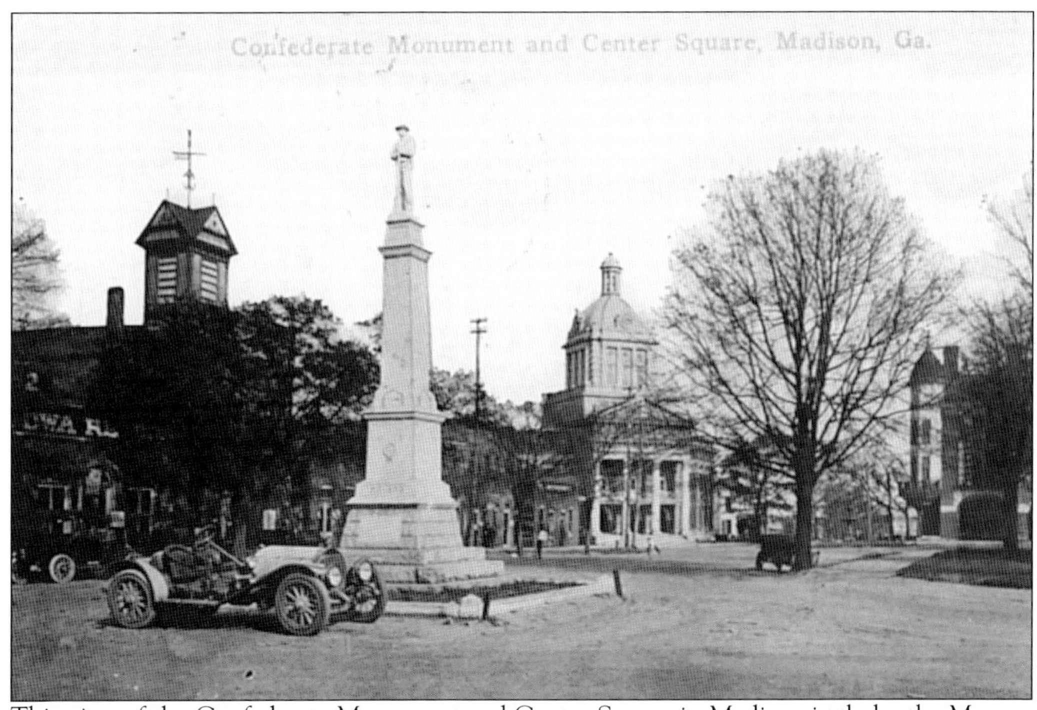

This view of the Confederate Monument and Center Square in Madison includes the Morgan County courthouse. The Confederate Monument is seen here in its original location where it was unveiled April 26, 1909. Increased traffic over the years forced its removal to Hill Park. The courthouse was built in 1905 and is still in service.

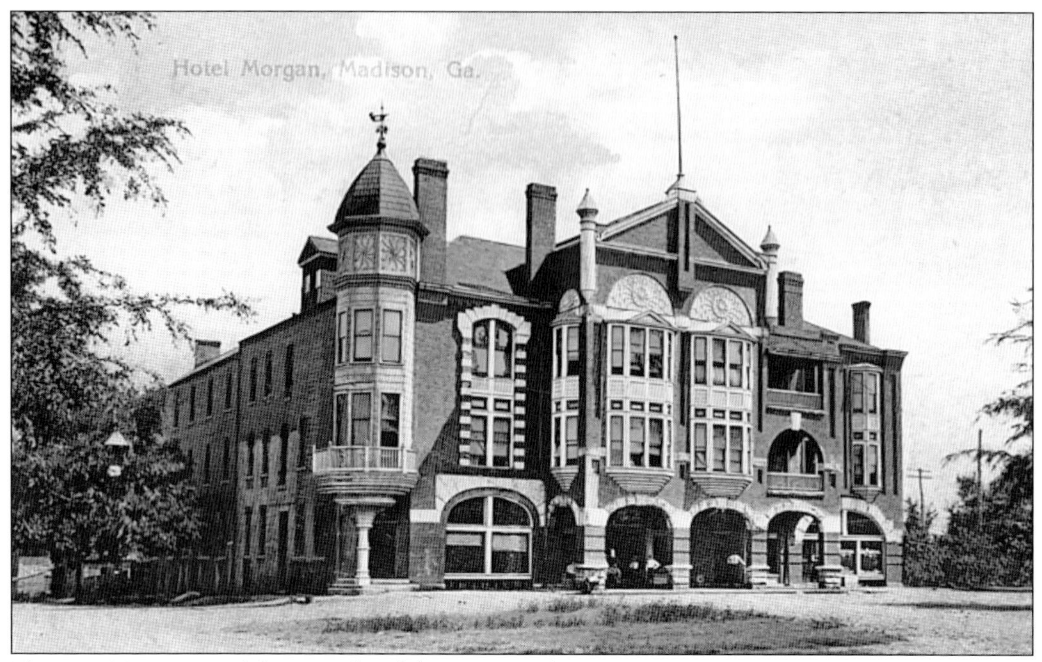

This *c.* 1909 post card features the elaborate Hotel Morgan in Madison.

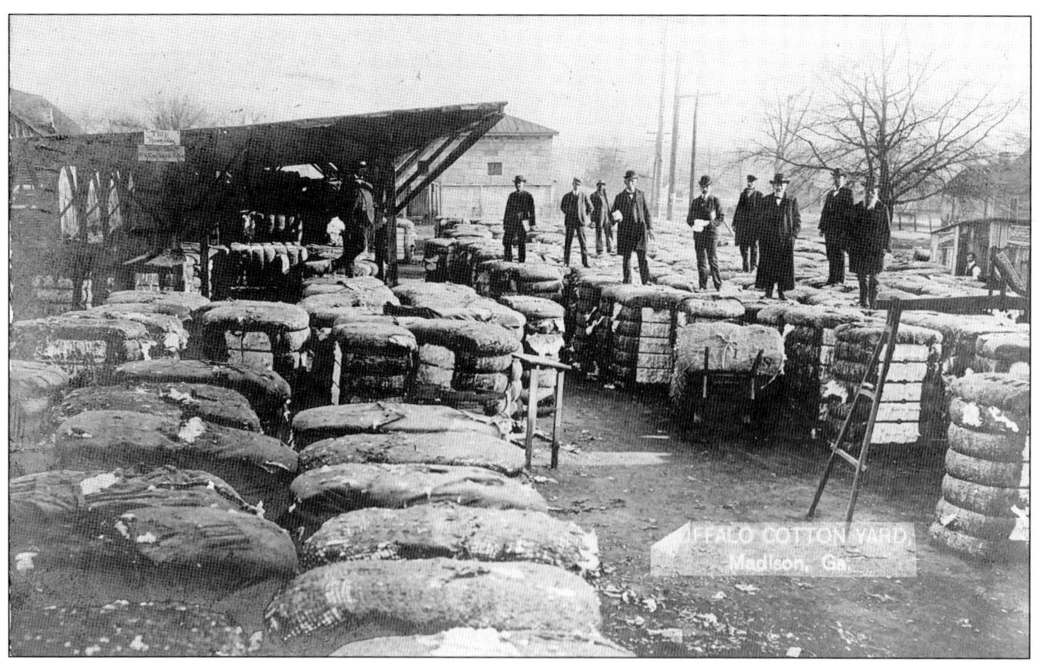

Well-dressed gentlemen stand on top of bales of cotton at the Buffalo Cotton Yard in Madison in 1907. They were probably cotton buyers inspecting that year's crop.

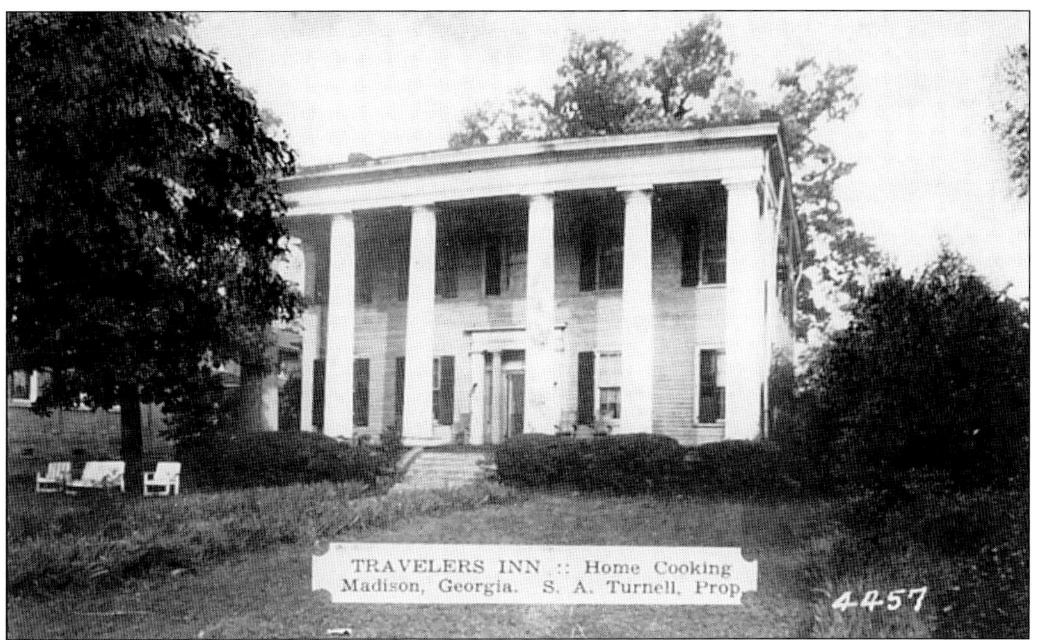

This is the Travelers Inn in Madison, which was owned by S.A. Turnell. The post card advertised the inn's home cooking.

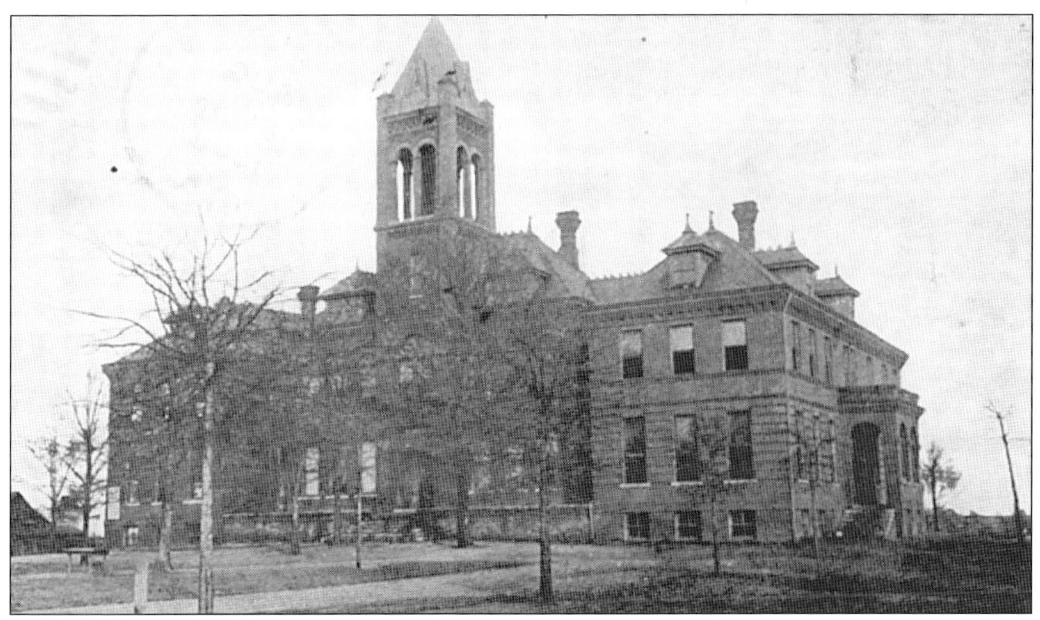

The high school in Madison, shown here *c.* 1908 , is now the Morgan County Cultural Center.

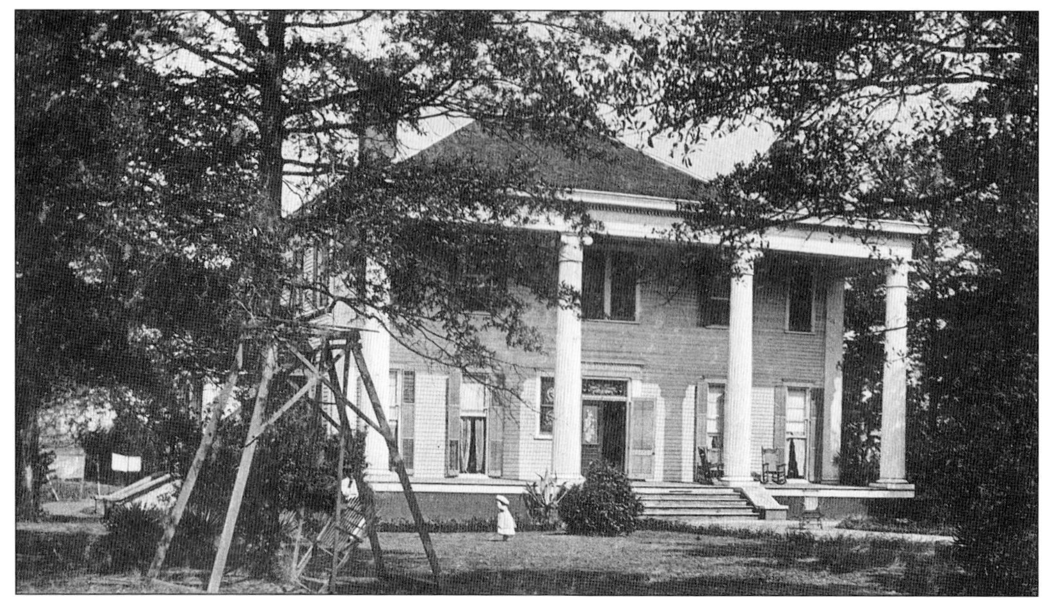

This card features the Lee Brammel home in Madison.

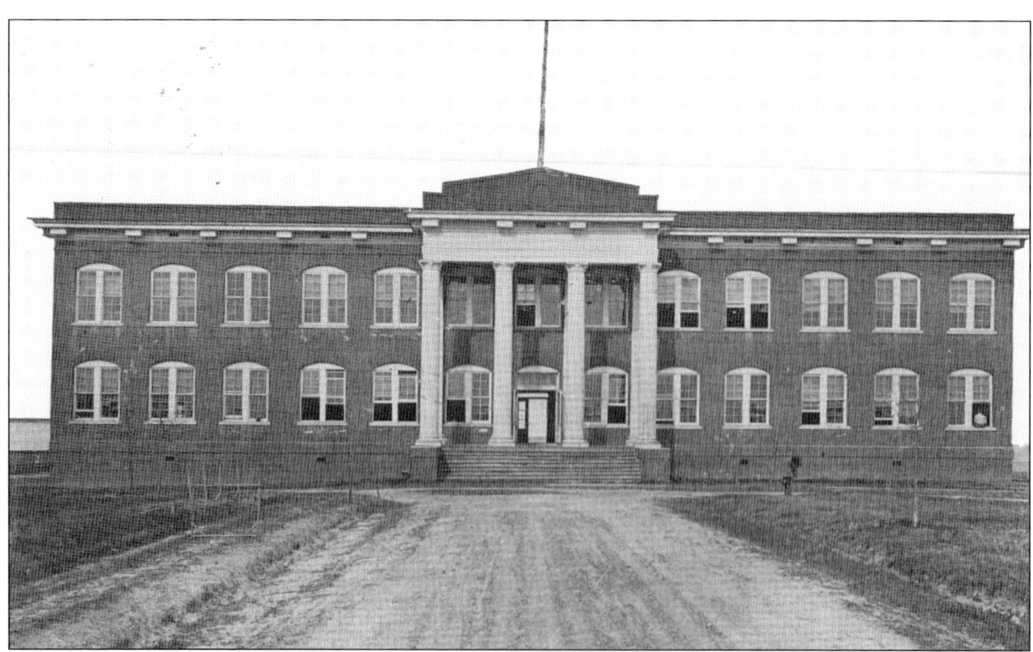

This *c.* 1913 post card features the main building of the agricultural college in Madison.

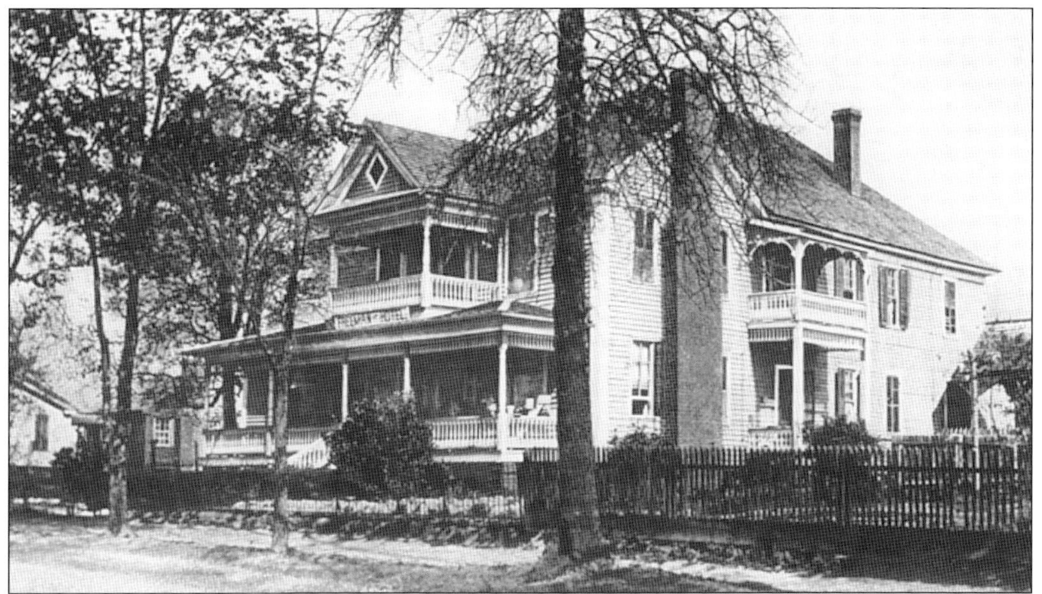

This view shows the Freeman house in Rutledge.

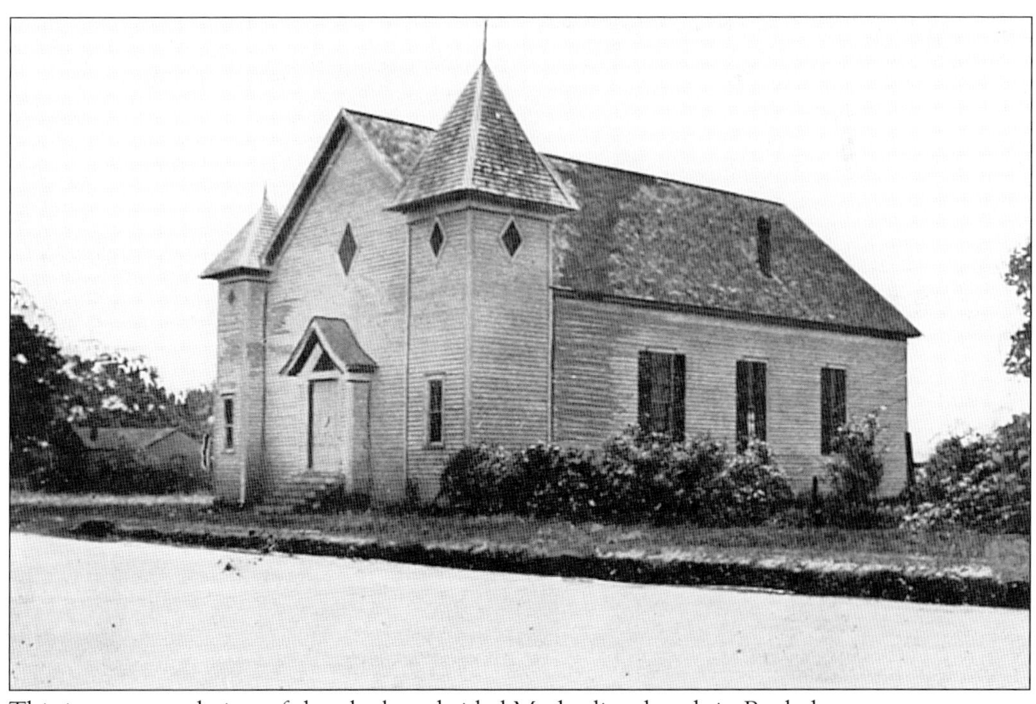

This is a post card view of the clapboard-sided Methodist church in Rutledge.

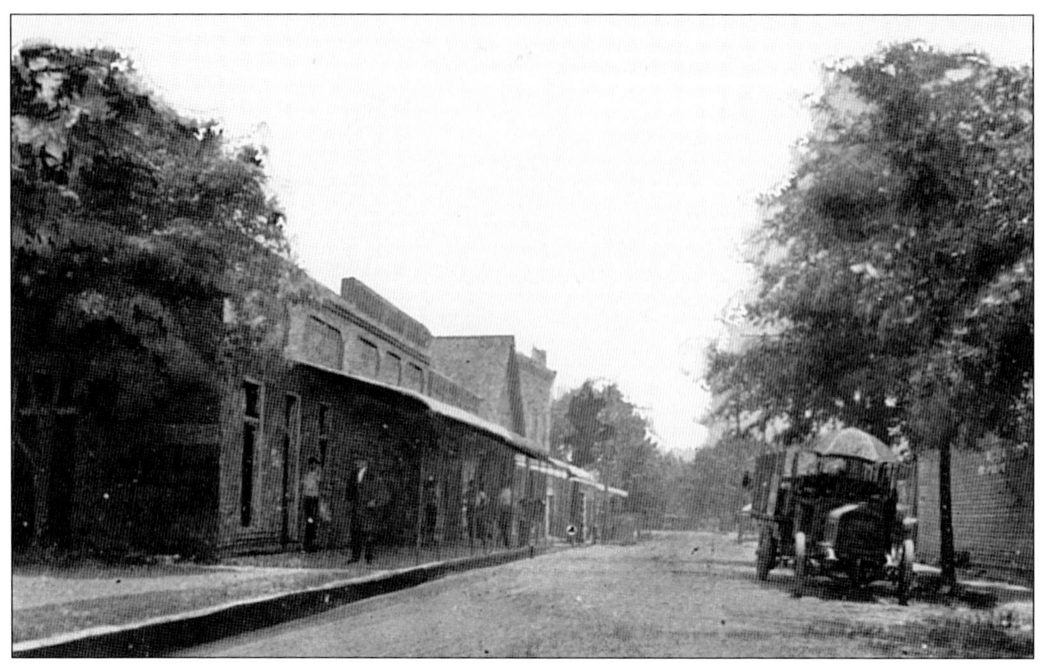

An early-model truck sits idle in this view of Main Street in Rutledge.

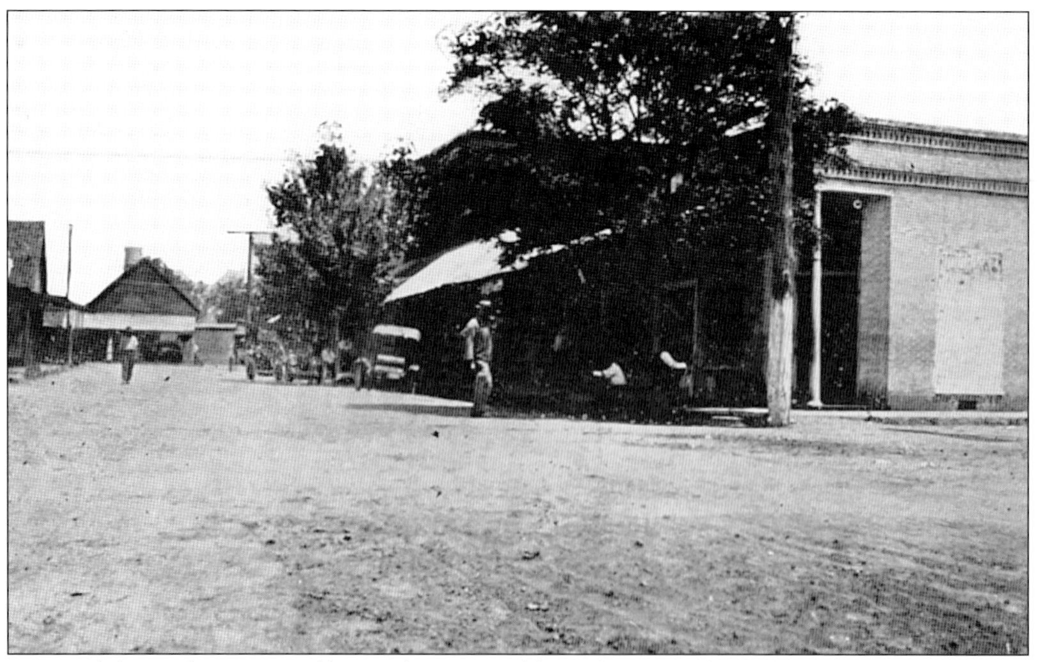

Automobiles, pedestrians, and bystanders are visible in this view of Fairplay Street in Rutledge.

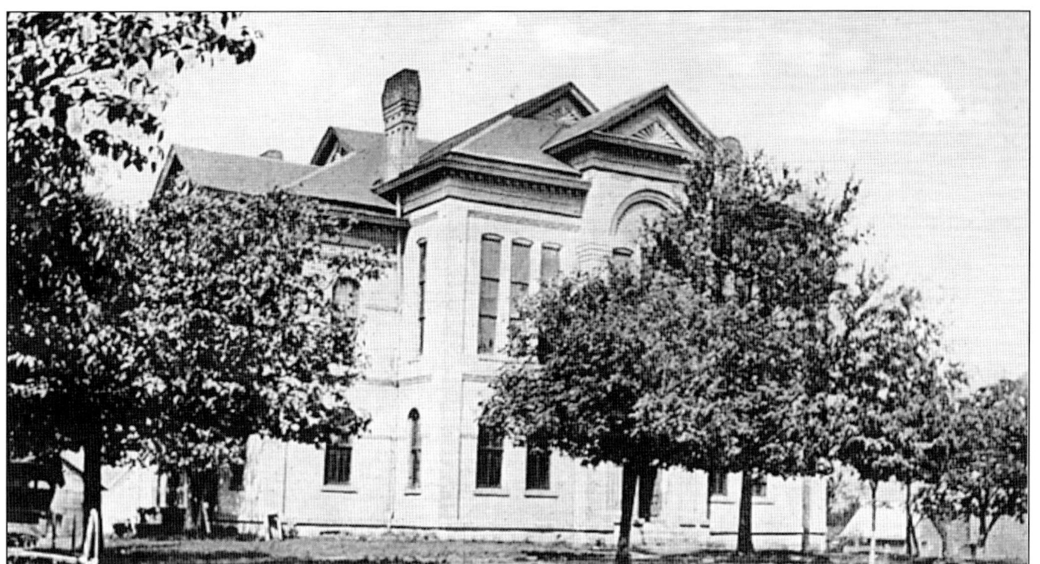

This courthouse in Watkinsville was built in 1888 and was destroyed by fire on May 6, 1938.

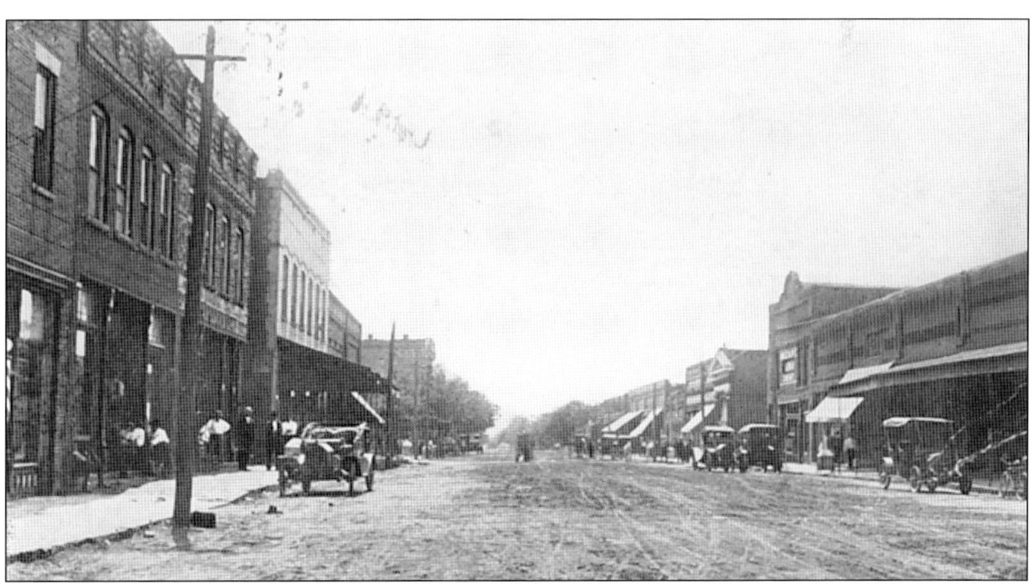

Automobile tracks criss-cross the dirt street in this 1910 view of Broad Street in Monroe.

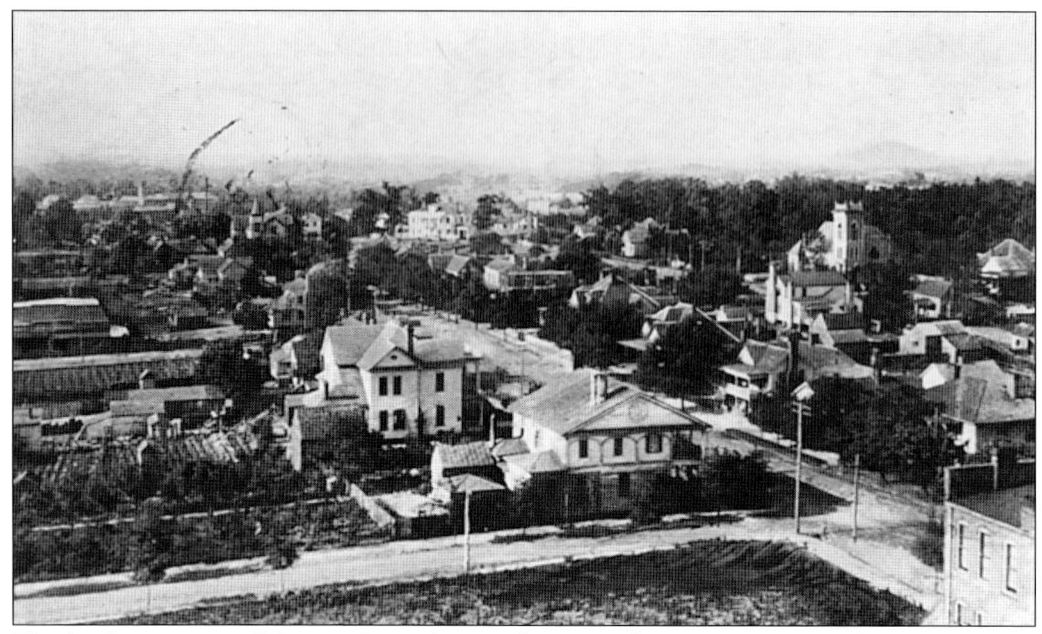

This bird's-eye view of Monroe shows the neat houses and numerous trees in the town.

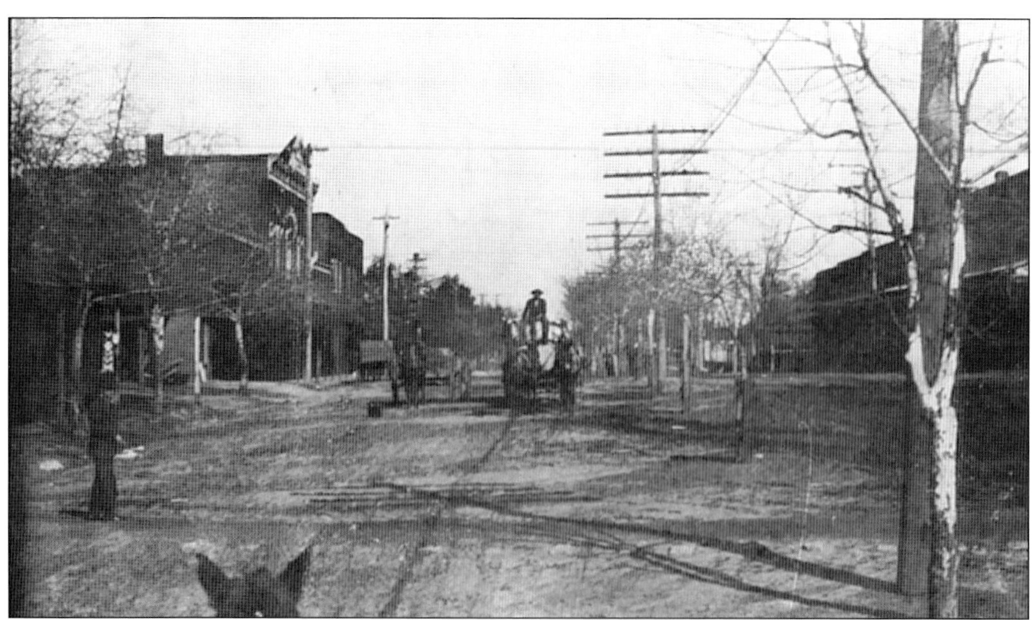

Horse-drawn vehicles were evidently still the norm when this *c.* 1908 view was photographed in Social Circle.

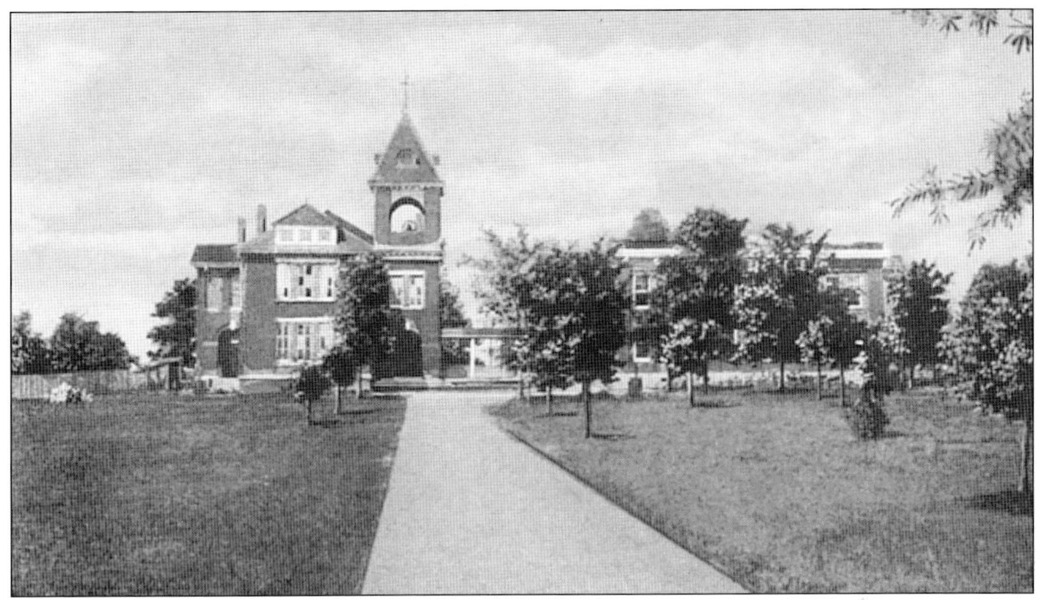

This card features the school in Social Circle.

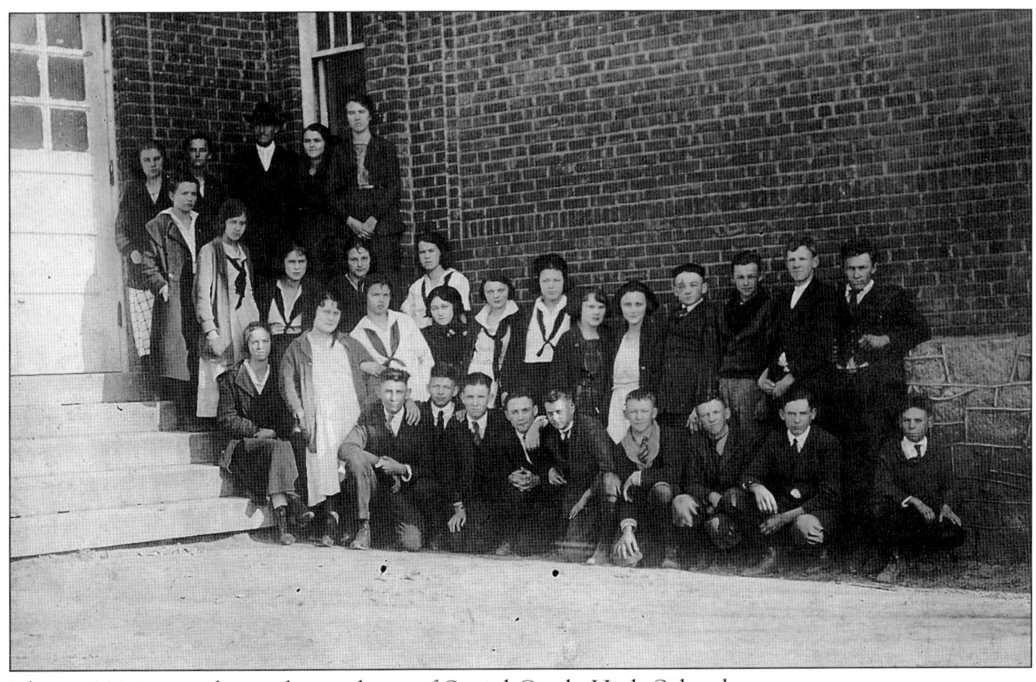

This *c.* 1914 view shows the students of Social Circle High School.

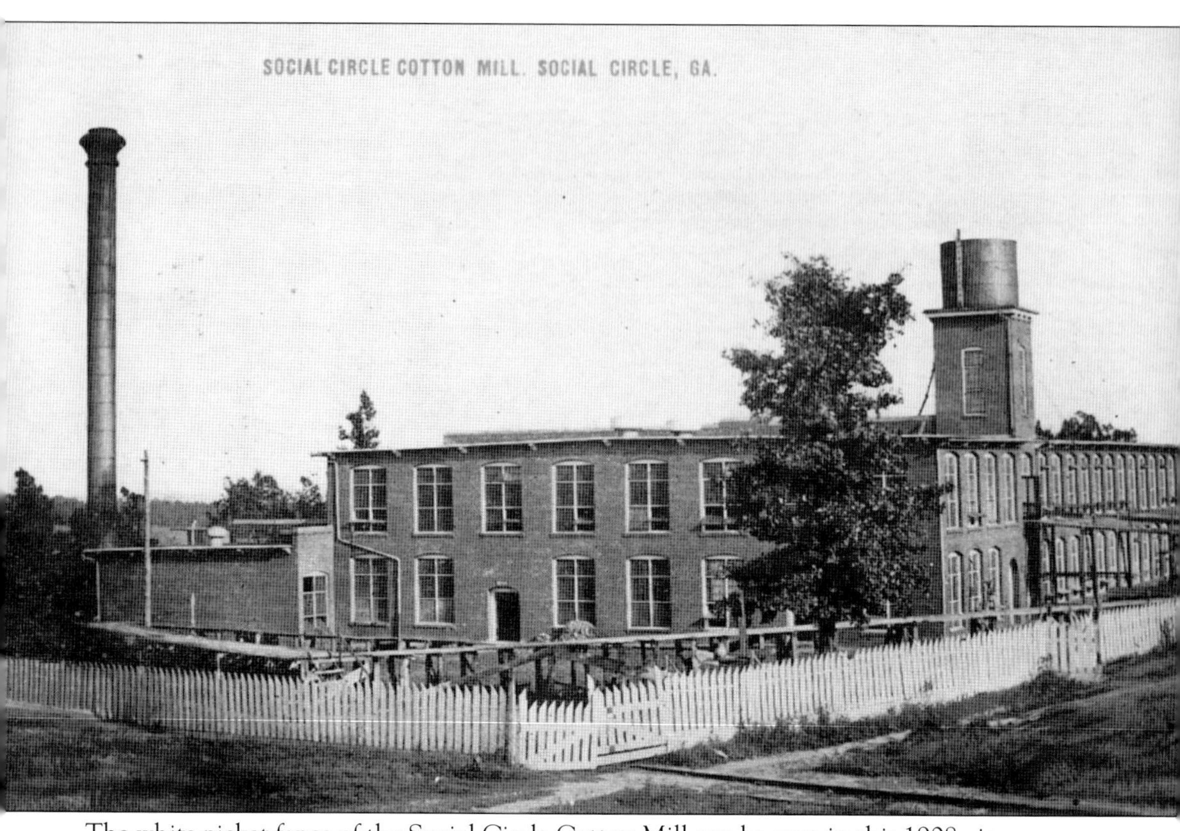

The white picket fence of the Social Circle Cotton Mill can be seen in this 1908 view.

Nine
Rabun County

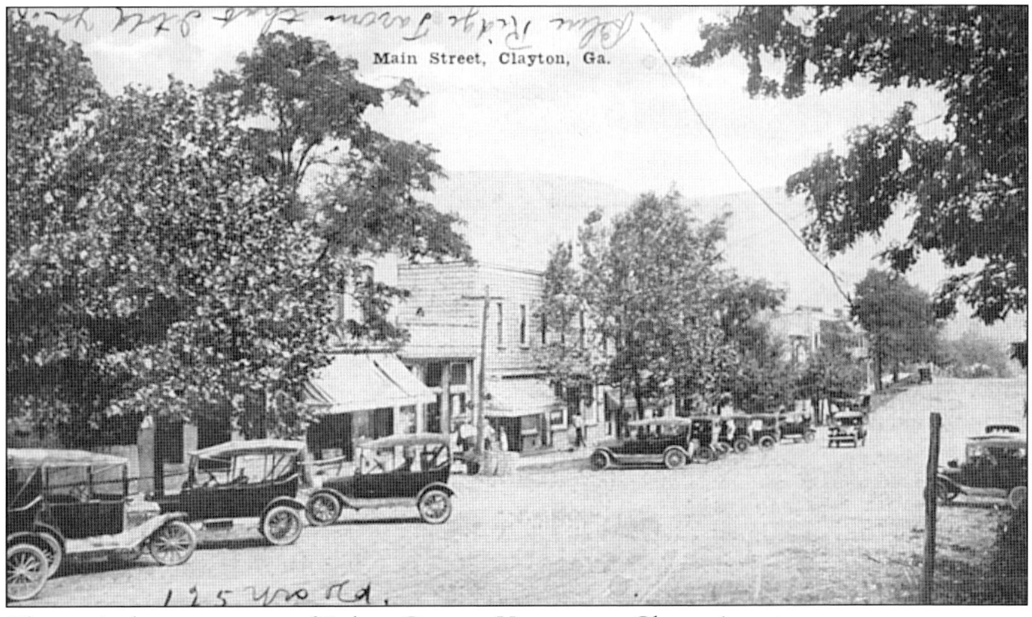

Clayton is the county seat of Rabun County. Here we see Clayton's main street.

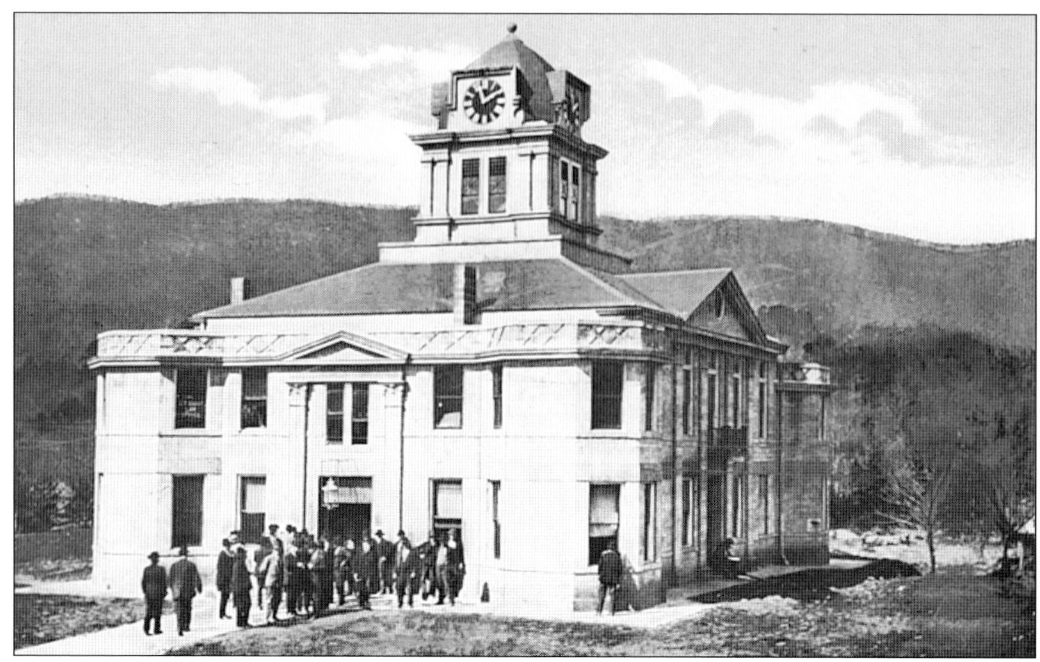

The old Rabun County Courthouse in Clayton was built in 1908.

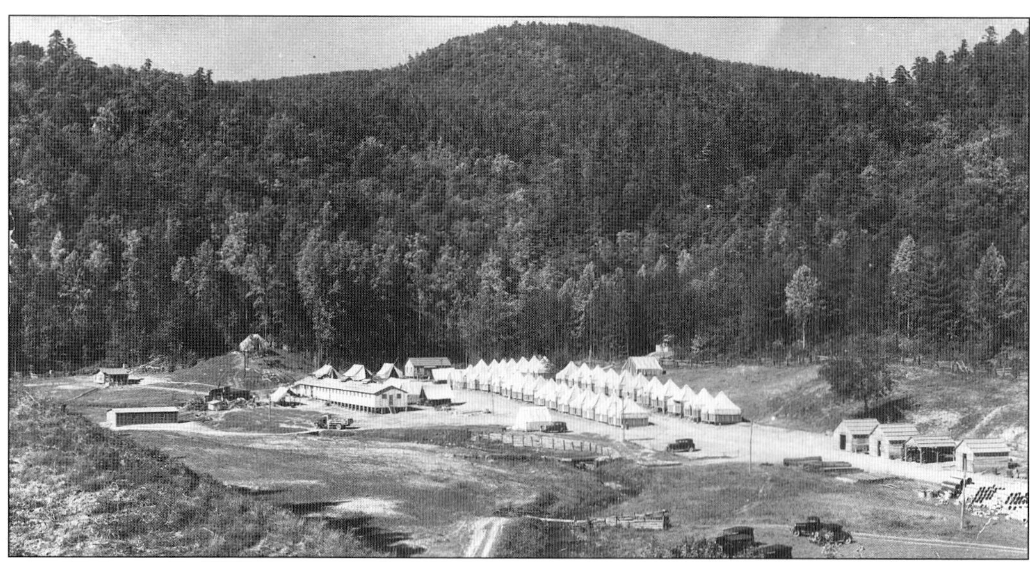

The Warwoman Creek Camp, at Clayton, was one of countless Civilian Conservation Corps settlements in the 1930s. The CCC, which provided employment for Depression-era workers, built many improvements to the country.

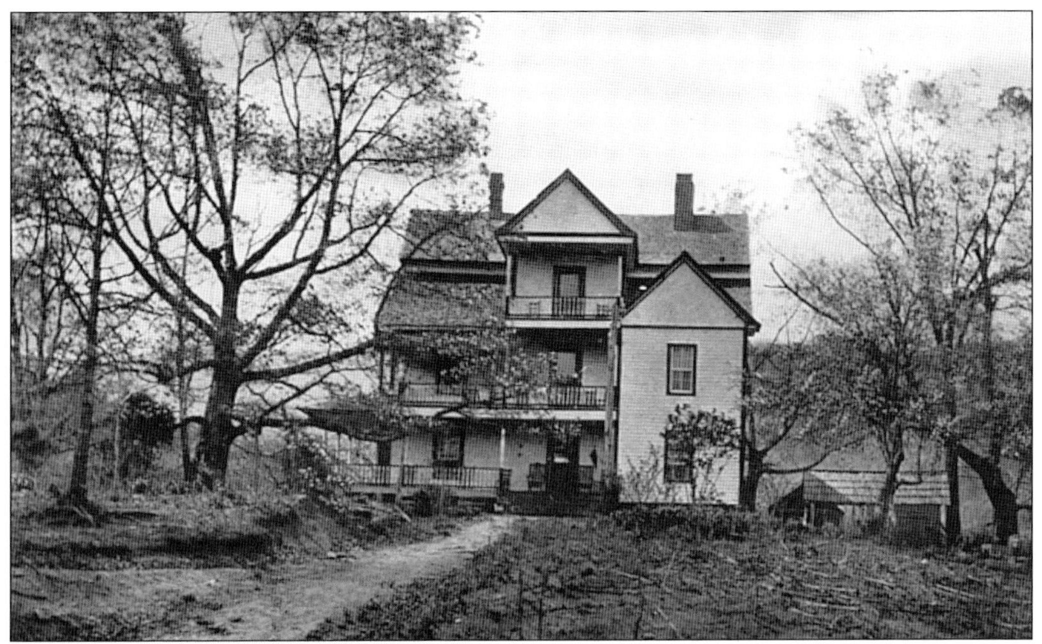

Oak Mount, a beautiful three-story structure, was tucked away in the hills of Clayton.

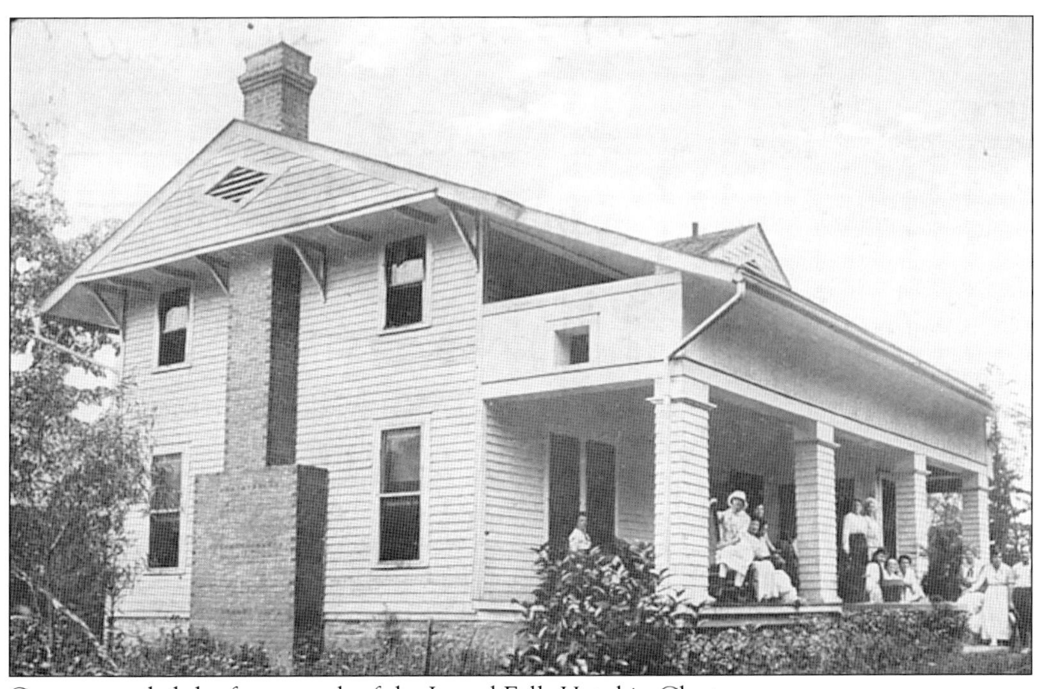

Guests crowded the front porch of the Laurel Falls Hotel in Clayton.

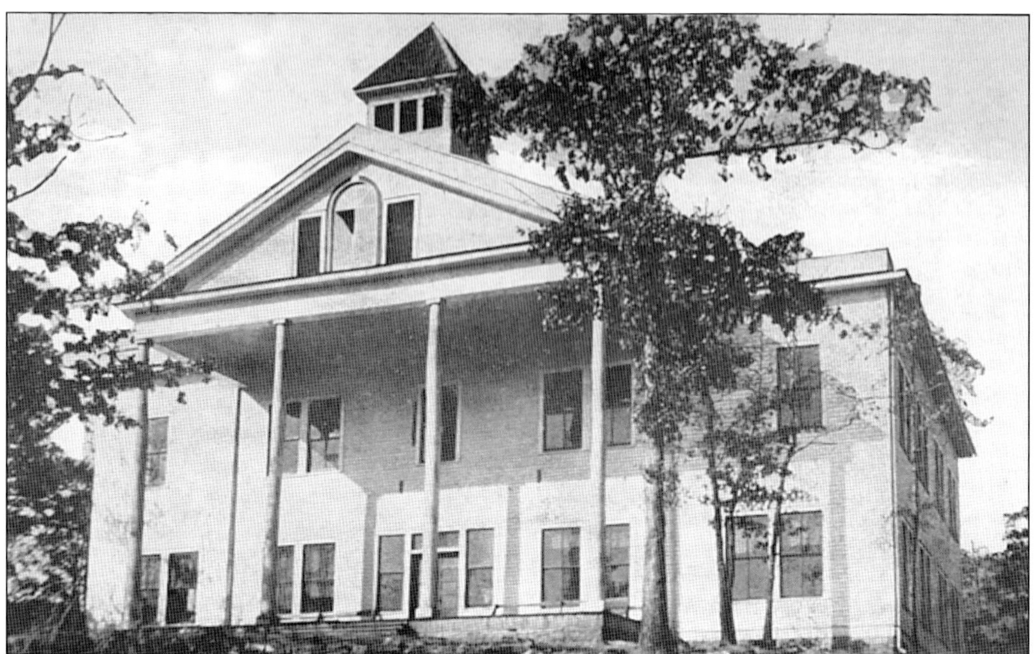

This is the public school building in Clayton.

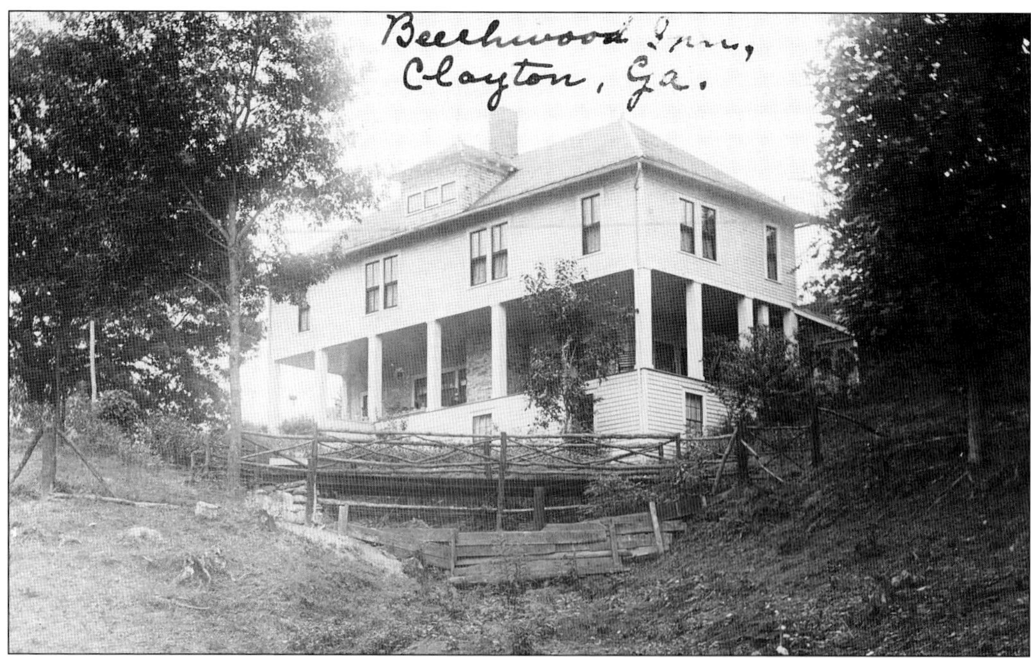

The sender of this card from the Beechwood Inn in Clayton could have written copy for advertisements about the inn. On the back, Mrs. L.E. Buchholz wrote, "All Modern Conveniences. Elevation 2,200 ft. Overlooking Clayton, Ga. Twelve minutes walk from depot or center of town. Cool, quiet, restful."

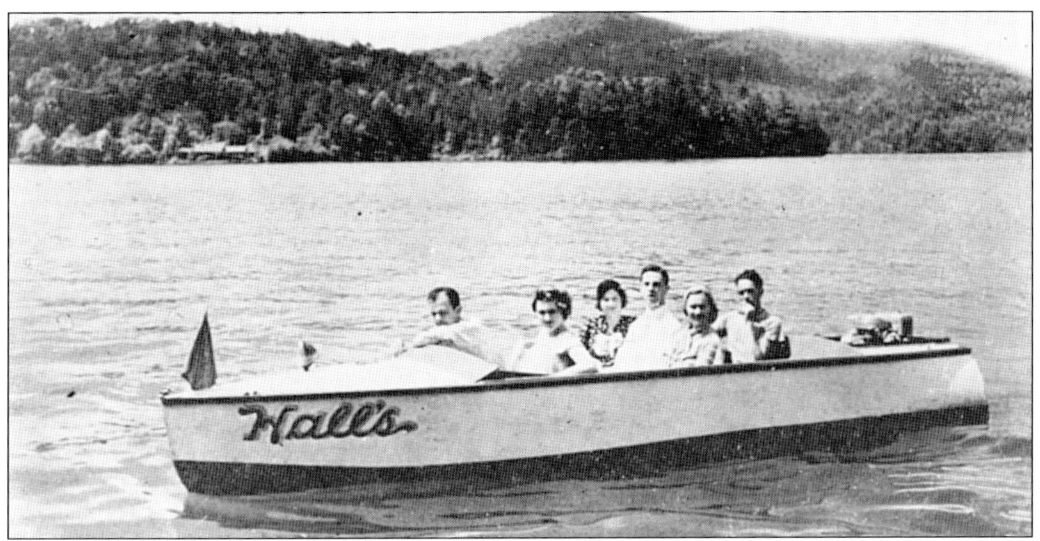

Boaters enjoy scenic Lake Rabun.

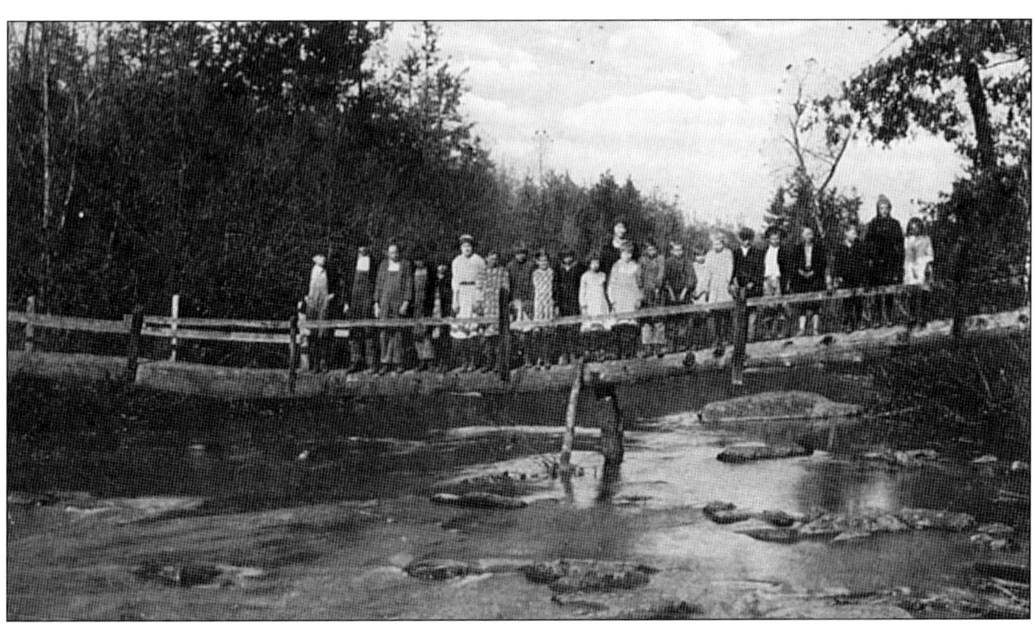

Traveling conditions were still somewhat primitive when this 1923 view was taken at Lakemont. Schoolchildren are shown crossing a creek on a log bridge.

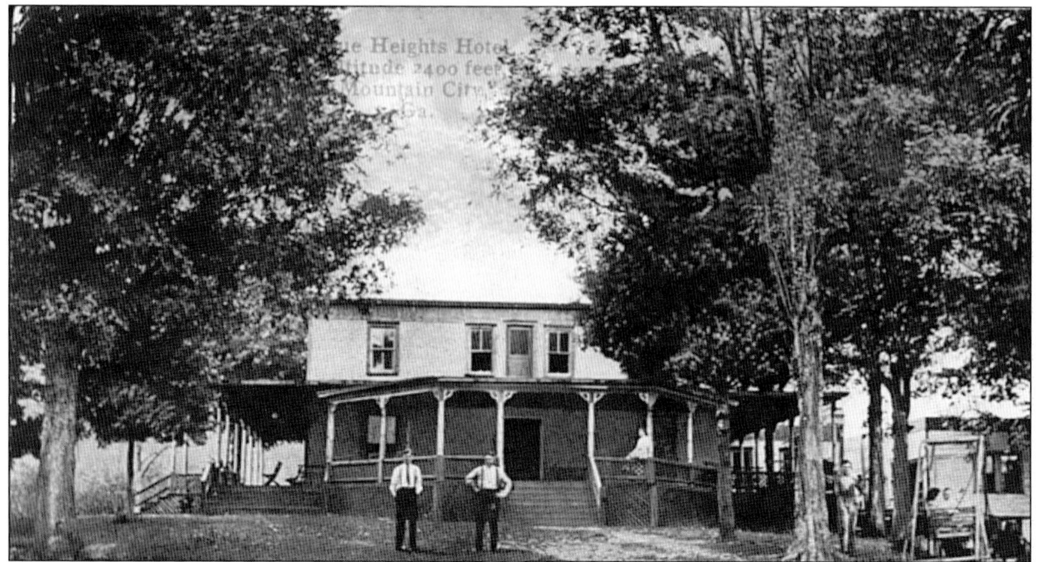

The Blue Heights Hotel at Mountain City was located at an altitude of 2,400 feet.

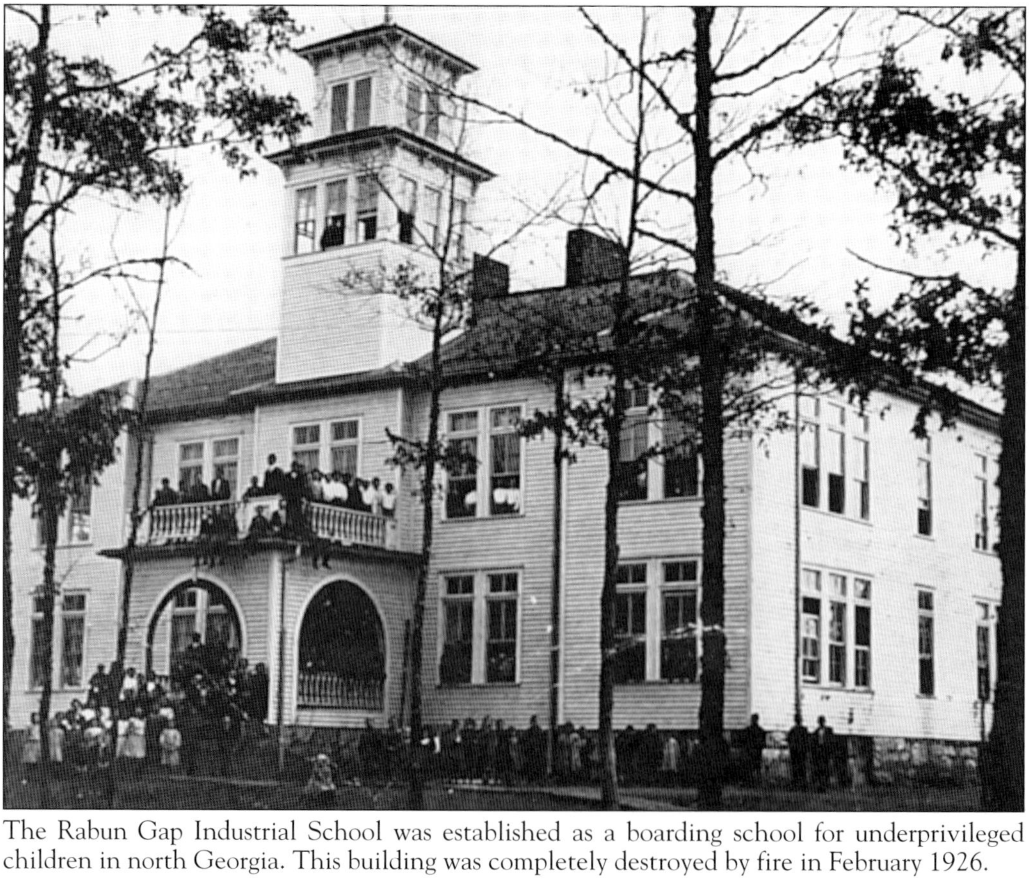

The Rabun Gap Industrial School was established as a boarding school for underprivileged children in north Georgia. This building was completely destroyed by fire in February 1926.

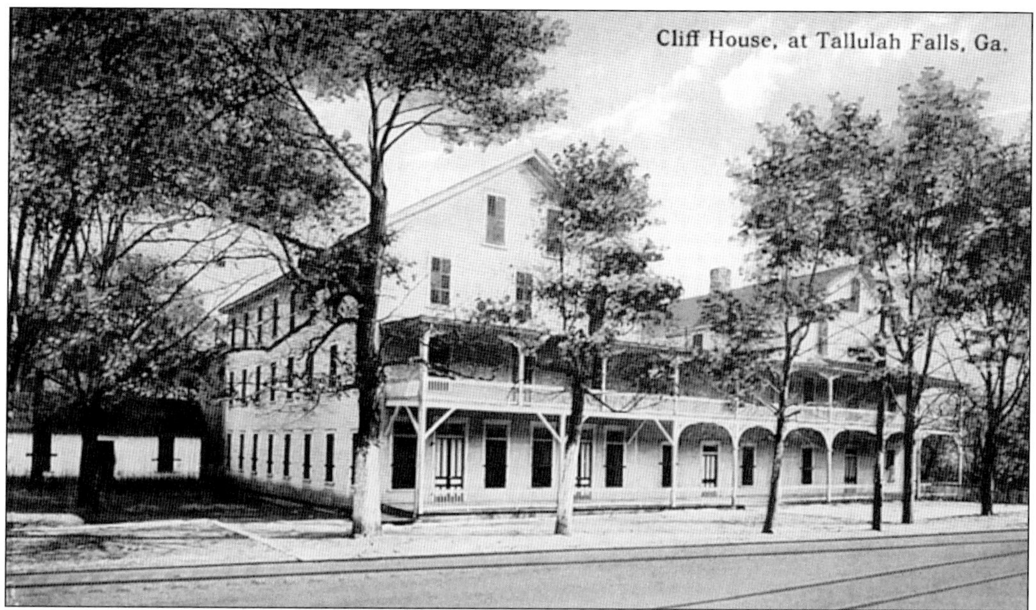

The printed message on the back of this view of the Cliff House in Tallulah Falls reads, "Cliff House at Tallulah Falls, GA. 100 miles Northeast of Atlanta. Special Sunday and week-end rates made by the Southern Railway. The Cliff House offers all modern conveniences at moderate prices, supports an excellent orchestra during Summer Season, and has accommodations for 250 people."

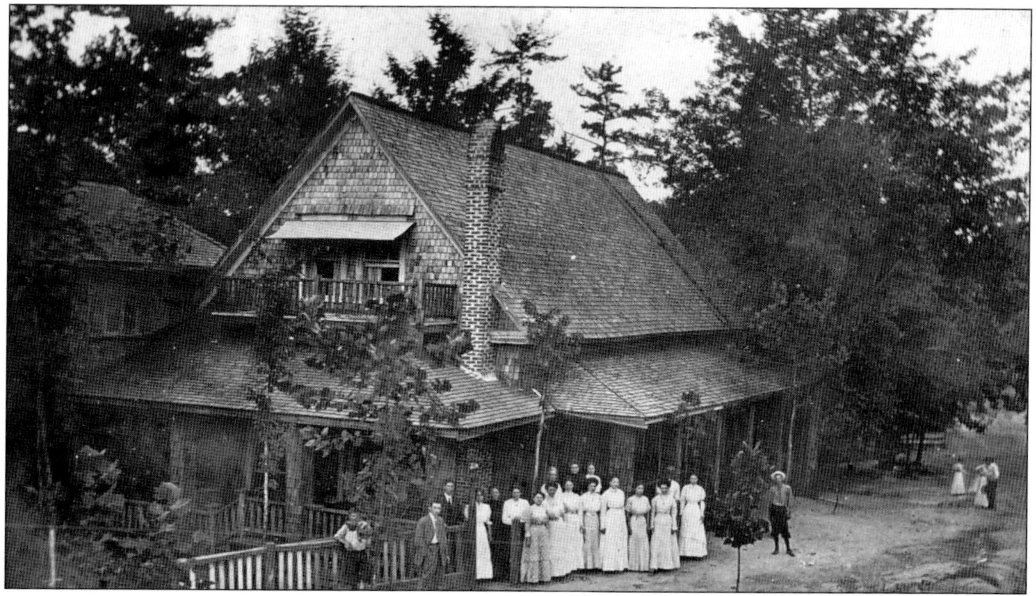

People are pictured outside the Chasm Brink Hotel in Tallulah Falls in 1910.

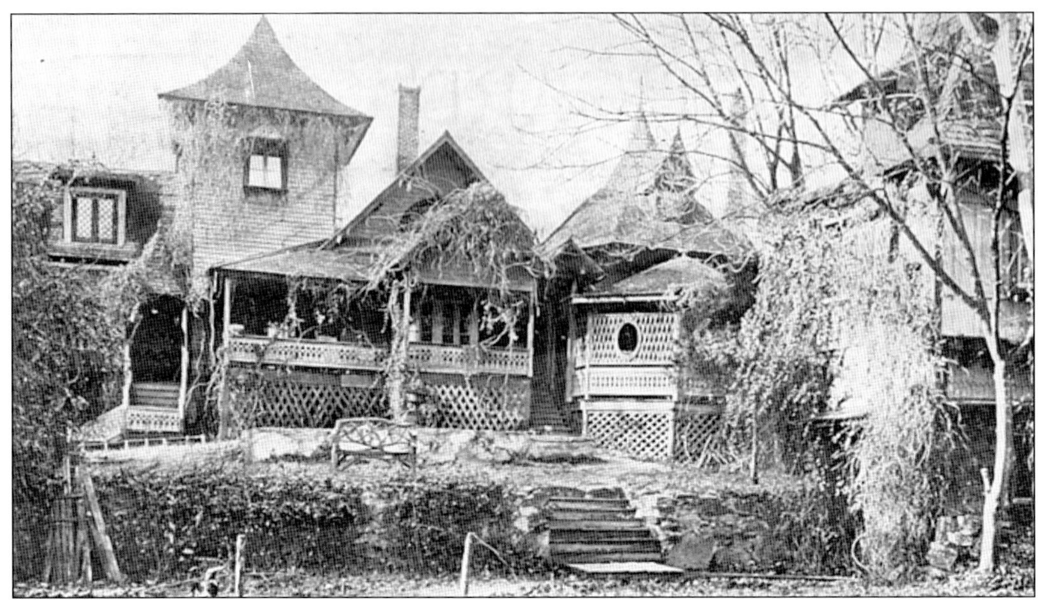

The vine-covered Glenbrook Hotel in Tallulah Falls seemed destined for ruin in this early view. However, the structure was preserved and has reopened in modern times.

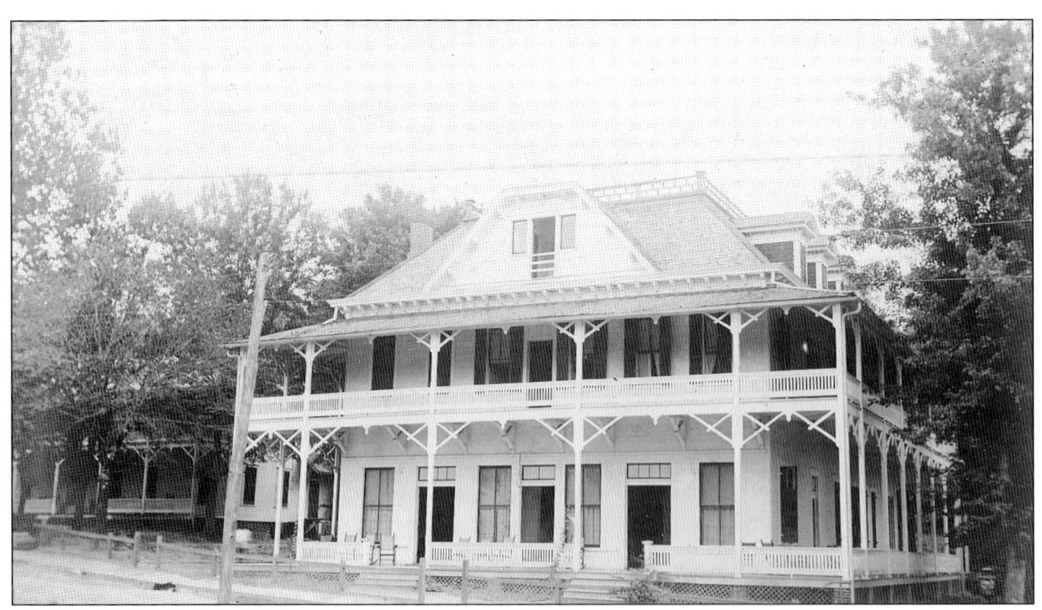

On the back of this postcard of the Maplewood Inn in Tallulah Falls, the sender wrote, "Do you recognize this? Have been hoping to hear that you and the children and Mother would come up here. How about it? Louise and children are here and having a pleasant time. Think we will stay a month. Much love to each of you."

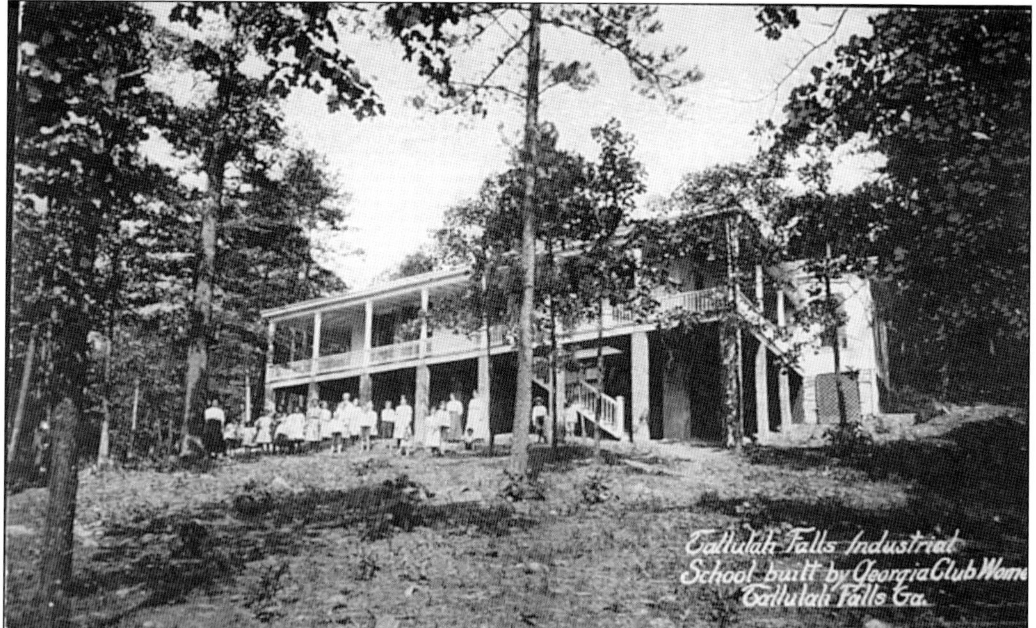

This card shows the Tallulah Falls Industrial School in 1911. The sender's message reads, "Our trip has certainly started out delightfully—hasn't been a 'hobble' so far. The scenery is beautiful. Please send Julia's skirts home—I forgot them. Don't forget to send my plumes too, hear. There's a pretty good crowd here, but not so many as I expected. More card playing and dancing going on than a little! I am enjoying the good music tho. With love, E.M.T."

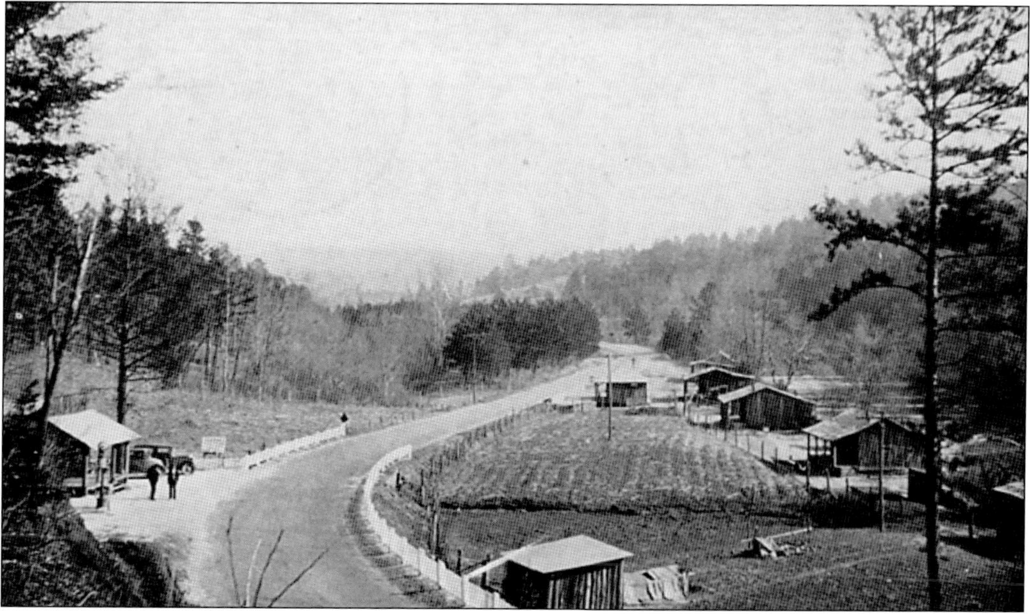

This is J.D. Wooddall's Riverside Camp on the main highway of Tallulah Falls.

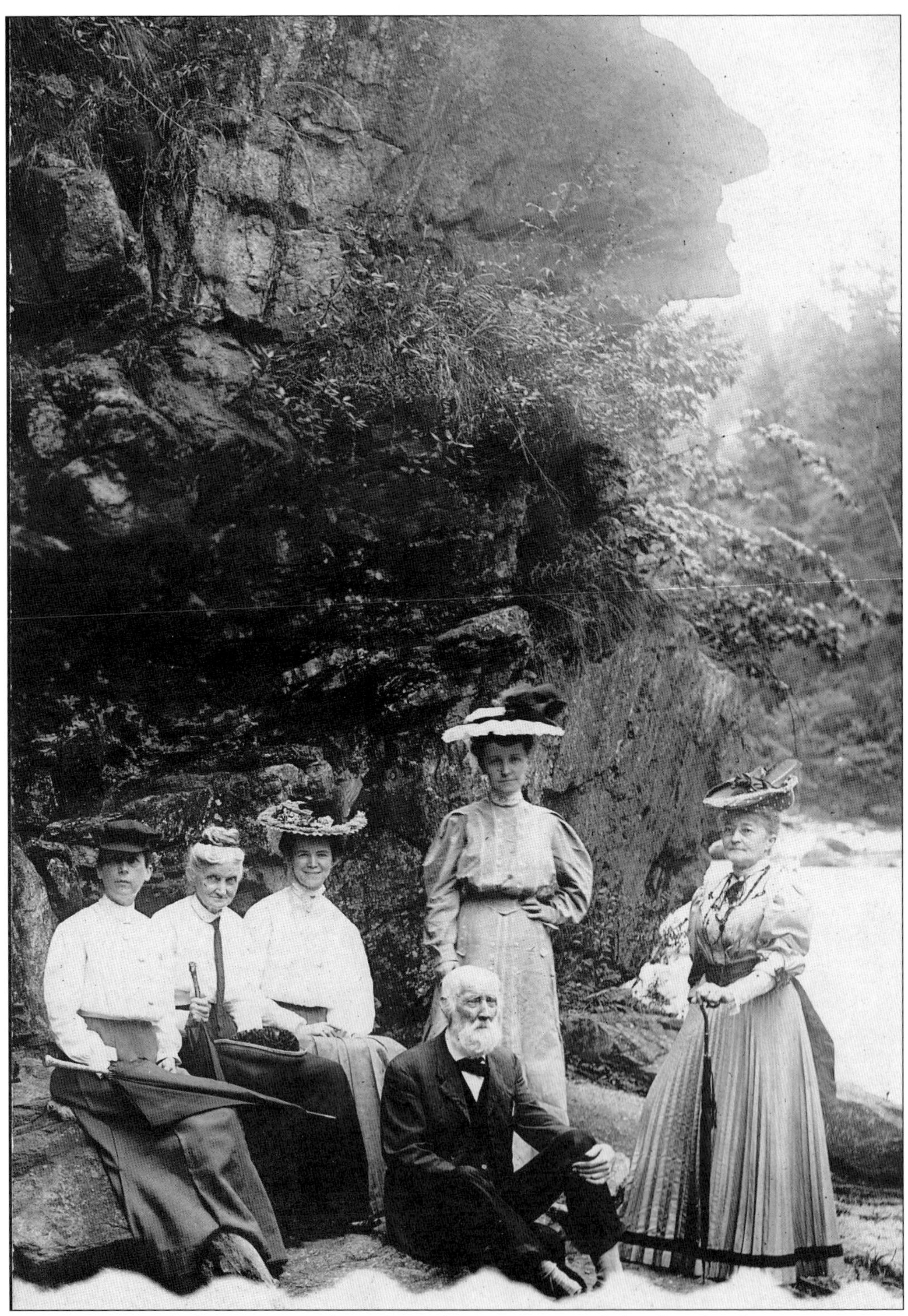

In this 1906 real-photo post card, Rufus Lafayette Moss and family of Athens are visiting Witch's Head at Tallulah Falls.

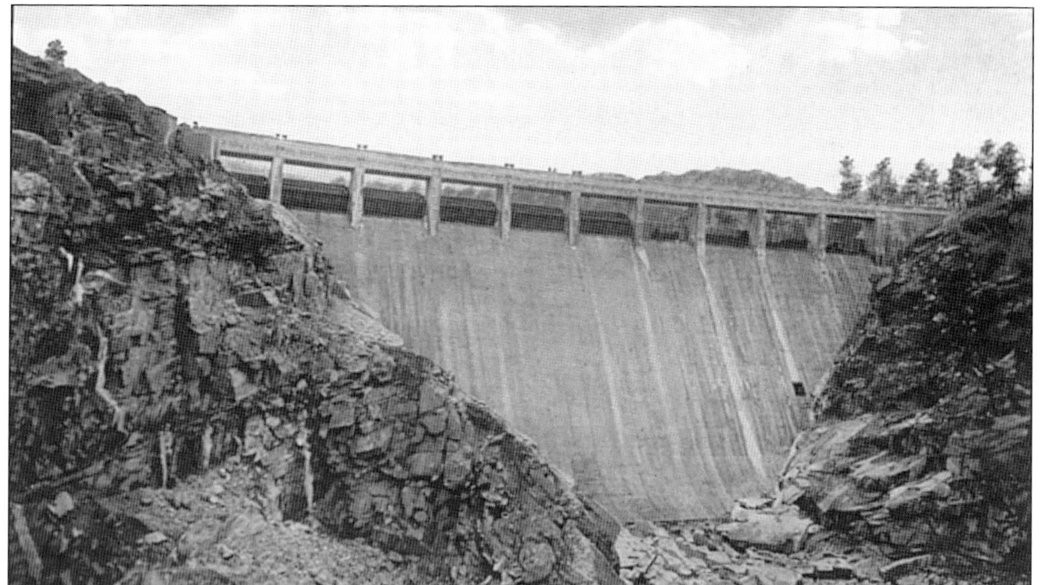

The back of this view of the Tallulah Falls dam reads, "The Tallulah Falls Dam at Tallulah Falls, GA. This Dam, which is one of the most marvelous feats of modern engineering, stands more than 100 feet above the river bed and is 53 feet in thickness at the base. This view shows the enormous proportions of this truly wonderful work. A few minutes walk from the Cliff House."

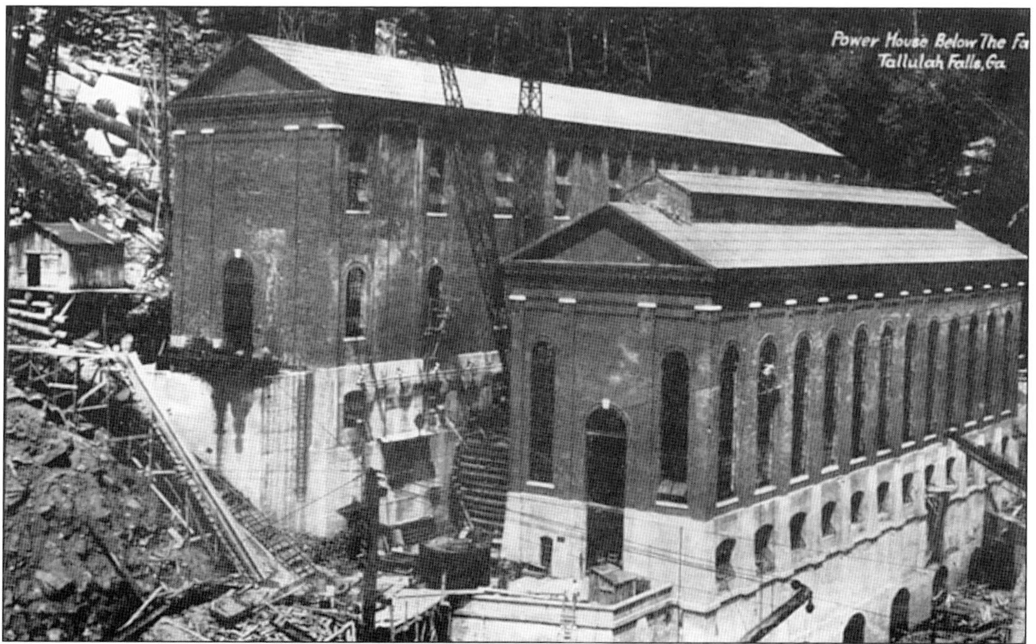

The massive scope of the powerhouse at Tallulah Falls is evident in this view.

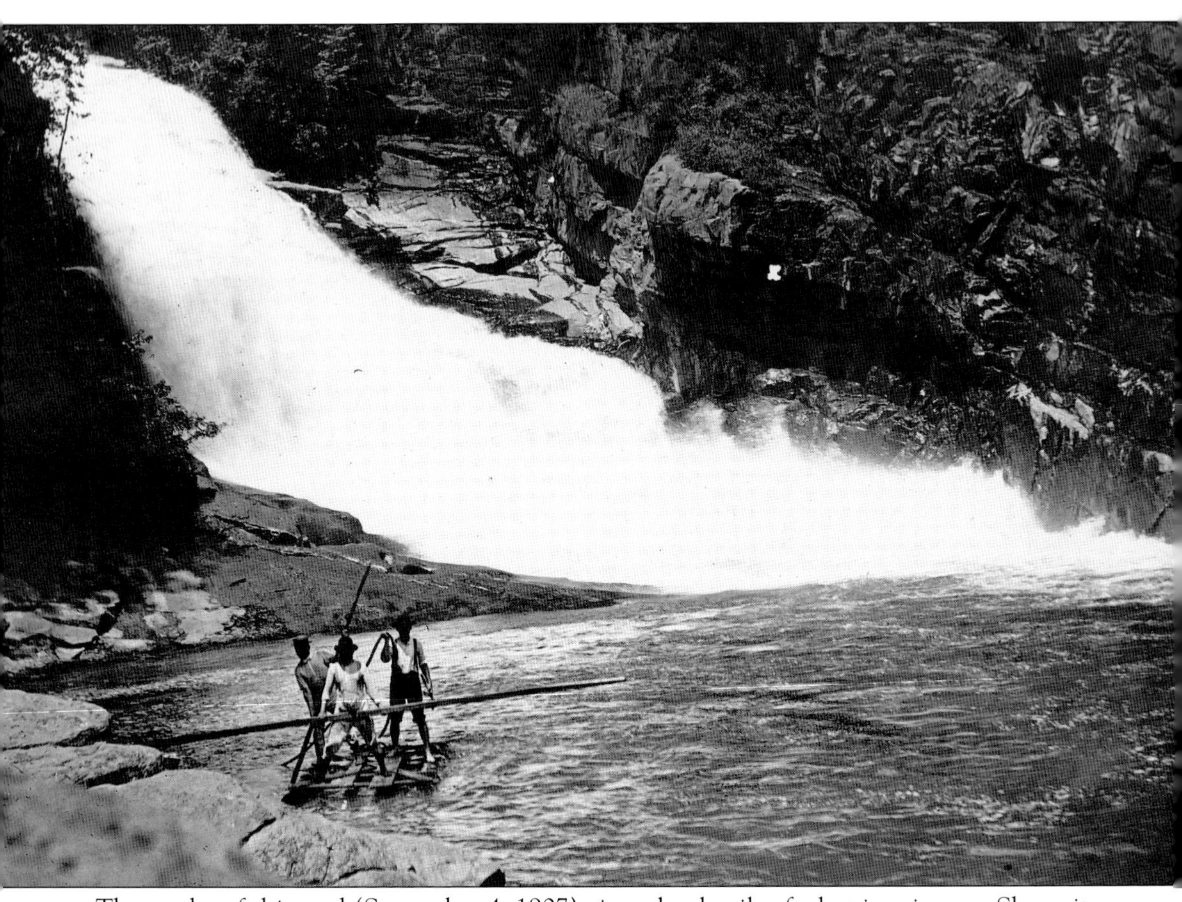

The sender of this card (September 4, 1907) gives the details of what is going on. She writes, "This is the place where Mr. Mangum was drowned. The men on the raft are looking for his body."

Bibliography

Anonymous. *1909–1910 Business and Professional Directory of the Cities and Towns of Georgia.* Atlanta, Georgia: Young and Company, 1910.

Jordan, Robert H. and J. Gregg Puster. *Courthouses in Georgia. Editing and Design by Patti Anderson and Mary Jackson.* Norcross, Georgia: The Harrison Company, 1984.

Krackow, Kenneth K. *Georgia Place-Names.* Macon, Georgia: Winship Press, 1975.

McKenny, Frank M. *The Standing Army: History of Georgia's County Confederate Monuments.* Alpharetta, Georgia: W.H. Wolfe Associates, 1993.

Winn, Les R. *Ghost Trains & Depots of Georgia (1833–1933).* Chamblee, Georgia: Big Shanty Publishing Company, 1995.

Index